Best Hikes Near
Columbus

JOHNNY MOLLOY

D1564753

FALCONGUIDES

GUILFORD, CONNECTICUT
HELENA, MONTANA

AN IMPRINT OF GLOBE PEQUOT PRESS

This book is for all the hikers who ply the trails of Columbus and the greater capital region.

To buy books in quantity for corporate use
or incentives, call **(800) 962-0973**
or e-mail **premiums@GlobePequot.com**.

FALCONGUIDES®

Copyright © 2013 Morris Book Publishing, LLC

ALL RIGHTS RESERVED. No part of this book may be reproduced or transmitted in any form by any means, electronic or mechanical, including photocopying and recording, or by any information storage and retrieval system, except as may be expressly permitted in writing from the publisher. Requests for permission should be addressed to Globe Pequot Press, Attn: Rights and Permissions Department, PO Box 480, Guilford, CT 06437.

FalconGuides is an imprint of Globe Pequot Press.
Falcon, FalconGuides, and Outfit Your Mind are registered trademarks of Morris Book Publishing, LLC.

Interior photos: Johnny Molloy
Maps: Hartdale Maps © Morris Book Publishing, LLC

Project editor: Julie Marsh
Text design: Sheryl P. Kober
Layout: Maggie Peterson

Library of Congress Cataloging-in-Publication data is available on file.

ISBN 978-0-7627-7174-5

Printed in the United States of America

10 9 8 7 6 5 4 3 2 1

The author and Globe Pequot Press assume no liability for accidents happening to, or injuries sustained by, readers who engage in the activities described in this book.

Contents

Overview

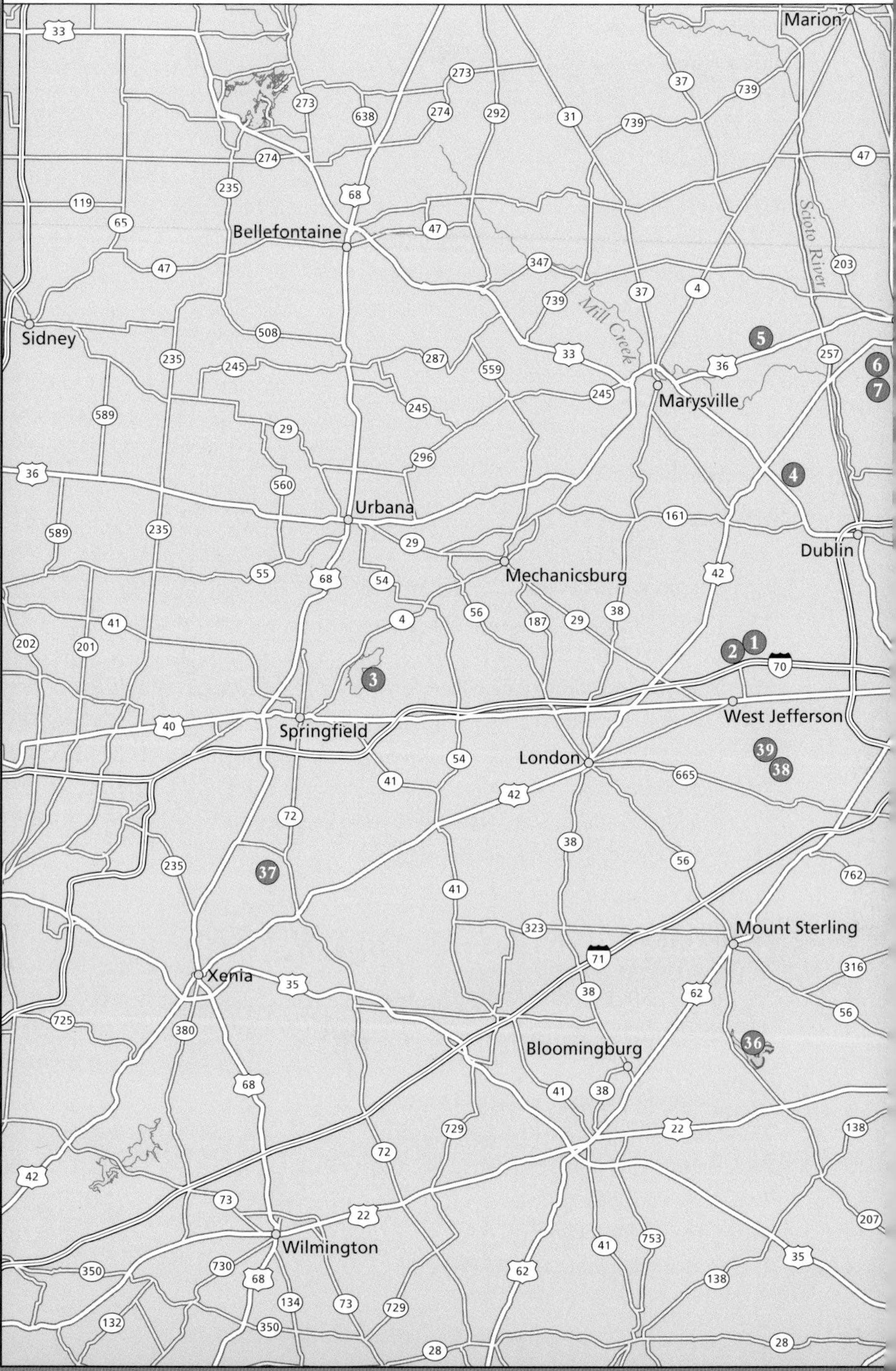

Marion
Bellefontaine
Sidney
Scioto River
Mill Creek
Marysville
Urbana
Dublin
Mechanicsburg
Springfield
West Jefferson
London
Mount Sterling
Xenia
Bloomingburg
Wilmington

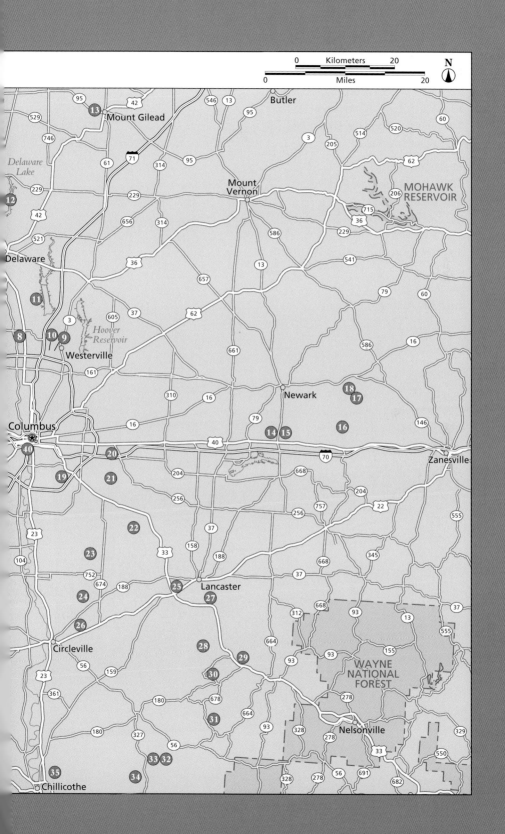

A curious white-tailed deer browses near the trail.

Acknowledgments

Thanks to all the people of Columbus who shared their favorite places to hike, including Jerry Urse and Ross Long. Thanks to Merrell for providing me with great hiking boots, hiking shoes, and sandals for the trail. Thanks to DeLorme for the fine GPS used to create maps for this book. Thanks also to the folks at Falcon-Guides/GPP, especially Jess Haberman and Katie Benoit.

Even fungi can be a beautiful woodland surprise.

HELP US KEEP THIS GUIDE UP TO DATE

Every effort has been made by the author and editors to make this guide as accurate and useful as possible. However, many things can change after a guide is published—trails are rerouted, regulations change, techniques evolve, facilities come under new management, etc.

We would appreciate hearing from you concerning your experiences with this guide and how you feel it could be improved and kept up to date. While we may not be able to respond to all comments and suggestions, we'll take them to heart, and we'll also make certain to share them with the author. Please send your comments and suggestions to the following address:

Globe Pequot Press
Reader Response/Editorial Department
PO Box 480
Guilford, CT 06437

Or you may e-mail us at: editorial@GlobePequot.com

Thanks for your input, and happy trails!

Introduction

Greater Columbus is blessed with a range of hikes that explore Ohio's biodiversity. It all starts with area residents acknowledging and preserving this scenic beauty in the capital region and points beyond. The citizenry could see that the special places would remain special if they were held by the public for the public to use and enjoy. In 1945 the Metro Parks system began a tradition of creating parks. Other parks and preserves were expanded or came to be, from the eight-decades-old Blacklick Woods to newer parks such as Walnut Woods, and trails became part of these natural oases.

Set on the banks of the Scioto River in the heart of Ohio, Columbus hikers can immerse themselves in the state's physiographic regions and the attendant biodiversity contained within each province. The unglaciated Appalachian Plateau is easiest to identify: Think of the Hocking Hills southeast of town—a land of deep valleys, sandstone ridges, and rough topography. In this area you can hike to Rockbridge—Ohio's largest natural arch—or visit the amazing gorge of Conkles Hollow. To the east stands another section of the Appalachian Plateau, except it was swept over by glaciers. Sheets of ice worked over its hills and vales: Recall Blackhand Gorge State Nature Preserve.

Franklin County, the heart of greater Columbus, mostly lies within what is known as the Till Plains. Glaciers deposited rich soil and sculpted gentle hills in this land. Glacier Ridge Metro Park exemplifies the region. Stretching west of town, glacial outwash carved local gorges that are some of Ohio's best hiking destinations. Think Clifton Gorge, with its sheer stone bluffs shading huge mossy boulders astride a crystalline stream. This meeting of physiographic regions gives greater Columbus a varied landscape where the flora and fauna meld into a mosaic of nature.

The recipe for great central Ohio hiking starts with this varied landscape. Next, add a layer of quality parks: Metro parks come to mind first. Preserves of this quality and variety—and full of trails—aren't in every city. I applaud Columbians for their foresight in establishing these natural gems, such as Clear Creek, with its streamside wildflower-filled meadows; Three Creeks Park, with a mix of primitive trails, asphalt paths, and other facilities overlain where Alum Creek and two of its tributaries meet in moist, rich bottoms; and Prairie Oaks Park, where Big Darby Creek flows through woods and field. Battelle Darby Creek Metro Park also features a stretch of Big Darby Creek—and lakes, and vertical terrain, and an ancient village site, and on and on. Then there's Slate Run Park, with its living-history farm and miles of trails coursing through wetlands, woodlands, hills, and steep-sided creeks. These wetlands are of special note, since they attract waterfowl and support fish and other aquatic creatures.

Additionally, the state of Ohio has established several state parks within easy striking distance of greater Columbus, such as Delaware State Park and Deer Creek State Park. The establishment of some preserves extends back to the Great Depression of the 1930s, when the Civilian Conservation Corps came in and built campgrounds, picnic shelters, and other facilities to enhance the already verdant beauty in what became the state parks. Of course, they built hiking trails to explore hills and valleys, vistas and waterfalls. In addition, Ohio's state nature preserve program protects a collection of natural gems, from the largest natural arch in Ohio at Rockbridge State Nature Preserve to rugged Clifton Gorge. Today we hikers benefit from a cornucopia of parkland throughout the capital region. It all adds up to an impressive array of hiking destinations!

It is in Columbus and this greater region where the hikes in this book are found. After having the privilege of researching potential hikes for this book, following the routes, taking photographs, determining which hikes made the grade (and the ones that didn't), exploring the parks beyond the trails, mapping the hikes, then actually writing and completing this compendium, I couldn't help but reflect on the wealth of places found within the guide's scope. For instance I think

At Blackhand Gorge State Nature Preserve (hike 17), the trail traces an old railroad grade blasted through sheer rock.

about Cantwell Cliffs, one of the most famous area landmarks, with its rock houses, stone bluffs, clear streams, and fascinating geological formations.

From atop a bluff at Cantwell Cliffs, I looked out and reflected on other destinations, recounting all the scenic hikes of greater Columbus. I thought of quiet Blues Creek Preserve, with its restored sun-splashed prairie, rife with colorful wildflowers in summer. Speaking of sun, I can still see ol' Sol reflecting off Delaware Lake from a trailside vista. Highbanks Park came to mind, where trails visited vistas and aboriginal mounds and earthworks amid woods with everywhere-you-look beauty. The high knobs of Shallenberger State Nature Preserve provided vertical variation, wildflowers, and impressive trees near Lancaster. The hills aren't quite as high at Lancaster's Alley Park, but the trail network there can be physically challenging.

My legs got a little sore remembering the 2,000 feet of ascent and descent while hiking an 8-mile loop near Mount Ives and Lick Run at Great Seal State Park. And the rock formations there . . . the abrupt hills, the wildflower-rich hollows— what sights! The Hargus Lake Loop at A. W. Marion State Park circled completely around the impoundment there, allowing watery views of the lake and of the numerous clear streams that feed it.

I came again to the scene at hand, Cantwell Cliffs, and considered the preserved gorge admired by generations past and present, as will those of the future. Ohioans from the distant past knew this as a special spot in the Hocking Hills. Today the city of Columbus forms the heart of Ohio, a place where trail-laden parks overlay an area enriched by an abundance of natural features. I hope the trails offered in this book will help you explore, understand, and appreciate the natural and human history of the greater Columbus region. Enjoy!

Weather

Columbus experiences all four seasons in their entirety. Summer can be warm, with occasional downright hot spells. Morning hikers can avoid the high temperatures and the common afternoon thunderstorms. A smart phone equipped with Internet access allows hikers to monitor storms as they arise.

Hikers increase in numbers when the first northerly fronts of fall sweep cool, clear air across the mid-state. Crisp mornings, great for vigorous treks, give way to warm afternoons, which are more conducive to family strolls. Fall is drier than summer.

Winter will bring frigid subfreezing days along with chilling rains and snows— and far fewer hours of daylight. However, a brisk hiking pace and wise time management will keep you warm and walking while the sun is still above the horizon. Each cold month has a few days of mild weather. Make the most of them.

Spring will be more variable. A warm day can be followed by a cold one. Extensive spring rains bring regrowth but also keep hikers indoors. Any avid hiker, however, will find more good hiking days than they will have time for in spring—and every other season for that matter.

A good way to plan your hiking is to check the average high and low temperatures and precipitation for each month. The table below shows Columbus's monthly averages and will give you a good idea of what to expect.

Month	Average High (Fahrenheit)	Average Low (Fahrenheit)	Precipitation (Inches)
January	37°	19°	2.9
February	42°	22°	2.4
March	52°	29°	3.0
April	65°	40°	3.1
May	75°	50°	3.8
June	83°	60°	3.7
July	86°	64°	4.4
August	85°	61°	3.1
September	78°	55°	3.0
October	67°	41°	2.7
November	54°	32°	3.3
December	42°	23°	3.1

Flora and Fauna

The landscape of Ohio's heart varies from the sharp wooded knolls and hollows of the Hocking Hills and the Appalachian foothills, to wooded reservoirs and water-carved gorges, to flatland forests and meadows stretching toward the horizon. A wide variety of wildlife calls these dissimilar landscapes home.

Deer will be the land animal you most likely will see while hiking Columbus's trails. They can be found throughout the capital region. Deer in some of the parks are remarkably tame and may linger on or close to the trail as you approach. A quiet hiker may also spot turkeys, raccoons, or even a coyote. Don't be surprised if you see beavers, muskrats, or a playful otter along streams and lakes. If you feel uncomfortable when encountering any critter, keep your distance, and they will generally keep theirs.

Overhead, many raptors will be plying the skies for food, including hawks, falcons, and owls. Depending upon where you are, other birds you may spot range from kingfishers to woodpeckers. Look for waterfowl in lakes. Songbirds are abundant no matter the habitat.

The flora offers just as much variety. Along the trails you will find verdant hardwood forests. In cooler north-facing areas you will see maple, beech, cherry, and other northern hardwoods. Pawpaws will be found under the shade of them. South-facing woods will have more oaks and hickories. Sycamores and cottonwoods predominate in moister areas and thrive along nearly every stream in greater Columbus. Wildflowers will be found in spring, summer, and fall along watercourses and in drier site-specific situations. Restored prairies are special wildflower enclaves. Wetlands provide unique habitats and occur naturally and with a little help from park personnel.

Wilderness Restrictions/Regulations

Hiking in greater Columbus is done primarily in city, county, and state parks, in addition to nature preserves and US Army Corps of Engineers land. Greater Columbus has one of the finest park systems in the country, known as Metro Parks. They are well-run, well-maintained facilities with a little bit of everything for everyone, from hiking to camping to golfing. Entrance is free, and visitor guidelines keep the parks in the best shape possible.

Coneflowers brighten the trailside vegetation.

Ohio state parks offer natural getaways with an emphasis on recreation. They also protect special areas such as the nature preserves within them. Area state parks—Delaware State Park, for example—are often centered around a reservoir built by the Army Corps of Engineers. These man-made lakes were built primarily for flood control and water storage. The recreation aspect of the lakes is an important but secondary function. Trails are laid upon the shoreline of the reservoirs. Entrance to state parks and their trails is free, but you will have to pay to golf, camp, or overnight in a cabin. As a whole, the state park trail systems are in good shape.

Then there are the nature preserves. Ohio has a special program whereby land is set aside for protection. These lands usually have unique ecological characteristics that deem them worthy of saving. The preserves are the most restricted in terms of usage. Luckily for us, hiking is considered passive recreation. Camping is generally not allowed on these lands.

Getting Around

Area Codes
The Columbus area code is 614. Areas east and north of Columbus are 740. The area code west of town is 937.

Roads
For the purposes of this guide, the best hikes near Columbus are confined to a one-hour drive from the greater metro region. Southeasterly, this stretches to the town of Logan, north to Mount Gilead, west to Clifton, and south to Chillicothe. The entire hiking area is considered the heart of Ohio, with Columbus its epicenter.

A number of major interstates converge in Columbus. Directions to trailheads are given from these arteries. They include I-70, I-71, I-670, and I-270—the main loop around Columbus.

By Air
Port Columbus International Airport (CMH) is 6 miles east of downtown Columbus, off I-270 and I-670, near Gahanna, Ohio.

To book reservations online, check out your favorite airline's website or search one of the following travel sites for the best price: cheaptickets.com, expedia.com, previewtravel.com, orbitz.com, priceline.com, travel.yahoo.com, travelocity.com, or trip.com—just to name a few.

By Bus

Central Ohio Transit Authority (known as "COTA") operates bus service through-out Columbus and its suburbs. Visit www.cota.com or call (614) 228-1776. In addition to COTA, Greyhound serves many towns in the region; visit www.grey hound.com for more information.

Visitor Information

For general information on Columbus, visit the official website of the Greater Columbus Convention and Visitors Bureau, www.experiencecolumbus.com, or call (614) 221-6623. This covers the central Ohio area, beyond the city of Columbus.

Even snakes like the trails of Pickerington Ponds Metro Park (hike 21).

How to Use This Guide

Take a close enough look, and you'll find that this guide contains just about everything you'll ever need to choose, plan for, enjoy, and survive a hike near Columbus. Stuffed with useful central Ohio–area information, *Best Hikes Near Columbus* features forty mapped and cued hikes. To organize the location of the hikes throughout the Columbus area, I grouped them into four geographic quadrants that neatly fit with greater Columbus's road system radiating from downtown: "Northwest" covers hikes north of I-70 and west of US 23; "Northeast" details hikes north of I-70 and east of US 23; "Southeast" harbors hikes south of I-70 and east of US 23; and "Southwest" details hikes south of I-70 and west of US 23.

Each hike starts with a short **summary** of the hike's highlights. These quick overviews give you a taste of the hiking adventures to follow. You'll learn about the trail terrain and what surprises each route has to offer.

Following the overview you'll find the **hike specs**—quick, nitty-gritty details of the hike. Here's what you'll find:

Start: This locates the trailhead.

Distance: The total distance of the recommended route—one-way for loops or round-trip for out-and-back sections of trail. Options detail alternate routes along the given hike. The options may shorten the route or describe spur trails to add more highlights to the hike.

Hiking time: The average time it will take to cover the route. It is based on the total distance, elevation gain, and condition and difficulty of the trail. Your fitness level will also affect your time.

Difficulty: Each hike has been assigned a level of difficulty. The rating system was developed from several sources and personal experience. These levels are meant to be a guideline only—hikes may prove easier or harder for different people depending on ability and physical fitness.

Easy: 5 miles or less total trip distance in one day, with minimal elevation gain and paved or smooth-surfaced dirt trail.

Moderate: up to 10 miles total trip distance in one day, with moderate elevation gain and potentially rough terrain.

Difficult: more than 10 miles total trip distance in one day, with strenuous elevation gain and rough and/or rocky terrain.

Trail surface: General information about what to expect underfoot.

Best season: General information on the best time of year to hike.

Other trail users: Such as horseback riders, mountain bikers, joggers, etc.

Canine compatibility: Know the trail regulations before you take your dog hiking with you. Dogs are not allowed on several trails in this book.

Land status: Metro Parks, county park, state nature preserve, etc.

Fees and permits: Indicates whether you need to carry any money with you for park entrance fees and permits.

Schedule: Season, days, and hours that trails are accessible.

Maps: This is a list of other maps to supplement the maps in this book. USGS maps are the best source for accurate topographical information, but the local park map may show more recent trails. Use both.

Trail contact: This is the address, phone number, and website for the local land manager(s) in charge of the trails within the selected hike. Get trail access information before you head out, or contact the land manager after your visit if you see problems with trail erosion, damage, or misuse.

The **Finding the trailhead** section gives you dependable driving directions to where you'll want to park. **The Hike** is the meat of the chapter. Detailed and honest, it's a carefully researched impression of the trail. It also often includes lots of area history, both natural and human. Under **Miles and Directions,** mileage cues identify all turns and trail name changes, as well as points of interest. **Options** are also given for many hikes to make your journey shorter or longer depending

Black-eyed Susans color the creekside prairie (hike 28).

on the amount of time you have. Don't feel restricted to the routes and trails that are mapped here. Be adventurous and use this guide as a platform to discover new routes for yourself.

Green Tips are included to help you help the environment we all share.

Sidebars can also be found throughout the book. These include interesting information about the area or trail that doesn't necessarily pertain to the specific hike but gives you some human or natural tidbit that may pique your interest to explore beyond the simple mechanics of the trek.

Enjoy your time in the outdoors, and remember to pack out what you pack in.

How to Use the Maps

Overview map: This map shows the location of each hike in the area by hike number.

Route map: This is your primary guide to each hike. It shows all of the accessible roads and trails, points of interest, water, landmarks, and geographical features. It also distinguishes trails from roads, and paved roads from unpaved roads. The selected route is highlighted, and directional arrows point the way.

Fall's glory surrounds a hiker's boots.

Trail Finder

Hike No.	Hike Name	Best Hikes for Waterfalls	Best Hikes for Great Views	Best Hikes for Children	Best Hikes for Dogs	Best Hikes for Stream Lovers	Best Hikes for Lake Lovers	Best Hikes for Nature Lovers	Best Hikes for History Lovers
1	Lakes and Plains of Prairie Oaks Metro Park		●		●	●	●		
2	Coneflower Trail at Prairie Oaks Metro Park			●		●		●	
3	Buck Creek State Park Shoreline Ramble		●	●			●		
4	Glacier Ridge Hike			●	●			●	
5	Blues Creek Preserve			●		●		●	
6	Stratford Ecological Center Hike			●		●		●	
7	Deer Haven Preserve Hike			●				●	
8	Highbanks Hike		●				●		●
9	Hikes of Blendon Woods		●	●	●	●	●	●	
10	Sharon Woods Loops		●	●	●	●	●		
11	Hiking Network of Alum Creek State Park		●	●	●		●		
12	Delaware State Park Loop		●		●		●		
13	Mount Gilead State Park Hike			●		●	●		

Trail Finder

Hike No.	Hike Name	Best Hikes for Waterfalls	Best Hikes for Great Views	Best Hikes for Children	Best Hikes for Dogs	Best Hikes for Stream Lovers	Best Hikes for Lake Lovers	Best Hikes for Nature Lovers	Best Hikes for History Lovers
14	Dawes Arboretum		●	●				●	●
15	Dawes Arboretum East			●			●	●	
16	Flint Ridge State Memorial			●		●		●	●
17	Blackhand Gorge State Nature Preserve		●			●		●	●
18	Marie Hickey Trail at Blackhand Gorge	●	●	●		●			●
19	Three Creeks Hike		●	●	●	●			
20	Blacklick Woods Hike			●				●	●
21	Hikes of Pickerington Ponds Metro Park		●	●	●		●	●	
22	Chestnut Ridge Hike		●	●					●
23	Slate Run Hike		●						●
24	Stages Pond State Nature Preserve			●		●	●	●	
25	Shallenberger State Nature Preserve			●			●	●	
26	Hargus Lake Loop at A. W. Marion State Park		●		●	●	●		

Trail Finder

Hike No.	Hike Name	Best Hikes for Waterfalls	Best Hikes for Great Views	Best Hikes for Children	Best Hikes for Dogs	Best Hikes for Stream Lovers	Best Hikes for Lake Lovers	Best Hikes for Nature Lovers	Best Hikes for History Lovers
27	Alley Park Hike						•	•	
28	Clear Creek Loop		•		•	•		•	•
29	Rockbridge State Nature Preserve			•		•		•	
30	Cantwell Cliffs Loops	•	•	•		•		•	
31	Conkles Hollow Hike	•		•		•			
32	Ross Hollow Loop			•	•	•			
33	North Loop of the Logan Trail		•			•		•	
34	South Loop of the Logan Trail		•			•		•	
35	Great Seal State Park Loop							•	
36	Deer Creek State Park Vistas		•	•	•		•		
37	Clifton Gorge	•	•			•		•	•
38	Battelle Darby Double Loop			•	•	•			•
39	Dyer Mill Loop			•	•		•		
40	Scioto Audubon Metro Park Walk		•	•	•	•			

Map Legend

Transportation

- ⬭70⬭ Freeway/Interstate Highway
- ⬭321⬭ US Highway
- ⬭656⬭ State Highway
- ⬭CR 24⬭ County/Paved/Improved Road
- ==== Unpaved Road
- +—+—+ Railroad

Trails

- ▬▬▬▬ Selected Route
- - - - - - Trail
- → Direction of Route

Water Features

- Body of Water
- Swamp/Marsh
- River or Creek
- Intermittent Stream
- Waterfall

Land Management

- National Forest/Monument
- State/Local Park
- Wilderness Boundary

Symbols

- ||||||| Boardwalk
- Boat Ramp/Launch
- ⎵ Bridge
- ▪ Building/Point of Interest
- ⛺ Campground
- ▲ Campsite (backcountry)
- ✪ Capital
- ○ City/Town
- Firetower
- •—• Gate
- P Parking
- ▲ Peak/Hill
- Picnic Area
- Ranger Station
- Restroom
- Scenic View/Overlook
- ① Trailhead
- ? Visitor/Information Center

Northwest Hikes

Looking over the swim beach at Buck Creek State Park (hike 3).

This area offers quality hikes in city parks, state parks, county ecological preserves, and even a private nature preserve, covering western Franklin County, western Delaware County, Madison County, and Union County. Big Darby Creek cuts a scenic swath through the land, along with other tributaries of the Scioto River.

Prairie Oaks Metro Park features two treks among its scattering of woods and fields astride Big Darby Creek. As if a state scenic river isn't enough to see, you can also wander past several lakes. And if hiking through flower-studded prairies doesn't light your fire, then walk in deep woods on undulating terrain—and that's just on one hike! The well-marked Coneflower Trail at Prairie Oaks presents mostly level trailway, allowing you to view Big Darby Creek and enjoy prairie as it changes with the seasons, while simultaneously holding a conversation with your hiking partner.

Hike along the shore of impressive C. J. Brown Reservoir at Buck Creek State Park. Excellent for summer, cruise the shoreline to find the campground swim beach. It offers views and a place to take a dip! Be sure to make a side trip to the Crabill Homestead.

Glacier Ridge Metro Park is a modern park incarnation, mixing preservation and recreation. The 1,036 acres were restored to a natural state of woodlands, meadows, wetlands, and prairies. A wetland education center and a wind/solar demonstration area add an environmental education component. A mix of paved and natural paths let you roam Glacier Ridge and the adjoining neighborhoods.

Blues Creek Preserve in Delaware County is also a newer-style nature park. Get back to nature on nature's terms, where the park facilities are integrated into the landscape. It offers a superlative native prairie wildflower display in summer. Explore Blues Creek, then parallel field and forest, with an emphasis on learning. Between 2 and 4 percent of Ohio's landmass was prairie prior to American settlement, and Blues Creek Preserve highlights this colorful part of the Buckeye State.

At the Stratford Ecological Center, you can visit a living farm, experiencing agricultural practices close up. Part of the walk enters adjacent Stratford Woods State Nature Preserve, where excellent spring wildflower displays are a sight to behold. Deer Haven Preserve, another Delaware County preservation park, mixes its trail system with traditional Havener Park. The preserve presents meadows, restored prairie, a steep ridge, and big trees.

Some hikers argue that Highbanks Park has the most highlights of any central Ohio trek. Begin by hiking along steep shale ravines and through changing landscapes to see a homesite and re-created cemetery of early area settlers. Next, wander by prehistoric earthworks from aboriginal Ohioans, and gaze from an observation deck 110 feet above the Olentangy State Scenic River. Finally, visit a wildlife blind astride a restored wetland, then stop by a burial mound left by the ancient Adena Indians. And the hike isn't even long!

Green Tip:
Go out of your way to avoid birds and animals that are mating or taking care of their young.

Lakes and Plains of Prairie Oaks Metro Park

This hike covers many diverse sites and scenery at big Prairie Oaks Metro Park. First it travels past several lakes that are part of an old reclaimed surface-mine pit where sand was once extracted. The hike straddles an elevated berm with Big Darby Creek on one side and the Darby Bend Lakes on the other—talk about a watery walk!—then explores woods along lower Big Darby Creek. Visit creekside lowlands before climbing to the Sycamore Plains, a restored upland prairie displaying yet another ecosystem. Head back north toward the Darby Bend Lakes for more still-water scenery before reaching the trailhead.

Start: Darby Bend Lakes entrance road
Distance: 5.6 miles in multiple loops
Hiking time: About 3.5 to 4.5 hours
Difficulty: Moderate; does have some hills
Trail surface: Gravel and natural surface
Best season: Year-round; spring and fall for wildflowers
Other trail users: Joggers and bicyclists on Darby Creek Greenway Trail

Canine compatibility: Leashed dogs permitted
Land status: Metro Parks
Fees and permits: None
Schedule: Open daily year-round, 6:30 a.m. to dark
Maps: Prairie Oaks Metro Park; USGS West Jefferson, Galloway, Plain City
Trail contact: Metro Parks, 1069 W. Main St., Westerville, OH 43081; (614) 891-0700; www.metroparks.net

Finding the trailhead: From exit 85 on I-70, west of downtown Columbus, take Plain City–Georgesville Road north for 2.1 miles to Lucas Road, which becomes Beach Road. (Do not turn into the main park entrance on the west side of Prairie Oaks Park.) Follow Lucas/Beach Road 0.7 mile to reach Amity Road. Turn right on Amity Road and follow it 0.4 mile to the Darby Bend Lakes entrance of Prairie Oaks Metro Park. At 0.1 mile, park on your right. Trailhead GPS: N39 59.610'/W83 15.541'

THE HIKE

What I like about this hike is the ever-changing scenery. It's not just miles and miles of walking through endless forest, or open grasslands, or hill after hill; rather it is the fluctuating settings on many different trails, yet the way is clear and well-marked. Speaking of trails, even they are different from one another. At one point you may be on a wide gravel track, while at other times your trail will be grassy or composed of rocks and roots and other natural ingredients. So strap on your hiking boots and get ready for a multiplicity of environments on this hike.

Water is a big part of this adventure. It isn't long before you are walking alongside the shore of the Darby Bend Lakes on the Mound Trail. Yes, there's even a relic

Fall colors border the grassy track.

Indian mound that you can visit. Historic burial mounds, such as this one, are found throughout central Ohio and look like low hills of dirt grown over with grass and/or trees. Some have been systematically excavated, while others have not. Some have been torn apart by amateurs looking for something valuable. So even though you see what looks like a nondescript hill, having this mound inside a park increases its likelihood for long-term preservation.

Four impoundments comprise the Darby Bend Lakes. The most northerly of the lakes are open to fishing and nonmotorized boating, meaning canoeing or kayaking, but anglers may be seen in johnboats vying for fish. The smallest and centermost lake is open to angling for children only. The southernmost lake is open to everyone for fishing.

The aquatic adventure increases when you come alongside Big Darby Creek. It is not often the hiker can walk a trail with a lake on one side and a moving stream on the other, especially when there's not a flood! You will stay alongside Big Darby Creek for a couple of miles, utilizing several different trails. At first the hike takes you around the actual Darby Bend. It was this pronounced curve in the creek that indirectly caused this park to be. Historically, in times of flood, sediment-filled water would cut across the bend, depositing sand with each high-water event. Later, the sand deposit was seen as an extractable resource and was mined. The trail travels atop a berm that was constructed to keep Big Darby Creek from flooding the mine pit. Ironically, this berm is now part of the trail system, after being lowered to allow flood waters into the Darby Bend Lakes. But after the mine was given up, it was purchased by the Metro Parks system and became part of Prairie Oaks Metro Park. We will never know, but perhaps this particular area might not have ended up a park if it wasn't mined for sand first.

Be sure to detour to the bridge over Big Darby Creek, near the Alder Trail junction. Good stream views can be had here. Once on the Alder Trail, walk beneath pawpaw, sycamore, ash, walnut, and honey locust. These creekside lowlands may be flooded in spring. You will enjoy prolonged looks at Big Darby Creek, though you do occasionally pull away from the stream in the wettest of areas. A portion of the Sycamore Plains trail network keeps you cruising along Big Darby Creek in big woods. Eventually you turn back away from the creek and climb up to the actual Sycamore Plains, a prairie area that is also growing up with young sycamore trees. The hike here is scenic, but the noise from I-70 can be loud with a south wind.

It isn't long before you have left the Sycamore Plains trail network and are resuming a northbound track back on the Alder Trail. Your final new path takes you astride the most southeasterly of the Darby Bend Lakes to complete the trek.

Lakes and Plains of Prairie Oaks Metro Park

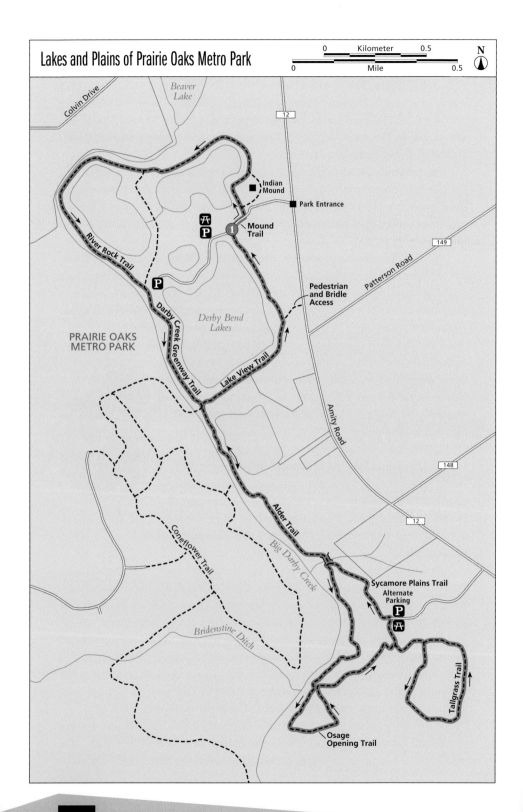

Beaver Lake

Colvin Drive

12

Indian Mound

Park Entrance

Mound Trail

1

River Rock Trail

Darby Creek Greenway Trail

P

149

Patterson Road

Pedestrian and Bridle Access

Derby Bend Lakes

PRAIRIE OAKS METRO PARK

Lake View Trail

Amity Road

148

Coneflower Trail

12

Alder Trail

Big Darby Creek

Sycamore Plains Trail

Alternate Parking

P

Bridenstine Ditch

Tallgrass Trail

Osage Opening Trail

0   Kilometer   0.5

0   Mile   0.5

N

MILES AND DIRECTIONS

0.0 Start on the Mound Trail as it leaves the Darby Bend Lakes entrance road. Join a northbound pea-gravel track.

0.1 An arm of the Mound Trail goes right and circles around an old Adena Indian mound. Stay straight on the main arm of the Mound Trail, walking alongside the most northeasterly of the greater Darby Bend Lakes.

0.2 Reunite with the other end of the alternate arm of the Mound Trail. Keep straight, with one of the Darby Bend Lakes to your left.

0.3 Turn left on the wide, gravel Darby Creek Greenway Trail. Walk an elevated margin with a lake to your left and Big Darby Creek to your right.

0.6 Turn right, joining the River Rock Trail, bordered by many cottonwood trees. The margin of this path is even narrower and is decidedly pinched in by the lake to your left and creek to your right. The trail curves along the actual Darby Bend, which gave this area its name. Enjoy the interpretive information detailing the mining history of the park.

1.2 The Darby Creek Greenway Trail comes in on your left. There is an alternate parking area here. Stay right, rejoining the Darby Creek Greenway Trail. Big Darby Creek remains to your right and you are now on a higher levee.

1.6 Come to a four-way trail junction. The Darby Creek Greenway Trail leaves right and bridges the creek, connecting to the west end of the park. To your left the Lake View Trail heads back to the trailhead. Keep straight, joining the Alder Trail as it continues downstream along Big Darby Creek.

2.2 Reach the Sycamore Plains trail network just after bridging a streamlet. Turn right here, staying along Big Darby Creek.

2.6 Come to a four-way trail junction. Stay right on the Osage Opening Trail. You will return to this junction later.

2.8 Turn away from Big Darby Creek, then climb to an Osage orange grove and dip back to the creek.

3.0 Complete the Osage Opening Trail, returning to the four-way junction on Big Darby Creek. This time turn right, heading away from Big Darby Creek again on the Sycamore Plains Trail. Open onto restored prairie rife with young sycamores along with prairie grasses.

3.3 Reach the sub-loop of the Sycamore Plains Trail, the Tallgrass Trail. Take a right here. The loop makes a mostly level circuit through fields with a small copse of trees. I-70 is within sight, and songbirds compete with the interstate for audio supremacy.

4.0 Complete the loop portion of the Tallgrass Trail. Backtrack to the main Sycamore Plains Trail, still on the Tallgrass Trail.

4.1 Turn right on the Sycamore Plains Trail.

4.2 Come to the Sycamore Plains parking area after passing through a line of trees. There is a shaded picnic table here for resting or picnicking. Stay left, toward the north end of the park.

4.4 Return to the Alder Trail. Bridge the small streamlet, then continue backtracking through flatwoods and successional meadow.

5.0 Complete the Alder Trail a second time. The bridge over Big Darby Creek is just to your left. Turn right here on the Lake View Trail and enjoy a waterside walk.

5.4 A trail leads right; this is the pedestrian and bridle trail entrance. Stay left on a grassy track, still the Lake View Trail.

5.6 Arrive back at the Darby Bend Lakes entrance road, completing the hike.

🌿 Green Tip:
Never feed wild animals under any circumstances. This includes everything from birds to chipmunks to raccoons to deer. You may damage their health and expose yourself (and them) to danger.

Coneflower Trail at Prairie Oaks Metro Park

You will be exploring both meadow and woods on this hike. Leave the Whispering Oaks Picnic Area and begin a loop that leads to the banks of Big Darby Creek, a state scenic river. A spur trail visits the waterway to admire the aquatic splendor. The hike then continues downstream through a mosaic of tall trees, prairies, and a mix of the two. Come alongside a tributary of Big Darby Creek before returning to the trailhead. The well-marked and maintained trail is mostly level and makes for a pleasant track enjoyed by all.

Start: Whispering Oaks Picnic Area

Distance: 2.3-mile loop

Hiking time: About 1.5 to 2 hours

Difficulty: Easy to moderate; trails are mostly level

Trail surface: Gravel and natural surface

Best season: Year-round; spring and fall for wildflowers

Other trail users: Joggers and bicyclists on Darby Creek Greenway Trail

Canine compatibility: Leashed dogs permitted

Land status: Metro Parks

Fees and permits: None

Schedule: Open daily year-round, 6:30 a.m. to dark

Maps: Prairie Oaks Metro Park; USGS West Jefferson, Galloway

Trail contact: Metro Parks, 1069 W. Main St., Westerville, OH 43081; (614) 891-0700; www .metroparks.net

Finding the trailhead: From exit 85 on I-70, west of downtown Columbus, take Plain City–Georgesville Road north (OH 142 goes south from the exit) for 0.7 mile. Turn right into Prairie Oaks Park and follow the main park road 0.9 mile to a dead end at the Whispering Oaks Picnic Area. Trailhead GPS: N39 59.610'/W83 15.541'

THE HIKE

When establishing parks for the greater Columbus area, the Metro Parks system develops them not only for recreation but also for restoration. Prairie Oaks Metro Park has plenty of room for both. The 1,782-acre preserve is situated along Big Darby Creek. This valley was once home to a vast prairie known as the Darby Plains, with grassland species native to the Buckeye State. Today over 400 acres of the preserve have been restored in Ohio prairie plants. This hike travels through some of the restored prairies. In fact, the trail takes its name from an important prairie plant, the coneflower.

You will start your hike at the Whispering Oaks Picnic Area. Despite the name, the picnic area is short on trees but has a covered shelter to protect you from the sun. It also has a restroom. A spur trail leads to the Darby Creek Greenway Trail, which runs in conjunction with the Coneflower Trail. At 3.4 miles, the Darby Creek Greenway Trail is the park's longest walking path and connects with just about every other hiking trail here. The Bridle Trail (not shown on the map) is the longest path of them all, but it is open only to equestrians. Please stay off this trail. You will intersect the Bridle Trail a few times during your hike, and a couple of times the

An OSU fan cruises the gravely Coneflower Trail.

equestrian trail will run in conjunction with the Coneflower Trail. However, these junctions are not confusing, as the trail network as a whole is well marked and maintained. The Darby Creek Greenway Trail is a multiuse path and is open to bicyclists as well.

The Darby Creek Greenway Trail and the Coneflower Trail travel a wide gravel track that first turns north before curving back south to reach a grassy meadow. Here the Coneflower Trail goes its own way along the margin of the meadow and a walnut-rich forest. The path changes to grass and is easy on the feet. You soon enter a successional prairie, where grasses and trees are growing together. Note the honey locust trees here, a common pioneer tree that reforests clearings. This successional prairie adds another habitat to complement pure prairie and pure forest.

Big Darby Creek quietly flows through the trees to your left. You finally get an opportunity to come right along the waterway when a spur trail leads to the water's edge. The normally clear stream stretches about 30 to 40 feet wide. Occasional riffles break up the quiet pools. The waterway is known for its biodiversity, with over 100 species of fish and 43 species of mussels.

The Coneflower Trail carries on down the valley, with sycamores and sumacs complementing the high grasses. The farther south you go, the more likely you may get a little windborne traffic noise from I-70. The trail might be a little wet when you come alongside Bridenstine Ditch, which meets Big Darby Creek inside the park.

The hike turns back north and the Coneflower Trail once again meets the Darby Creek Greenway Trail. To extend your hike, follow the Darby Creek Greenway Trail as it crosses Bridenstine Ditch and meanders to the south boundary of Prairie Oaks Metro Park at I-70. It is about a mile each way, thus you would add around 2 miles to your hike. Otherwise continue north on the Coneflower Trail. Ahead, a spur leads left to the park's other picnic locale—Prairie View. It also has a covered shelter and restroom. All too soon the hike ends at the Whispering Oaks Picnic Area.

MILES AND DIRECTIONS

0.0 From the Whispering Oaks Picnic Area, pick up the gravel track leading southeast from the lower parking area. Follow the path a short distance to meet the Darby Creek Greenway Trail. Turn left here on a wide gravel track. At this point the Darby Creek Greenway Trail runs in conjunction with the Coneflower Trail. A couple of short spurs cut back to the Whispering Oaks Picnic Area.

0.3 The Darby Creek Greenway Trail and the Coneflower Trail split. Stay on the Coneflower Trail. (The Darby Creek Greenway Trail continues straight, then comes alongside Darby Creek to bridge the stream and continue through the park's east end.)

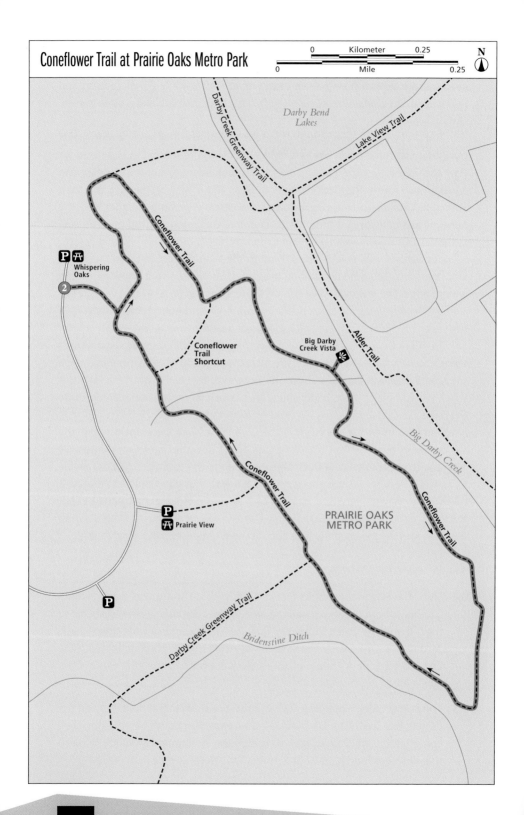

0   Kilometer   0.25

0   Mile   0.25

N

Darby Bend Lakes

Lake View Trail

Darby Creek Greenway Trail

Coneflower Trail

Whispering Oaks

2

Coneflower Trail Shortcut

Big Darby Creek Vista

Alder Trail

Big Darby Creek

Coneflower Trail

Prairie View

Coneflower Trail

PRAIRIE OAKS METRO PARK

Coneflower Trail

Darby Creek Greenway Trail

Bridenstine Ditch

0.5 Pass through a strip of woods and reach a trail junction. Here the Coneflower Trail Shortcut leaves right. Stay left with the Coneflower Trail. Travel through a successional prairie, where trees are growing up amid the grasses.

0.8 A spur trail leads left through the trees to the bank of Big Darby Creek. This is a good opportunity to appreciate this state scenic river.

1.4 The Coneflower Trail reaches its most southerly point in damp woods. The path now turns back northwest, traveling alongside the unusually named Bridenstine Ditch, a tributary of Big Darby Creek. Continue along the nexus of forest and field.

1.8 The Darby Creek Greenway Trail comes in on your left. Keep straight as the greenway and the Coneflower Trail run in conjunction.

1.9 A spur trail leads left to the Prairie View Picnic Area. Keep straight on the Coneflower Trail.

2.1 The Coneflower Shortcut comes in on your right. Stay straight.

2.2 Complete the loop portion of the hike and head left for the Whispering Oaks Picnic Area.

2.3 Arrive back at the trailhead.

🌿 **Green Tip:**
For rest stops, go off-trail so others won't have to get around you. Head for resilient surfaces without vegetation if possible.

Big Darby State Scenic River

Big Darby Creek and its major tributary, Little Darby Creek, were incorporated into the Ohio state scenic river system in 1984. The two streams together make for 84 miles of protected waterway. Located west of Columbus, Big Darby Creek is born among the wooded hills of southeastern Logan County. Even up here, the state has purchased parcels within the watershed, keeping its banks wooded and natural and its waters clean. Big Darby continues aiming toward Columbus, picking up tributaries in Union County. The stream turns due south after passing through Plains City, keeping greater Columbus to its east. This upper part of the Darby primarily travels through farmland.

Big Darby Creek enters Prairie Oaks Metro Park as a paddleable stream. The uppermost segment of the park includes a paddler access for canoes and kayaks. Skill level is Class I, with mostly easy riffles along with a few more lively shoals. There are outfitters in the area if you want to float the river. Trapper Johns Canoe Livery offers trips of varied lengths and distances along Big Darby Creek in the Prairie Oaks/Battelle Darby parks vicinity. Packages include shuttle and canoe or kayak rental. For more information, visit www.trapper johnscanoeing.com.

The natural shoreline of Prairie Oaks Metro Park helps keep the stream clean. The wooded lands can absorb floodwaters more readily, which prevents more devastating floods downstream. Also, the vegetated stream banks are less likely to erode, reducing sedimentary runoff and loss of topsoil.

The watershed of Big Darby encompasses over 550 square miles. Below I-70 Big Darby Creek cuts a deeper valley, with more extensive waterside woods. Little Darby Creek meets its mother stream in another protected area—Battelle Darby Metro Park. The now-bigger Big Darby Creek angles southeasterly again, eventually giving its waters to the Scioto River at Circleville. So whether you are hiking or paddling, the waters of Big Darby Creek—and its tributary Little Darby Creek—are a natural asset to greater Columbus.

Buck Creek State Park Shoreline Ramble

This out-and-back trek wanders the east shore of big C. J. Brown Reservoir, within the boundaries of Buck Creek State Park. Start near the park marina and enjoy immediate vistas of the lake. Undulate in woods, passing the park's cottages. Pass near the campground before ending at the campground swim beach, a swath of white sand that overlooks the biggest part of the impoundment. Consider adding water recreation or camping to your walk at this state park near Springfield.

Start: State park marina

Distance: 2.4 miles out and back

Hiking time: About 1.5 to 2 hours

Difficulty: Easy to moderate

Trail surface: Natural surface

Best season: Year-round

Other trail users: None

Canine compatibility: Leashed dogs permitted

Land status: Ohio state park

Fees and permits: None

Schedule: Open daily year-round

Maps: Buck Creek State Park; USGS New Moorefield

Trail Contact: Buck Creek State Park, 1901 Buck Creek Ln., Springfield, OH 45502; (937) 322-5284; www.dnr.state.ohio.us

Finding the trailhead: From exit 62 on I-70, west of downtown Columbus, near the town of Springfield, take US 40 west for 2.5 miles to a traffic light and Bird Road. Turn right on Bird Road and follow it 1.1 miles to a traffic light and Old Columbus Road. Keep straight at the light as the road you are driving changes to Buck Creek Road. Drive 0.9 mile farther, then turn right on Park Road 2, following signs for the marina. Drive 2 miles, then turn left and follow the park road 0.4 mile. Veer right to the north side of the marina, where you will see a sign on your right for the Lakeview Trail. Trailhead GPS: N39 57.434'/W83 43.205'

THE HIKE

The Buck Creek State Park website advertises over 9 miles of hiking trails, plus additional bridle trails. However, in reality their trail system is on the decline. This is unfortunate, since the setting of Buck Creek State Park is a fine one—the shoreline of C. J. Brown Reservoir, a large lake coming in at 2,100 acres. The state park has plenty of room to roam within its 1,800 land acres.

The park's longest trail, the 7.5-mile Buckhorn Trail on the west side of the lake, has not been maintained. The hike this trail follows, the Lakeview Trail, is advertised as 2 miles one way, but the upper portion of the path has disintegrated to an unmaintained track. Just as new trails become old, old trails can be revitalized. What we need to do is pester Ohio State Parks and tell them that we want more trails and we want the already existing trails kept in good condition. And we can help them do it. The squeaky wheel does get the grease in a lot of these parks. Due to the aquatic domination of this area, hiking trails have been placed on the back burner. It's a shame, since the park has wonderful potential hiking opportunities. That's why the trails were built in the first place.

The Lakeview Trail makes a wide path as it leaves the marina and travels north with the impoundment to your left and surprisingly high hills rising to your right. The water and slopes add scenic value to the hike. It's just a matter of feet before you come to a gravel beach on your left, with waves gently lapping on the shore.

The author overlooks rolling waves on a fine summer day.

The beach presents rewarding panoramas of the lake and is often used by bank fishermen. Unfortunately, they will sometimes leave litter. You will still appreciate the size of the impoundment as it stretches far to the western horizon. C. J. Brown Reservoir is one of Ohio's prettiest lakes, in my estimation.

The lake is more than just a pretty body of water, however. It prevents floods and also stores drinking water for the capital region's ever-expanding population. Also, it brings in tourist dollars, from hikers like us to anglers and swimmers and campers. The lake was named for a longtime politician from the area whose first job was Ohio State Statistician, back in 1916. (Who knew there was such a job?) He later served in the US House of Representatives. The congressional body, upon his death in 1965, voted to name the lake after him.

Oak, maple, and walnut trees shade the path as it traces the shoreline. Cottonwoods are some of the bigger trees you will see, along with white oaks. Other places will be evolving from field to forest. Blackberries and tangled brush border the track here.

The hike soon comes in proximity to the park campground. The large camping area avails sizable and scenic electric and non-electric campsites. I have camped here myself. An overnighter adds to the Buck Creek State Park experience. Views of the far lakeshore open in this area, and it is here where you will see old farm remnants, from fence lines to crumbling asphalt roads. The well-maintained part of the trail ends at a grassy area and the campground swim beach. The white sand and water have appeal during summer. A road leads from the campground to the beach, which is only open to campers. The main park has a separate day-use beach.

From here the Lakeview Trail once curved around the peninsula upon which the campground sits, then went on to meet the equestrian trails east of the lake. In the future the path may be cleared again. If so, you could add mileage to this hike and also potentially make a loop using the equestrian trails. User-created trails snake between the swim beach and the campground.

MILES AND DIRECTIONS

0.0 Start on the north end of the marina parking area. Pick up the Lakeview Trail as it enters woods, northbound. The lake is to your left. Soon come upon a gravel beach. Ahead, a grassy spur leads right uphill to a nearby picnic area.

0.4 Trails leave left to the water and right uphill to the park's rental cottages. The Lakeview Trail keeps straight, with the lake to your left.

0.5 After climbing a low hill, cross a road with park cottages along it.

0.8 The Lakeview Trail reaches the park campground. Campsites are easily within view. Turn left here, coming to an old concrete gate shaded by cherry, honey locust, and river birch.

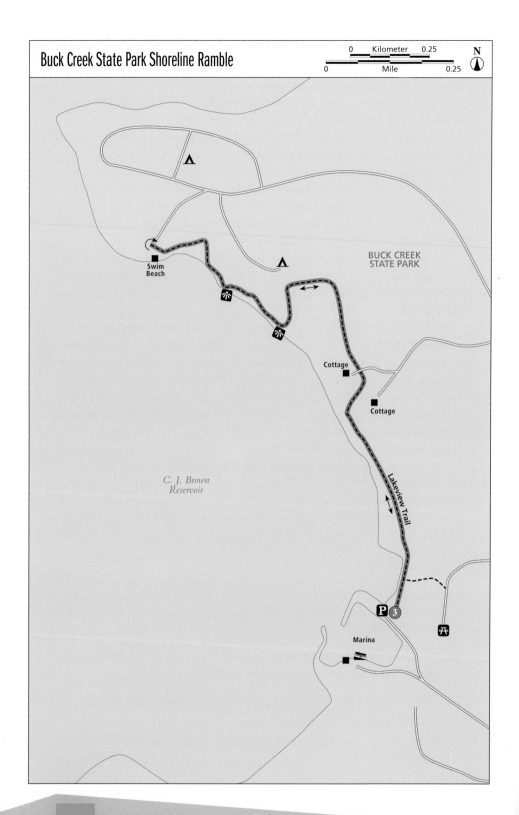

Buck Creek State Park Shoreline Ramble

0 Kilometer 0.25
0 Mile 0.25

N

Swim
Beach

BUCK CREEK
STATE PARK

Cottage

Cottage

C. J. Brown
Reservoir

Lakeview Trail

P 3

Marina

0.9 Come alongside the reservoir and open onto a view. Look back to the lake marina where you started. Continue along the lakeshore.

1.0 Come to another good view. Here you can gaze south at the lake dam.

1.2 Open onto the campground swim beach, which offers warm-weather swimming and broad lake panoramas. From here backtrack to the marina.

2.4 Complete the hike, arriving back at the state park marina.

The Crabill Homestead

On the west side of C. J. Brown Reservoir, opposite this hike, stands the Crabill Homestead. Constructed in the early 1820s and officially on the state tax rolls in 1826, the redbrick structure still stands regal and proud after nearly 200 years.

The landscape and means of travel were a little different back then—no paved roads and no lake for that matter—but somehow ol' David and Barbara Crabill drove a wagon here to what was then the northwestern frontier, leaving Virginia behind. After working on other Ohioans' farms, they finally scraped up the money to buy some acreage and built the house you see today. Imagine life on the farm back then, with the Crabills and their twelve children living in the house!

The Crabill family and their descendants occupied the Federal-style dwelling, now on the National Register of Historic Places, until the early 1900s. It sat forlorn for three score until the establishment of Buck Creek Lake. The US Army Corps of Engineers obtained the Crabill house and the land upon which it sat through eminent domain. The corps slated the house for demolition, but that didn't sit well with area residents. The Clark County Historical Society stepped in to save the day, funding the work needed to stabilize and preserve the house. Even after this first restoration, the home went through another period of neglect, but the George Rogers Clark Heritage Association has taken the Crabill House under its wing and things are looking up again.

Today living-history weekends are held on the homestead. The home and its outbuildings are worth a visit, and worth preserving. You can be a part of this volunteer effort. Home tours are held the third weekend of each month May through October from 1 to 3 p.m. For more information, visit www.crabill homestead.org.

Glacier Ridge Hike

Two trails add up to a varied experience at this Columbus Metro Park. Take the Red Oak Trail on a gravel path, exploring deciduous flatwoods, then join the asphalt Marsh Hawk Trail, looping through fields and meadows as well as woods. The first-rate, easy-to-follow trail system has little vertical variation, making for a relaxing trek used by locals for their daily exercise.

Start: Red Oak trailhead
Distance: 3.3-mile multiple loops
Hiking time: About 1.5 to 2.5 hours
Difficulty: Easy to moderate
Trail surface: Gravel and asphalt
Best season: Sept through May; can be hot in summer
Other trail users: Joggers and bicyclists
Canine compatibility: Leashed dogs permitted on Marsh Hawk Trail

Land status: Metro Parks
Fees and permits: None
Schedule: Open daily year-round, 6:30 a.m. to dark
Maps: Glacier Ridge Metro Park; USGS Shawnee Hills
Trail contact: Metro Parks, 1069 W. Main St., Westerville, OH 43081; (614) 891-0700; www.metroparks.net

Finding the trailhead: From exit 17 on I-270, northwest of downtown Columbus, take US 33 west to the Post Road/Plain City exit. Turn right on Post Road and follow it 0.1 mile, then turn left on Hyland Croy Road. Follow Hyland Croy Road for 3.2 miles (do not turn into the lower end of Glacier Ridge Park at the Honda Wetland Education Center) to the main entrance of Glacier Ridge Park. Pass the barn on your left, then circle right around the auto loop, reaching the Red Oak Trail parking area on the south side of the auto loop at 0.9 mile from the park entrance. Trailhead GPS: N40 9.267'/W83 11.613'

THE HIKE

I t is hard to believe that the first Columbus metro park was established back in 1945. How prescient that was, to begin setting aside land for residents of greater Columbus to enjoy and explore while simultaneously preserving the natural qualities of these parks. Today the Metro Parks system presents fifteen parks covering over 23,000 acres in seven counties in and around Columbus.

Columbus continues to grow, and the area between Dublin and Marysville, once farms and villages, is fast morphing into houses and shopping centers. Luckily, Metro Parks established Glacier Ridge Park in 2002. The 1,036-acre preserve is managed toward restoring its natural amenities, including woodlands, meadows, wetlands, and prairies. A wetland education center and a wind/solar demonstration area provide environmental education. Traditional picnic shelters and playgrounds round out the amenities. Located in four distinct parcels (though the three biggest are connected by narrow land strips), the park melds into the schools and neighborhoods growing around them.

The good news is these varied tracts are all connected by a trail system. The trails, mostly asphalt greenways, not only tie the various tracts of the park together

Ironweed rises beside the trail.

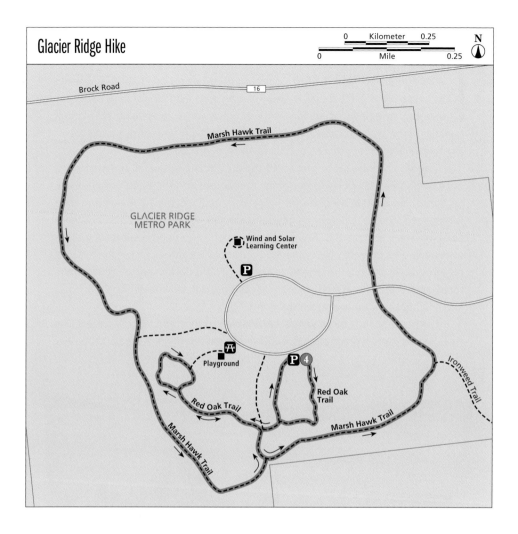

0   Kilometer   0.25

0   Mile   0.25

N

Brock Road   16

Marsh Hawk Trail

GLACIER RIDGE
METRO PARK

Wind and Solar
Learning Center

P

Playground

P 4

Red Oak
Trail

Red Oak Trail

Marsh Hawk Trail

Ironweed Trail

Marsh Hawk Trail

as one, but also bond the park and nearby schools through neighborhood greenways. This way walkers, joggers, and bicyclists can get around the vicinity while
crossing a minimum number of roads.

This hike sticks to the northernmost parcel of Glacier Ridge Park, so named for
the low ridge that remained after ancient glaciers melted. Here the park is working
to restore native grasslands and prairie to the landscape, giving wildlife a home.
You will first wander the shady woods via the hiker-only Red Oak Trail. Deciduous
flatwoods with plenty of maple, beech, and red oak grow tall, creating a high canopy. The Red Oak Trail takes you to another section of woods after passing through
successional terrain. Watch for a huge red oak to the left of the trail while looping
near the picnic shelters.

The next part your hike joins the Marsh Hawk Trail. While it does travel through some woodlands, it primarily tours meadow and prairie. The Marsh Hawk Trail is a good trail choice when natural-surface trails become muddy. It can also be a favorable wintertime hike, especially on a sunny day. Consider taking this trail in the morning or evening during the heat of summer. Civilization is visible, but such views make the park all the more valuable. Along the way you will pass the Iron-weed Trail, which links this area to the other parts of the park. If you want to extend your hike, the Ironweed Trail will do the trick.

The Marsh Hawk Trail circles around the north side of the park. The wind tur-bine of the wind/solar learning center is visible to your left. Hike among prairie grasses, then turn south past wetlands and woodlands. The shade is a nice change from the open prairie. The hike finally leads back to the Red Oak Trail and a short section of gravel path that returns to the parking area.

MILES AND DIRECTIONS

0.0 Facing south from the parking area, you will see two branches of the Red Oak Trail entering the woods. Take the trail on your left, or easterly side, heading south into the woods. A disc golf course leaves from the most southeasterly end of this parking area.

0.2 Reach a trail intersection. Here a branch of the Red Oak Trail leaves right for the parking area where you started. Stay left with another branch of the Red Oak Trail. Just ahead, cross an asphalt branch of the Marsh Hawk Trail. Keep straight on the Red Oak Trail and open onto a meadow.

0.3 Pass through a strip of oaks and pines, then enter successional habitat tran-sitioning from field to trees.

0.4 Begin the loop portion of the Red Oak Trail, reentering full-blown forest, traveling clockwise. Along the way, pass a spur leading to the playground and picnic shelter. Complete the loop and begin backtracking.

0.8 Return to the branch of the asphalt Marsh Hawk Trail and turn right, soon beginning the loop portion of the Marsh Hawk Trail. Turn left this time, now going counterclockwise. The path enters forest. You will see the equestrian trail nearby. Please stay off this trail—it is open only to horseback riders. Open onto meadow. You can see parts of the park's disc golf course here.

1.3 The Ironweed Trail leaves right for points south in Glacier Ridge Park. The Marsh Hawk Trail keeps north in open terrain.

1.4 Cross the park entrance road.

1.8 The Marsh Hawk Trail turns west.

2.3 The Marsh Hawk Trail turns south. Pass a cattail-lined wetland before reentering forest.

2.7 An asphalt spur trail leads left to the auto loop near the picnic shelter.

3.1 An asphalt spur leads left, north, to soon reach the Red Oak Trail. Turn right onto the Red Oak Trail. Pass the spur to the mini-loop then continue straight toward the trailhead.

3.3 Open onto the parking area where you started, completing the hike.

Wind and Solar: Pieces of the Energy Puzzle

Here at Glacier Ridge Park you can see upclose a demonstration of wind and solar energy systems. The solar panels and wind turbine were erected to educate the public on these two forms of American energy generation.

The wind turbine stands atop a 120-foot metal tower. You will see this tower during most of your hike. The tower was ahead of its time, erected in 2002, and was the first publicly owned wind turbine in the Buckeye State. Notice the tower's placement, in open terrain, away from trees, to maximize the wind. Over the course of a year, wind speeds at the tower average 13 to 15 mile per hour, a little below the average desired for the large-scale turbines coming into increasing use. Ohio's strongest winds come off Lake Erie to the north, and this is where the future of the state's plant-scale wind energy development will be.

The solar panels and the battery storage system display another component of energy generation. The power from this solar system, along with the wind turbine, lights the park's restrooms and picnic shelter. Excess power is sold back to the energy utility that manages the area's power, Union Rural Electric.

In the future solar panels will be a regular component of stand-alone, single-household energy generation systems. While on a mission trip in Haiti, I saw how a country without central energy generation and management systems is going the route of individual home energy systems. As solar and wind energy, as well as the battery systems used to store the energy, become more efficient, the more it will be used, becoming a bigger piece in our national energy puzzle.

Blues Creek Preserve

This hike at a nature-oriented Delaware County park explores a patchwork of stream, woodlands, wetlands, and hills, as well as restored prairie, all on well-marked and maintained trails that make for an ideal casual walk. Start at the preserve's north end, visiting Blues Creek and adjacent riparian lands. The hike then turns into tall forest and makes a loop into a prairie before visiting a managed wetland. Reach the main area of the park, a large restored prairie mixed with small wetlands, enhancing wildlife habitat. Finally, tour the picnic area and a fishing pond on your return trip.

Start: Trailhead parking just off Fontanelle Road

Distance: 2.8-mile triple loop

Hiking time: About 1.5 to 2.5 hours

Difficulty: Moderate

Trail surface: Gravel and natural surface

Best season: Year-round; July and Aug for prairie wildflowers

Other trail users: None

Canine compatibility: Leashed dogs permitted

Land status: Delaware County preservation park

Fees and permits: None

Schedule: Open daily year-round, 8 a.m. to sunset

Maps: Blues Creek Preserve; USGS Ostrander

Trail contact: Preservation Parks of Delaware County, 2656 Hogback Rd., Sunbury, OH 43074; (740) 524-8600; www.preservation parks.com

Finding the trailhead: From exit 17 on I-270, northwest of downtown Columbus, take US 33 north to US 42. Turn right on US 42 and follow it north 3.7 miles to Jerome Road. Turn left on Jerome Road and follow it 0.8 mile to Watkins Road. Turn left on Watkins Road and follow it 0.3 mile to State Road. Turn right on State Road and follow it north as it becomes Main Street as it passes through the village of Ostrander, then becomes Ostrander Road north of town. Drive a total of 5 miles from Watkins Road to Fontanelle Road. Turn left on Fontanelle Road and follow it 1.1 miles to reach Blues Creek Preserve on your left. After turning into the preserve, immediately look for a parking area on the right. The hike starts on the south side of the park entrance road. Trailhead GPS: N40 16.997'/W83 14.442'

THE HIKE

lues Creek Preserve is a newer-style nature park. Rather than being simply a recreation park with your typical ball fields, tennis courts, disc golf course, and such, these nature parks first and foremost emphasize preserving the natural landscape and even improve the area, bringing it back to its historic natural state or restoring former ecosystems. The park facilities are then integrated into the land rather than the land conforming or otherwise being altered to fit the facilities.

This is especially important in fast-growing urban areas like greater Columbus. It was clear to many residents of Delaware County that some open spaces and

A bee explores a coneflower at Blues Creek Preserve.

natural lands should be preserved before greater Columbus gobbled up the whole county. Thus the preservation parks were established. They provide passive recreation activities while keeping development to a minimum. Trails are established to allow people to visit the parks without adversely impacting the natural ecosystems preserved within. The voters of Delaware County approved a property tax to pay for this program. With the help of donors, other monies, and the time of volunteers, these preservation parks are thriving.

What became Blues Creek Preserve was initially purchased in 1993. Today the park now totals nearly 140 acres. Hiking trails, a primary picnicking area, and a pond are the only developments to the park other than restoring ecosystems, such as the prairies that provide colorful wildflower viewing in July and August.

Your hike first explores the bottoms along Blues Creek, growing in succession from field to forest. Walnuts and locusts are leading the way for the trees. The path then arcs over the waterway on a graceful bridge. Head south on the Shagbark Loop Trail, tracing the margin of field and forest. Parts of the field are repopulating with trees. This process, known as periodic succession, will be favorable for different species of plants and animals as the composition changes, culminating in the beech-maple woodlands that once covered much of central Ohio. You'll pass the main park facilities on your right while heading for the rear of the preserve, literally the back 40 acres, acquired in 1999.

After nearing a wetland on your right, you will make two separate loops. The first loop travels through hardwoods dominated by shagbark hickory, giving the trail its name. The second loop travels through restored prairie, offering a total contrast to the first loop. You will then leave the back 40 and return to the main part of the park, making a circuit through the hilly restored prairie and wetlands. A well-timed hike in mid- to late July will reward you with incredible prairie wildflowers, thanks to the efforts at prairie restoration. Beyond the prairie ramble, take a tour of the picnic area and fishing pond before rejoining the Shagbark Loop Trail and backtracking to the trailhead.

MILES AND DIRECTIONS

0.0 Start across the road from the parking area. Walk south on a grassy connector trail amid low-slung woods. The trail soon splits; head left.

0.1 Cross the attractive curved iron bridge over Blues Creek. Continue walking south, now on a wide gravel track, the Shagbark Loop Trail.

0.2 A trail leaves right for the hilltop picnic area and will be your return route. Keep southbound on the Shagbark Loop Trail. Gain a look at the park's fishing pond.

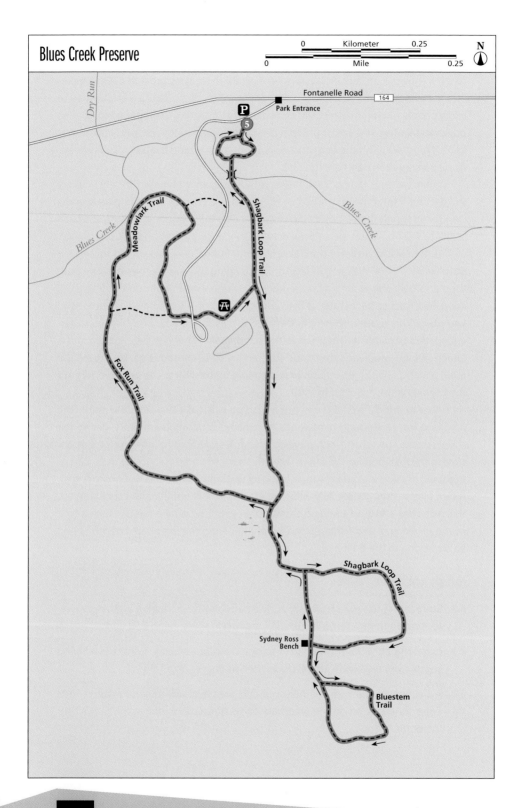

Blues Creek Preserve

0 — Kilometer — 0.25
0 — Mile — 0.25

N

Dry Run

Fontanelle Road
164
Park Entrance

P
5

Meadowlark Trail

Blues Creek

Blues Creek

Shagbark Loop Trail

Fox Run Trail

Shagbark Loop Trail

Sydney Ross Bench

Bluestem Trail

0.6 Reach a trail intersection. Here the path splits right to the prairie but keep straight, still southbound on the Shagbark Loop Trail, passing a wetland on your right.

0.7 Come to the loop portion of the Shagbark Loop Trail. Turn left here in a forest of ash, buckeye, and hickory, bridging a streambed. Begin wandering easterly, then south, crossing another boardwalk. Eventually turn west.

1.0 Complete the Shagbark Loop Trail. Note the bench at this trail intersection. It is dedicated to Sydney Ross, who loved wildflowers and strove to identify every one she saw. Turn left on the Bluestem Trail, a grassy track that leaves the woods for open prairie. Stay left at the loop portion of the Bluestem Trail. Note the bird boxes in the prairie grasses.

1.4 Return to the contemplation bench dedicated to Sydney Ross. From here hike northerly.

1.5 Complete the Shagbark Loop Trail. Backtrack past the wetland, now on your left.

1.6 Turn left, now on the Fox Run Trail. You are walking through mostly prairie but cross a thin strip of woods on a boardwalk before coming to the balance of the prairie. Look for small vernal pools amid the hilly grasses.

2.0 The Fox Run Trail leaves right to the picnic area. Keep straight on the grassy track, joining the Meadowlark Trail. It soon bisects a forest stand of hackberry and honey locust, then comes alongside the wooded margin of Blues Creek.

2.2 A spur trail leads left to the park access road. Stay right, rolling through hills and traveling south away from Blues Creek.

2.4 Turn left at an intersection. A spur leads right, to the nearby sledding hill. Shortly reach and pass through the picnic area, with its playground, shelters, and pond. Keep east toward the Shagbark Loop Trail.

2.5 Turn left on the Shagbark Loop Trail, backtracking to the bridge over Blues Creek. Beyond the bridge, head left, picking up a short segment of new trail.

2.8 Arrive back at the trailhead, completing the hike.

Restoring Ohio's Prairies

Blues Creek Preserve is but one place where Ohio's prairies are being restored. It is estimated that between 2 and 4 percent of Ohio's landmass was prairie prior to American settlement. Ohio's prairies are covered with special grasses and flowers native to such openings. Big bluestem is the main grass. You have seen but maybe not identified prairie wildflowers—purple coneflower, New England aster, and stiff goldenrod to name a few.

Interestingly, Ohio's prairies simply wouldn't be except for the intervention of man. Prairies are normally found in dry regions to the west. Around 5,000 years ago Ohio's climate was much drier and thus not completely wooded over, but then the climate became moister and forests threatened to overtake the prairie. Ohio's native people recognized the value of prairies and thus regularly burned them, prohibiting the encroachment of forests. These prairies attracted wildlife, especially deer, which feasted on the rich grasses. American Indians were dependent upon deer not only for food but also for other things obtained from the carcass, such as leather from the hide and tools from the antlers.

From the Indians we learned that the deep-rooted grasses and wildflowers not only can withstand fire, but fires are necessary for the perpetuation of the prairie species. Regular burning is done here at Blues Creek Preserve to enrich the prairie and restore it to a natural state. Prescribed burns are undertaken in winter or spring, when the prairie growth is dead, waiting to emerge during the warm season. Also, wildlife such as fox and deer are less likely to be roaming the prairie during the colder seasons, when the prairie is dormant.

Stratford Ecological Center Hike

Visit a living farm, where you can hike and experience agricultural practices up close. Visitors can even buy farm products in season! The hike itself is a very rewarding one. Start on the Swamp Trail and enter the 95-acre Stratford Woods State Nature Preserve. Explore a buttonbush swamp before turning back south. Here the Well Loop Trail leads along a creek where excellent spring wildflowers carpet the forest floor. See acres of trillium blooming in spring, and pass an old well from days gone by. Continue working downstream and join the Sugar Shack Trail. Here you will pass a maple syrup–making operation. The Cemetery Trail leads uphill to where early Delaware County residents are interred. From here the Hush Trail opens to a pond. Work your way back through the demonstration farm, completing the trek.

Start: Visitor center parking area

Distance: 2.4-mile loop

Hiking time: About 1.5 to 2 hours

Difficulty: Moderate

Trail surface: Natural surface

Best seasons: Spring for wildflowers, summer and fall for farming fun

Other trail users: None

Canine compatibility: Pets not permitted in preserve

Land status: Private ecological preserve

Fees and permits: None; donation requested

Schedule: Open Mon through Fri 9 a.m. to 5 p.m., Sat 9 a.m. to 1 p.m.; closed Sun and holidays

Maps: Stratford Ecological Center; USGS Delaware

Trail contact: Stratford Ecological Center, 3083 Liberty Rd., Delaware, OH 43015; (740) 363-2548; www.stratfordecologicalcenter.org

Finding the trailhead: From exit 23 on I-270, north of downtown Columbus, take US 23 north for 10.3 miles to OH 315 / Olentangy River Road and a traffic light. Follow OH 315 for 0.2 mile to Bunty Station Road. Turn right on Bunty Station Road and follow it 1 mile to Liberty Road. Turn right on Liberty Road and follow it 0.2 mile to Stratford Ecological Center on your right. Enter the preserve and drive 0.4 mile. Park near the visitor center. Trailhead GPS: N39 40.916' / W82 34.560'

6

THE HIKE

t took many twists of fate for the Stratford Ecological Center to evolve into what it is today. Back in the early 1980s, one Gale Warner interned at a demonstration farm and environmental education facility in California. Her experience was profound, and she shared the event with her mother, Louise Warner. It just so happened Louise had inherited 236 acres from her father, who had bought the land as investment property. But after Gale shared her vision of a living farm, what was to be a golf course bordered with houses would instead become the Stratford Ecological Center, a place of environmental education and farming education, as in city kids learning about where food actually comes from.

Unfortunately, young Gale was struck down by cancer before the center came to be, but in her mother's eyes, Gale's passing cemented the notion of establishing the ecological center. Louise Warner saw this part of Delaware County as an expanding development area, with greater Columbus heading north and the town of Delaware moving south. In hopes of protecting the land long-term, Louise brought out state officials to examine the tract for unique qualities that might result in its preservation as a state nature preserve. On a first visit, officials saw nothing special about the property to warrant state nature preserve status, but Louise didn't give up. She had the state DNR people come out in spring, when the

Spring wildflowers border the Well Loop Trail.

wildflowers were in bloom. This superlative wildflower display, along with a wetland buttonbush swamp, convinced the state to declare 95 acres of the property a state nature preserve. This strengthened the long-term possibilities of keeping this area in a primitive condition.

Over time an education center was built for visitors, and personnel began guiding schoolkids and other youth groups throughout the demonstration farm and the preserve's natural areas. The tours became a hit, and they go on to this day. You will see the fields that produce the farm products that are for sale, which not only provide a tangential link from farm to market, but also creates revenue for this private preserve. So when you come here, make sure to buy something and/or make a donation to help keep this jewel of greater Columbus up and running.

The hike itself is enough of a draw without the demonstration farm even being here. You will start on the foreboding-sounding Swamp Trail. Yes, it might be a little sloppy in spring, but the Swamp Trail offers a chance to view a wooded wetland with vernal pools. The trail will be a little drier from late summer through fall. The hike along creek bottoms will be a cornucopia of color in spring. A visit to the cemetery adds a time perspective to the land. Finally, a walk through the demo farm will be enlightening.

Maple Syrup—the Pioneer Sweetener

Stratford Ecological Center has what is known as a sugar shack—a building where maple sap is converted to maple syrup. American pioneers used whatever resources they could find in the great forests of the eighteenth and nineteenth centuries. They couldn't go to the grocery and get raw sugar or the myriad forms of artificial sweeteners we take for granted today. If they couldn't grow it or create it, they likely did without it. Today when looking at a sugar maple, we see a pretty tree producing golden leaves in autumn. The pioneers saw sugar and a trade product.

Even today maple syrup is made in Ohio, primarily in the northeast part of the state. Over 100,000 gallons are produced each year. First the sap must be tapped from the maple trees during the "sugar season," which runs from February through the middle of March in the Buckeye State. This is when the sap begins to move through the tree. It is collected in buckets (though hoses are used in the modern process) then boiled, removing the excess water, at the "sugar house" such as the one you pass on this hike. The liquid is then lowered to a precise temperature before being put in containers. You then have good stuff not only to pour over pancakes but also to flavor sweet treats, make candy, and make granulated maple sugar. Next time you are at the market, check the label to buy Ohio-made maple sugar products.

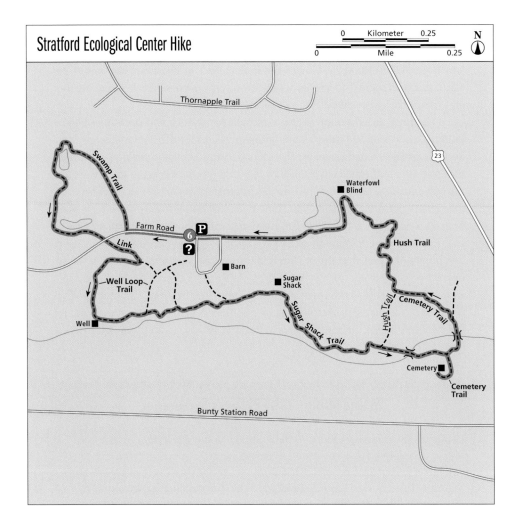

Stratford Ecological Center Hike

Thornapple Trail

Swamp Trail

Waterfowl Blind

23

Farm Road

P

6

?

Link

Hush Trail

Well Loop Trail

Barn

Sugar Shack

Well

Sugar Shack Trail

Hush Trail

Cemetery Trail

Cemetery

Cemetery Trail

Bunty Station Road

0 Kilometer 0.25

0 Mile 0.25

N

MILES AND DIRECTIONS

0.0 Start by walking back down the entrance road. When you reach a line of woods, look for the signed Swamp Trail leading right, northbound. Follow the singletrack path into maple, ash oak, and hickory woods.

0.3 Come to a vernal pond and begin curving around the seasonal buttonbush swamp. Circle around the pond, turning back south on a potentially muddy track. Curve past a second wetland.

0.5 Cross to the south side of the park entrance road and join the Link Trail. Continue cruising tall flatwoods with a light understory.

0.7 Turn right on the Well Loop Trail and hike toward the unnamed creek south of the demonstration farm. The forest will be carpeted with violets, Solomon seal, and mayapple in spring. Bridge a tributary twice while dipping toward the main stream, which drains into the nearby Olentangy River.

0.8 Pass the stoned-in well for which the Well Loop Trail is named. It lies in bottomland beside the creek, which indicates that the main creek south of the farm will dry up during summer and fall. However, in spring the streamside will be a riot of color, including purple phlox, maroon bent trillium, and white trillium.

0.9 The Well Loop Trail leaves left for the visitor center. Stay right and join the Creek Trail, continuing through moist woods near the creek.

1.1 Climb toward the farm barn, joining the Sugar Shack Trail. Walk behind the farm facilities.

1.4 Bridge a ravine and find the sugar shack, a maple syrup operation building. A grassy track leads left to fields. Stay right in the woods.

1.5 Come to another intersection. Here the Hush Trail leads left. Turn right with the Cemetery Trail, then drop off a hill to bridge the creek.

1.6 Turn right on the spur trail to reach the early Ohioan cemetery.

1.7 Top out on the hill at the cemetery. Most of the carved headstones are illegible due to weathering. Many of those interred here passed away in the early to mid-1800s, and the cemetery also includes Civil War veterans. Backtrack, then continue the loop, crossing the creek one last time. Watch for, then join a trail climbing the hill to your left. Do not take the wrong track, which keeps straight and opens to a grassy field. This can be a confusing area, but the correct path is singletrack.

1.9 Meet the Hush Trail, which comes in on your left. Stay right and meander through hills and hollows. The path can be a little overgrown here.

2.1 Open onto the east side of the farm field. You are near a pond. Look for wildlife through the blind, then head left, around the pond. Soon join a farm road heading west for the visitor center parking area. Watch for farm critters in the adjacent pens.

2.4 Arrive back at the visitor center parking area, finishing the hike.

Deer Haven Preserve

This hike combines trails at Deer Haven Preserve, a Delaware County preservation park, with paths at Havener Park, which also has traditional ball fields and such. You will cruise through the wooded watersheds of Havener Park before entering the preserve, where protection of the natural habitat is paramount. Walk through meadows, a restored prairie, and a steep ridge, and across the creek valleys. The hike also stops by an old pond where you can view wildlife from behind a blind. Big trees await out here and on the return journey.

Start: North end of parking area at Havener Park

Distance: 3.1-mile multiple loops

Hiking time: About 2 to 2.5 hours

Difficulty: Moderate

Trail surface: Pea gravel

Best season: Year-round

Other trail users: None

Canine compatibility: Leashed dogs permitted in Havener Park and at Deer Haven Preserve on the Pet Trail only

Land status: Delaware County park

Fees and permits: None

Schedule: Open daily year-round

Maps: Deer Haven Preserve; USGS Powell

Trail contact: Preservation Parks of Delaware County, 2556 Hogback Rd., Sunbury, OH 43074; (740) 524-8600; www.preservation parks.com

Finding the trailhead: From exit 23 on I-270, north of downtown Columbus, take US 23 north for 10.3 miles to OH 315/Olentangy River Road and a traffic light. Follow OH 315 for 0.2 mile to Bunty Station Road. Turn right on Bunty Station Road and follow it 1 mile to Liberty Road. Turn left on Liberty Road and follow it 0.6 mile to Havener Park on your left. Turn into the park, then make the first left and follow the road to the north end of the parking area, near some soccer fields on the park boundary. The Havener Park trails start here. Trailhead GPS: N40 14.739' / W83 4.858'

THE HIKE

I f you have two parks side-by-side and they both have trails, and both trail systems connect to one another, that can add up to a pretty decent hike. Here in Delaware County, a little west of the Olentangy River, Havener Park and Deer Haven Preserve sit side-by-side and are connected by trails. Though managed differently, the two parks complement each other and effectively double the available green space and trail mileage for this locale, situated just south of the town of Delaware. Since the elevation changes are fairly minimal and the trail system is tight and interconnected, it makes for a good family hike, especially if you have less-able trail trekkers, such as young children or senior citizens.

The hike starts out innocuous enough as it follows a mown path near some ball fields. It soon enters woods and comes alongside a creek. The two properties, Havener Park and Deer Haven Preserve, both feature streams draining easterly into the Olentangy River. These creeks cut little valleys, thus adding vertical variation to the terrain. As you loop along the north end of Havener Park, a farm provides contrast to the more natural parkland. However, as time goes on, this farm will likely become a subdivision, probably sooner rather than later. Such is life in a growing metropolitan area like greater Columbus. But that fact makes parks like this more

The early morning sun shines on a restored prairie at Deer Haven Preserve.

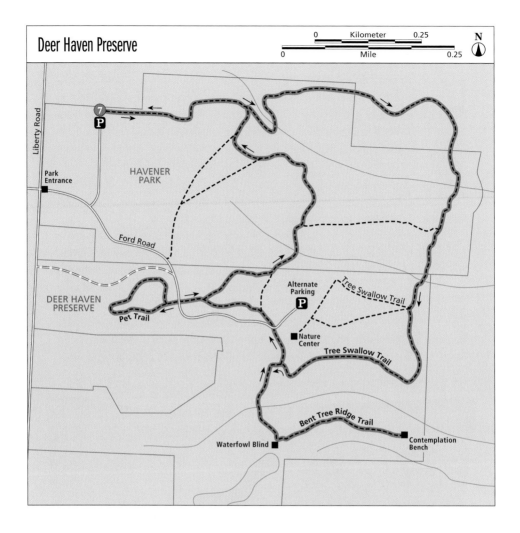

valuable and also validates the mission statement of the Delaware County preservation parks: "to protect open space and unique natural habitats for the public good."

The trail then passes through a meadow being restored to a prairie before turning south. Here it crosses a couple of the aforementioned streams. Wildflowers are abundant in these moist streamside areas. Look for purple phlox, white trillium, pale violets, and more in season. Then you reach Deer Haven Preserve. Environmental restoration and preservation is more intense here, as Delaware County works to reestablish the natural ecosystems, whether they are forest, wetlands, prairie, or something in between. Prescribed fire is even used at Deer Haven.

The preserve is the setting for environmental education for everybody from school groups to ordinary citizens. The preservation parks system is funded by a levy approved by Delaware County residents, much in the same way as Metro

Parks are funded in nearby Franklin County and other adjoining areas. Deer Haven Preserve stretches over 97 acres donated to the county by Phyllis A. Havener. Her family used the area as a summer retreat many decades ago, when this was but a rural backwater.

The hike passes through a restored prairie before curving onto a bluff in hardwoods. It then drops to a stream and cruises along a slender ridgeline that is a highlight of the hike. Here you pass a long-disused farm pond before heading out on this narrow hilltop, which spills into flower-laden hollows that offer beauty year-round. A contemplation bench lies at the trail's end and is a good place to reflect. After backtracking, reach the preservation park nature center. Hours vary but you can certainly learn more about the environmental character of Delaware County here. Next, pick up the Pet Trail as it heads out to another prairie. The last part of the hike returns you to Havener Park.

But just because you've left the preserve doesn't mean the beauty quits. In fact, some of the largest trees along the hike are found upon reentering Havener Park. All too soon the ball fields and parking area come into view. If you are like me, you'll be wishing the hike was a little longer, but at least we can appreciate these two parks being adjacent to one another, doubling the hiking mileage.

MILES AND DIRECTIONS

0.0 Start by walking a gravel track east, away from the Havener Park parking area. A farm stands to your left and ball fields stretch off to your right. Enter woods of ash, hickory, and oak.

0.2 The trail splits; stay left here, going for the maximum loop. Shortly dip to cross a stream by culvert. Keep easterly on the northern edge of the property.

0.5 Open onto a meadow undergoing reestablishment as a prairie, featuring switchgrass, Indian grass, and little bluegrass. This restoration is being done in open areas both here and at Deer Haven Preserve. The trail meanders through the heart of the prairie.

0.6 Look to your left for a partially filled farm pond beside which stands a massive old-growth oak.

0.7 Reenter woodlands, then bridge a creek.

0.8 Reach a trail intersection. Here a path (none of the trails in Havener Park are named) leads right to shortcut the loop. Keep straight, southbound, to soon enter Deer Haven Preserve, a designated bird sanctuary. Note the abundance of bird boxes about.

0.9 A boardwalk bridges a wetland. Note the cottonwoods. Just ahead come to another trail intersection. Here the Tree Swallow Trail leaves right toward the

Deer Haven Preserve nature center and left past an open prairie. Stay left, passing through the prairie to shortly reenter hardwoods.

1.3 Intersect the Bent Tree Ridge Trail very near the nature center. Turn left here and descend to bridge a stream.

1.4 Reach an old farm pond and wildlife blind. Peer through the slits in the wooden wall to observe waterfowl. From here keep easterly on the Bent Tree Ridge Trail. Sharp-sided stream valleys drop off on both sides of the pathway. Look for big beech trees, northern red oaks, and white oaks scattered in the forest.

1.6 Reach the end of the Bent Tree Ridge Trail. Take a moment for contemplation here in this scenic spot, then backtrack toward the nature center.

1.9 Reach the Tree Swallow Trail and turn left, passing the nature center. To continue the hike, cross the entrance road and look for a mown path leading left. Join the Pet Trail as another mown path leads right, north, back toward Havener Park.

2.0 Cross the preserve entrance road and make a loop through a restored prairie. In late summer the prairie will rise over your head. After recrossing the preserve entrance road, split left toward Havener Park.

2.5 Reenter Havener Park. Walk north under a tall canopy of old-growth trees, especially big oaks.

2.6 Stay left as a trail leads right.

2.9 Complete the loop portion of the hike at a trail intersection. Stay left here and backtrack to the trailhead.

3.1 Arrive back at the parking area at Havener Park, completing the hike.

> 🍂 **Green Tip:**
> *Leave old farm and homesite relics for others to discover and enjoy for themselves.*

Highbanks Hike

This hike visits most of the highlights at Highbanks Metro Park. From the nature center, walk along steep shale ravines and through forest to a meadow observation deck. Next, head past a homesite and re-created cemetery of early area settlers. Hike by prehistoric earthworks from aboriginal Ohioans before reaching an overlook 110 feet above the Olentangy State Scenic River, then visit a wildlife blind astride a wetland. Finally, stop by a burial mound left by the ancient Adena Indians. The well-marked and maintained trails are not too steep, making this hike doable by most trail enthusiasts.

Start: Highbanks Park Nature Center
Distance: 5.6-mile double loop with out-and-backs
Hiking time: About 3.5 to 4 hours
Difficulty: Moderate; does have some hills
Trail surface: Gravel, natural surface, and a little asphalt
Best season: Year-round
Other trail users: Joggers

Canine compatibility: Dogs not permitted on these trails
Land status: Metro Parks
Fees and permits: None
Schedule: Open daily year-round
Maps: Highbanks Metro Park; USGS Powell
Trail contact: Metro Parks, 1069 W. Main St., Westerville, OH 43081; (614) 891-0700; www .metroparks.net

Finding the trailhead: From exit 23 on I-270, north of downtown Columbus, take US 23 north for 2.7 miles, then turn left into Highbanks Park. Travel 0.3 mile and turn right into the nature center. Park here. Trailhead GPS: N40 9.103'/W83 1.464'

THE HIKE

This hike is a rolling highlight reel. Your first order of business is to visit the fine nature center, with its exhibits, library, and pertinent information concerning the park's human and natural history. You will learn about the land's past—both ancient and recent—from the people of the Cole Culture, who built the horseshoe-shaped earthworks bordered by the Olentangy River, to more recent settlers who farmed what is now the park. The park has reverted back to nature— and part of Highbanks is set aside as the Edward F. Hutchins Nature Preserve. This 206-acre tract within the Metro Park protects the fragile shale bluffs and attendant life along the Olentangy River. It is these bluffs that gave the park its name.

Fragile shale bluffs lie within Edward F. Hutchins State Nature Preserve.

You will see smaller versions of these shale bluffs at the hike's beginning, on the Dripping Rock Trail. Here ancient glacial melt cut through the shale, exposing crumbly rock walls. Your best views of shale bluffs will be when the path bridges ravines. Overhead, white oak, sugar maple, wild cherry, beech, and shagbark hickory trees shade the trail and display favorable fall color. The wide, lightly graveled path makes for user-friendly walking, so you won't be tangling with joggers and other hikers when encountering one another. The woodland walk is interrupted by a visit to a meadow and observation deck. Watch for deer in the morning and evening. Ahead, the path wanders through a "controlled succession area," nature-speak for a field being left to grow back to woods. This process can take a full five decades. These successional woods are especially favorable for birdlife, with habitats that are neither mono-field nor total forestation.

The path comes alongside more ravines, some so steep that trailside fences have been erected to prevent accidents. Skirt the Big Meadows Picnic Area and come close to the Olentangy River before climbing past more ravines. You then get into the potentially busy Oak Coves Picnic Area, the favorite outdoor dining spot at Highbanks Park.

The Overlook Trail takes you into the south end of Highbanks Park and its many highlights. The first is the spur to an old homesite and the re-created cemetery of the Pool family, which settled the area. Their headstones were found in the park but the actual grave sites were never established, so the stones were moved here. This is a rewarding area to explore and see Ohio's settler past firsthand. Look around the homesite and see if you can picture the location of the house and other buildings.

Ahead, enter the Edward F. Hutchins State Nature Preserve and come to remnants of aboriginal Ohioans—the earthworks of the Woodland Indians. The semi-circular earthworks are unmistakable, and the trail actually travels over the land relics on the way to the Olentangy River overlook. A wooden deck stretches out atop the high shale bluff and allows views down to the state scenic river flowing south. It is easy to see why this area was known as Highbanks.

Your next highlight takes an often-skipped spur to a shallow pond, managed as a wetland. A boardwalk steers you to a blind, where slits in the wooden structure allows viewing of migratory birds and other critters without their knowing. Most success will be had in the morning and evening. Your return trip leads to the more heavily used part of Highbanks and the Dripping Rock Trail. A final side trip takes you to an Adena burial mound. Though today the low mound seems a simple grassy knoll, understand that most mounds such as this have been erased over time, and Columbians are lucky to have this somber site preserved. From the mound it is but a short distance back to the nature center to finish the hike.

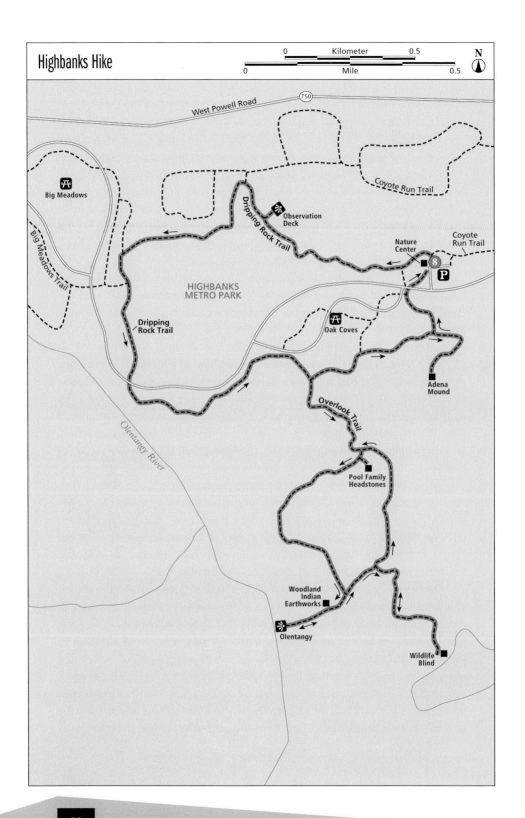

Highbanks Hike

Kilometer
0   0.5
Mile
0   0.5

N

West Powell Road
750

Big Meadows

Big Meadows Trail

Dripping Rock Trail

Observation Deck

Coyote Run Trail

Nature Center

Coyote Run Trail

8

P

HIGHBANKS METRO PARK

Dripping Rock Trail

Oak Coves

Adena Mound

Olentangy River

Overlook Trail

Pool Family Headstones

Woodland Indian Earthworks

Olentangy

Wildlife Blind

MILES AND DIRECTIONS

0.0 Start at the park nature center. As you face the nature center, take the gravel trail leading into the woods. Immediately come to an intersection. Head left here, swinging behind the nature center.

0.1 Come to an intersection. Stay right on the yellow-blazed Dripping Rock Trail, traveling westerly. Pass shale ravines ahead, crossing one on a bridge.

0.5 Though you are traveling through northern hardwoods, a spur trail leads right to an observation deck overlooking a meadow.

0.7 Reach an intersection. Here a connector trail leads right to the pet-friendly Coyote Run Trail. Keep straight on the Dripping Rock Trail, wandering through an edge community of forest and field.

1.1 Come near the Big Meadows Picnic Area after dropping off a hill. Stay left at the intersection here, as the trail heading right leads to the Big Meadows Path.

1.2 Arrive at a second intersection just after bridging a stream. Stay straight here, as the Big Meadows Trail leads right.

1.4 Cross the park road. You are near enough to the Olentangy River to see it through the trees to your right. Climb above a ravine.

1.8 Meet the Oak Coves Picnic Area after bridging a small ravine. Stay straight here, as the Dripping Rock Trail briefly becomes paved and the Oak Coves Path leaves left to meander amid the picnic sites. Reenter woods.

2.0 Leave the Dripping Rock Trail and turn right onto the Overlook Trail. You will come again to this intersection. For now, come alongside a meadow bordered by walnut trees and shortly reenter woods.

2.2 Come to the loop portion of the Overlook Trail after bridging a ravine. Turn right here, and soon find the spur trail leading left to the Pool family headstones and homesite. Notice the line of big trees marking an old roadbed. Look for other relics, such as rusty implements indicating human habitation, and leave them for others to discover.

2.8 Turn right at an intersection, heading toward the overlook of the Olentangy River.

2.9 The spur to the overlook traverses the curved mounds of the Woodland Indians. Absorb the interpretive information here to gain a better understanding of this culture.

3.0 Reach the Olentangy overlook deck, shaded by trees with built-in benches.

Enjoy glimpses of the river 110 feet below. Backtrack and resume the loop of the Overlook Trail by walking straight ahead.

3.3 Turn right on the spur to the wetland on a lesser-used path.

3.7 Reach the wetland and observation blind. Take a little time to see if you can spot waterbirds or other wildlife. Backtrack and turn right at the intersection to resume the loop part of the Overlook Trail.

4.4 Complete the loop portion of the Overlook Trail. Backtrack toward the Dripping Rock Trail.

4.6 Turn right at an intersection, rejoining the Dripping Rock Trail and heading easterly.

4.8 A spur trail turns left to reach the Oak Coves Picnic Area. Stay right.

5.0 Turn right to the Adena Mound on another lesser-used spur trail. Gypsy moths defoliated this area, and younger trees are sprouting amid the wooden skeletons.

5.2 Reach the Adena Mound, a low-slung rise covered in grass. Remember this is a burial site, even older than the Cole earthworks. Backtrack to the main Dripping Rock Trail and resume the loop to the right.

5.5 Cross the main park road and turn right toward the nature center parking area.

5.6 Reach the nature center parking area, completing the hike.

🌿 **Green Tip:**
Don't take souvenirs home with you. This means natural materials such as wildflowers, rocks, shells, and driftwood as well as historic artifacts such as fossils and arrowheads.

Bright green foliage greets the spring hiker (hike 10).

Hikes in the northeast section of greater Columbus feature a changing topography through changing historical eras. From Morrow County's Mount Gilead, to the lakes of eastern Delaware County, to the metro parks of eastern Franklin County and beyond to Licking County's Blackhand Gorge, hikers can experience an interesting geographical sampling.

Blendon Woods Metro Park presents a cornucopia of trailside environments and four different trails to explore. Since you start at the park's nature center, why not absorb a little environmental education while you are at it? The hike at Sharon Woods Metro Park also connects a series of nature trails, with a watery bent and virgin forest. Walk along Spring Creek Trail, passing a pond, streams, and wetlands, then head over to the Edward S. Thomas State Nature Preserve, with its amazing old-growth trees. Visit a final water feature, Schrock Lake, before completing a loop.

Alum Creek State Park presents a network of trails ambling along waters and wetlands large and small. Enjoy lakeside vistas that stretch for miles in addition to more intimate views of this natural area. Enthrall in fine lake vistas at Delaware State Park, where the Mink Run Trail carves its way through thick forest, emerging onto Delaware Reservoir. Soak in more forest and the stream of Mink Run. Mount Gilead State Park is an old-time, traditional state park, next to the town of Mount Gilead. Upon completing the hike, you will know the park, for the hike covers almost the entire grounds of the 181-acre park, passing nearly every recreational opportunity that lies within its boundaries.

Dawes Arboretum features two hikes at the 1,800-acre former country home and grounds of the Dawes family. The arboretum has over 15,000 living plants, 8 miles of trails, and a 4-mile auto tour, all initially established in 1929. Travel rolling terrain on garden-type paths, or head for the "back 40" where Mother Nature does the plant arranging. Either way, this private preserve will enhance your hiking experience. Many kids—and adults—take field trips to Flint Ridge State Memorial. Why not take your own? A historic hike heads to the source for flint—the ideal stone for making points for arrows, spears, and other tools. View former quarry pits and flint outcrops, where aboriginals came from hundreds of miles to obtain the essential stone. You'll also see big trees and impressive woods below the main quarry site.

Blackhand Gorge is one of those special places that make the case for state nature preserves. Not only is the place rich in geological features carved by the scenic Licking River, such as cliffs, rock overhangs, and boulder fields, it is also rich in vegetation, including wildflowers and diverse woodlands from xeric oak stands to bottomland hardwoods. Two hikes take place in this preserve. Start on the paved Blackhand Trail before venturing onto singletrack hilly paths, exploring deep woods and abandoned quarries. The Marie Hickey Loop is the forgotten hike of Blackhand Gorge. It oozes solitude amid deep, hilly woods on the north rim of Blackhand Gorge, where views await. Visit a dark hemlock copse through which a waterfall drops—and you likely won't see another soul along the way.

Hikes of Blendon Woods

Explore the whole of Blendon Woods Metro Park via a series of four shortish hikes that all emanate from the same trailhead. First, walk amid upland hardwoods on the Sugarbush Trail. Next, wander through fields and meadows with native prairie flowers on the Goldenrod Trail. After that head to Thoreau Lake, to hopefully see some wildlife, on the Pond Trail. Finally, make a loop in the Ripple Rock Creek valley, where you will visit bottomland woods stretched along the main watercourse that runs through Blendon Woods. Since the hikes start at the park nature center, you can easily add environmental education to the experience.

Start: Blendon Woods Nature Center

Distance: 5.4 miles on 4 short hikes

Hiking time: About 3 to 3.5 hours

Difficulty: Moderate

Trail surface: Natural surface, pea gravel, and a little asphalt

Best season: Year-round

Other trail users: None

Canine compatibility: Leashed dogs permitted only on the Goldenrod Trail

Land status: Metro Parks

Fees and permits: None

Schedule: Open daily year-round

Maps: Blendon Woods Metro Park; USGS New Albany, Northeast Columbus

Trail contact: Blendon Woods Metro Park, 4265 E. Dublin-Granville Rd., Westerville, OH 43081; (614) 891-0700; www.metroparks.net

Finding the trailhead: From exit 30B on I-270, northeast of downtown Columbus, take OH 161 east a short distance to the Little Turtle Way exit. Turn right on Little Turtle Way, then immediately turn right again on Cherry Bottom Road and follow it 0.4 mile to the park entrance on your left. Follow the main park road to the large parking area at the nature center. Trailhead GPS: N40 4.238'/W82 52.417'

THE HIKE

With so many trails emanating from one trailhead, you can tailor your hike at Blendon Woods Metro Park to any distance or difficulty you desire. You could walk just a short distance with your grandchildren to observe waterfowl at Thoreau Lake, or you could take your dog for a jaunt on the Goldenrod Trail. You might look for wildflowers on the Brookside Trail, or even check out the fall colors on the Sugarbush Trail. Or you might want to make an event of it and hike them all! Throw in a picnic and a visit to the park nature center. Consider creating a full day of outdoor pleasure—that is what I recommend!

To hit the trail "grand slam," park at the nature center, enabling access to all the major paths. Phase 1 of the grand slam will be on the Sugarbush Trail, whose name derives from a stand of sugar maples. In the old days when sugar maples were tapped for sap, and the sap then turned into maple syrup, the stand of trees that were tapped was known as a "sugarbush." As you can imagine, the forest here is full of sugar maples. However, the trail starts out in a mix of meadow and trees. The middle portion is mostly forested, while the loop on the west travels open terrain, where you will see prairie wildflowers extraordinaire toward summer's end.

A pair of Canada geese play on Thoreau Lake.

After backtracking to the trailhead, the Goldenrod Trail is the next phase of the grand slam. This path, the only one open to pets, cruises along the park edge, sometimes among trees but often in meadows. This is perhaps the best spot for prairie wildflowers at Blendon Woods.

The Pond Trail leads past the nature center to Thoreau Lake, the centerpiece of the 118-acre Walden Waterfowl Refuge. The shoreline habitat and surrounding wetlands have been enhanced for wildlife. Two individual wildlife-viewing blinds are outfitted with spotting scopes, enabling you to see waterfowl and other birds in detail as they go about their natural activities. This refuge is one of only eighty designated state watchable-wildlife areas as deemed by the Ohio Department of Natural Resources. Your best chances for viewing wildlife are in the morning and evening, during migratory times, and when things are quiet. You might not be lucky on a warm afternoon with a band of schoolkids running wild nearby. Patience is always the key with these wildlife blinds.

The final part of the grand slam leads you to Ripple Rock Creek. Here enter a bucolic valley and cruise along the stream, with wildflowers blooming in season. When you are at the bottom of this valley, it's hard to imagine that civilization encircles the park. It is truly a natural escape down along the stream. The second half of the loop climbs a ridge above Ripple Rock Creek. This upland view gives an alternate aspect of the valley. After you have visited Ripple Rock Creek, the Blendon Woods grand slam is complete.

MILES AND DIRECTIONS

0.0 Start by walking west away from the nature center. Pick up the Sugarbush Trail as it leaves the parking area on a wide, mostly level track.

0.2 Open onto a field, then shortly return to high-canopied hardwoods of ash, beech, hickory, and maple.

0.7 Cross the main park road just after passing through a white pine copse. Come to the loop portion of the Sugarbush Trail. Stay right, walking along the edge of a sown field. In late summer, prairie wildflowers will rise resplendent.

1.3 Finish the Sugarbush Trail loop and backtrack to the nature center trailhead.

2.0 Pick up the Goldenrod Trail as it leaves south from the nature center parking area. Open onto a field and stay left at all trail junctions as you execute a double loop.

2.2 Begin the clockwise lower loop of the Goldenrod Trail.

2.5 Complete the lower loop of the Goldenrod Trail. Keep north and begin the second loop, which travels through a large meadow.

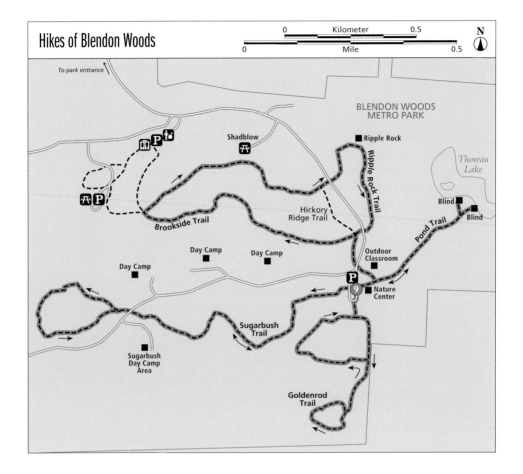

0   Kilometer   0.5

0   Mile   0.5

N

3.0 Reach the nature center parking area after finishing the Goldenrod Trail. Now head toward the nature center and pick up the Pond Trail. This is an asphalt path that leads easterly into tall woods.

3.1 Stay straight at a four-way junction near the park outdoor classroom.

3.4 The trail splits. You can go to either the east wildlife-viewing blind or the west one first, but make sure to visit both. Hopefully the birds will be cooperating. Backtrack toward the nature center after checking out the wildlife on Thoreau Lake.

3.7 Return to the four-way junction before reaching the nature center. Turn right, passing the park outdoor classroom, to cross the main park road and join the Hickory Ridge Trail.

3.9 Come to a four-way trail intersection. Turn left, joining the Brookside Trail, and begin your final loop. Cruise a gravel track in bottomland.

4.2 Bridge Ripple Rock Creek, which courses through the park from Thoreau Lake. This stream is a tributary of Big Walnut Creek to the west of the park. Enjoy a period of walking beside the stream through rich woods amid a quiet valley. This is arguably the prettiest part of Blendon Woods. A wooden fence runs along the trail here.

4.5 Come to another four-way junction. Turn right on the Overlook Trail, and walk easterly on a ridge running above the creek where you just were. The trail gets its name from the overlooks it provides of the waterway below. Ahead, pass near the Shadblow Picnic Shelter and dip into bottoms full of spring wildflowers.

4.8 Bridge Ripple Rock Creek, then rise to a bluff overlooking the stream below.

5.0 Arrive at a trail junction; keep straight, join-ing the Ripple Rock Trail. Just ahead, cross the main park road, then dive back down to Ripple Rock Creek. Note the rocky bluff across the stream before you turn away from the watercourse and climb.

5.3 Meet the Hickory Ridge Trail at a four-way intersection, just after crossing the main park road. Turn left here and cross the main park road one more time.

5.4 Reach the nature center trailhead.

🍂 Green Tip:
If you're driving to or from the trailhead, don't let any passenger throw garbage out the window. Keep a small bag in the car that you can empty properly at home, after recycling what you can.

Hickory Ridge

On part of this hike, you will walk the Hickory Ridge Trail. The shagbark hickory is a prominent component of central Ohio's forests. Shagbark hickories look like what their name implies: a tree with loose plated bark sloughing off the main trunk, looking like it could use a trim, much like a shaggy-haired human. The loose bark plates run vertically up the trunk of the tree.

Found all over the Buckeye State, shagbark hickories were once an important food source for aboriginal Ohioans, who sought out their surprisingly sweet nuts. The nuts were used by American pioneers much as you would use pecans. However, attempts at commercial propagation of the shagbark hickory have been unsuccessful. In the wild, nut production varies greatly year to year.

The thinner shell and greater amount of nutmeat make shagbark hickory nuts an attractive choice. Indians even made hickory nut soup. They also broke the nuts, collected the meat, and pounded it down, releasing the nut's oil. They would then form the meat into balls, with the oil keeping the pulverized nuts intact. These "nutballs" were an ideal way to store the food for later use, since they could be quickly and easily eaten, as opposed to breaking the shells and removing the meat. Bird and mammals competed with the Indians in getting to the sought-after nuts, especially during times when the shagbarks' nut production was down.

Shagbark hickories also aided the Indians in obtaining food another way. The strong wood was fashioned into bows, which they used to hunt game. Ohio pioneers used the tough yet resilient wood for everything from ax handles to wagon axles. The best time to collect the shell was soon after the acorns fell and before the first frost of autumn.

The big shagbark hickories you see on the Hickory Ridge Trail may seem like mere shade trees, but at second glance, they have been providing the peoples—and the beasts—of Ohio with a good food source for ages. Nutty, isn't it?

Sharon Woods Loops

This hike wanders throughout Sharon Woods Metro Park, using a collection of nature trails. First you will take the Spring Creek Trail along its namesake, passing a pond and wetlands, then you will head over to the Edward S. Thomas State Nature Preserve. This path explores a protected parcel of central Ohio with old-growth trees, the size of which will amaze. Next head for yet another water feature—Schrock Lake. Walk along this aquatic centerpiece of Sharon Woods before taking the long way back to the trailhead. As with most Metro Parks, Sharon Woods has bountiful picnic and play facilities, as well as the paved Multipurpose Trail, which completely encircles the park.

Start: Maple Grove Picnic Area
Distance: 3.9-mile double loop
Hiking time: About 2.5 to 3 hours
Difficulty: Moderate
Trail surface: Pea gravel and a little asphalt
Best season: Year-round
Other trail users: None
Canine compatibility: No pets allowed on nature trails

Land status: Metro Parks
Fees and permits: None
Schedule: Open daily year-round
Maps: Sharon Woods Metro Park; USGS Northeast Columbus
Trail contact: Sharon Woods Metro Park, 6911 Cleveland Ave., Westerville, OH 43081; (614) 891-0700; www.metroparks.net

Finding the trailhead: From exit 27 on I-270, north of downtown Columbus, take Cleveland Avenue north for 0.5 mile and a traffic light. Turn left to enter the park, drive 0.4 mile, then turn left and immediately park at the Maple Grove Picnic Area. The Spring Creek Trail starts on the north side of the main park road, just across from the left turn into the picnic area. Trailhead GPS: N40 6.726' / W82 57.330'

THE HIKE

Sharon Woods Metro Park packs a lot of features into its 760 acres, and you will see most of them on this hike. I bet if you don't fully enjoy the amenities here, such as the picnic areas, playgrounds, Schrock Lake, and the Multipurpose Trail, in addition to the nature trails on this hike, you will return again to maximize this Metro Park experience.

The hike starts on the Spring Creek Trail. From the trailhead it's almost all downhill to Spring Creek, where the forest morphs into wildflower-rich bottom-land woods of sycamore, cottonwood, and buckeye. On your walk look for glacial erratics, seemingly out-of-place rocks and boulders deposited here when glaciers stretched over Ohio, then receded. If a boulder stands alone without any other geological features nearby, it is likely an erratic.

The path bridges Spring Creek one more time before leaving this valley. Here the path meanders through a floodplain. Look for evidence of past high-water events, including limbs and brush piled against the upstream sides of trees, channels dug into the woods, and drying pools of water. The Spring Creek Trail then makes a sharp climb to a bluff overlooking the watercourse. Enjoy a view into the lands below, and watch for a huge trailside oak tree ahead, even though you haven't yet reached the state nature preserve.

Looking for wildlife from an observation deck.

The hike then opens into a meadow, which contrasts with the deep woods along Spring Creek, especially on a sunny summer or early fall afternoon. You will soon meet up with the Connector Trail, which does what its name implies, traveling west across the meadow and linking the Edward S. Thomas State Nature Preserve and the trail of the same name. You will then roam upland flatwoods and pass an elevated observation deck that overlooks meadow and field. Birders will sometimes be gathered here. The path next heads into the heart of the preserve in thick forest. Look for old-growth bur oaks and other giants standing out among the relatively smaller trees. A side trip on the Oak Openings Trail adds a little distance to the hike and a stroll through a white pine grove.

The atmosphere changes when you open onto Schrock Lake and the asphalt trails and picnic, fishing, and play areas that surround the 11-acre impoundment. This is where most park visitors gather and can be a hubbub of activity on a beautiful day. The lake was created in 1965 to provide fill for the nearby interstates, and the park itself came to be three years later. Civilization has now encircled Sharon Woods.

The hike takes you to the water's edge to soak in some aquatic views and check out some of the lakeside action. You could shortcut your hike around the south side of Schrock Lake, but I recommend rejoining the Edward S. Thomas Trail and taking the long way back to the trailhead. This way you will enjoy more natural park scenery before coming to the Apple Ridge Picnic Area, another popular spot. After negotiating a few more trail junctions with the picnic area paths, the Spring Creek Trail leads back to the Maple Grove Picnic Area and the hike's end.

MILES AND DIRECTIONS

0.0 Start on the Spring Creek Trail, which leaves north from the main park road intersection with the turn into the Maple Grove Picnic Area. Pick up a pea-gravel path, descending through field and forest.

0.1 The Spring Creek Trail splits. Leave right, descending off a hill to cross the Apple Ridge Picnic Area access road. Soon enter full-blown woods.

0.2 Stay right as a spur trail leads left to an outdoor classroom. You are descending toward Spring Creek. Watch for a woodland pond on your right, most likely a relic from when Sharon Woods was farmed many decades ago. Keep working downhill, running alongside a ditch.

0.4 Reach and cross Spring Creek underneath sycamores aplenty. Buckeye has a strong presence, too—no surprise here in the heart of the Buckeye State. Cottonwoods rise in these bottoms as well.

0.7 Bridge Spring Creek a second time and travel through flood-prone bottoms.

Sharon Woods Loops

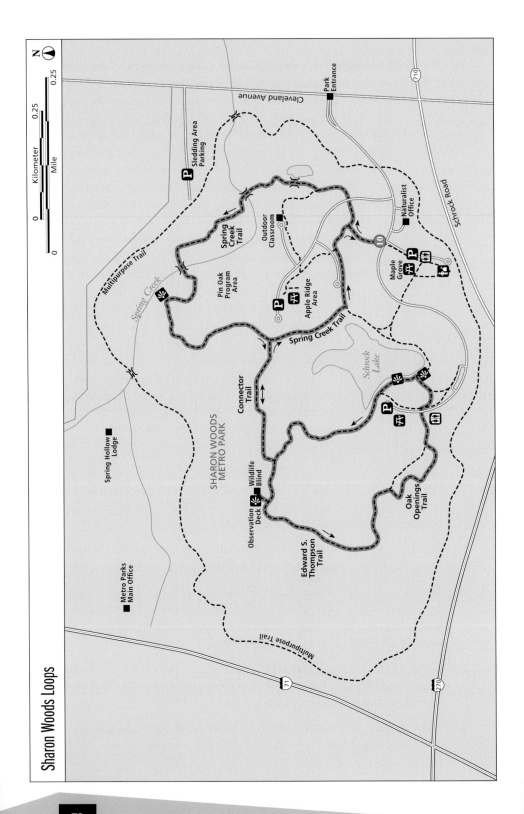

0.8 Meet a bluff-top overlook after rising steeply from Spring Creek. Contemplation benches beckon a seat, as does the challenge of the just-finished climb.

1.2 Reach a trail intersection, where you will see a sign indicating the Edward S. Thomas Trail. Turn right, following the grassy Connector Trail west through a field alongside a strip of woods. If you miss this junction, a trail leads left just ahead to the Apple Ridge Picnic Area.

1.6 Meet the Edward S. Thomas Trail after reentering woods. Turn right, beginning a counterclockwise loop in tall trees. You are now inside the 320-acre state nature preserve.

1.7 Turn right and follow a short path to reach the elevated wildlife-observation deck, which looks over a large meadow bordered by forest. Return to the Edward S. Thomas Trail, continuing counterclockwise. Large trees, mostly oaks, begin to appear in the forest. The girth of some of the tree trunks is amazing.

2.2 Turn right onto the Oak Openings Trail. Ahead, watch for a lone hemlock tree beside the path.

2.4 Return to the Edward S. Thomas Trail. Turn right and soon reach the large and potentially busy Schrock Lake area. Cross the picnic area access road, joining an asphalt track that immediately splits. Stay right, then curve left past a play area, heading for Schrock Lake.

2.6 Come to Schrock Lake at a fishing dock. These fishing areas are reserved for those under 15 and over 60 years old. Nevertheless, the docks are quality lake-observation areas as well. Turn left, northbound, along the west shore of Schrock Lake, passing a couple more fishing docks before rejoining the gravel Edward S. Thomas Trail. Hikers can use the asphalt paths to shortcut back to the trailhead around the south side of Schrock Lake if they choose.

3.1 Complete the Edward S. Thomas Trail. Backtrack right on the Connector Trail.

3.4 Return to the Spring Creek Trail. Turn right, southbound, passing a spur to the Apple Ridge Picnic Area.

3.6 The gravel portion of the Spring Creek Trail ends at an intersection with a path coming from Schrock Lake. Turn left, now walking on asphalt alongside the Apple Ridge Picnic Area.

3.7 Stay right as another asphalt path comes in from Apple Ridge.

3.8 Complete the loop portion of the Spring Creek Trail. Backtrack right (south) toward the Maple Grove Picnic Area.

3.9 Reach the Maple Grove Picnic Area, completing the hike.

Hiking Network of Alum Creek State Park

From the park office of Alum Creek State Park, explore a network of trails that ramble along waters and wetlands large and small, as well as hills and hollows. First, head south on the Marina Trail to surmount ridges dividing streamlets flowing to Alum Creek Lake. Turn around at Hollenback Road or dare to go on. Sooner or later you can turn back to the park office trails and enter a close-knit network of interconnected paths that explore the surprisingly varied terrain of this shoreline. Enjoy both lakeside vistas that stretch for miles and intimate views of a serene cattail-lined pond. At other points you will walk through meadows and evergreen woods as well as upland hardwoods. Hiking mileage can vary from the suggested hike with the amount of effort and exploration you want to engage.

Start: Alum Creek State Park office

Distance: 2.7 miles out and back with options

Hiking time: About 1 to 3 hours

Difficulty: Easy to moderate

Trail surface: Natural surface

Best seasons: Fall and winter for best views

Other trail users: None

Canine compatibility: Leashed dogs permitted

Land status: Ohio state park

Fees and permits: None

Schedule: Open daily year-round

Maps: Alum Creek State Park, Park Office Hiking Trails; USGS Galena

Trail contact: Alum Creek State Park, 3615 S. Old State Rd., Delaware, OH 43015; (740) 548-4631; www.dnr.state.ohio.us

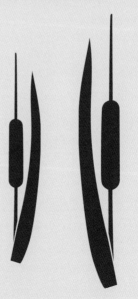

Finding the trailhead: From exit 23 on I-270, north of downtown Columbus, take US 23 north for 6 miles to Lewis Center Road and a traffic light. Turn right on Lewis Center Road and follow it 2 miles to S. Old State Road. Turn left on S. Old State Road and follow it north 1.9 miles to the Alum Creek State Park office, near the intersection with Peachblow Road. Turn right and reach the park office and a parking area at 0.1 mile. Trailhead GPS: N40 13.647'/W82 58.792'

THE HIKE

Alum Creek State Park is a very long preserve. It basically encircles all of 3,387-acre Alum Creek Lake, a slender impoundment situated in the heart of Delaware County. The park itself has an additional 4,630 acres of land along its shores. When you add together the equestrian trails, hiking trails, mountain-biking trails, and multiuse trails, there are over 50 miles of pathways at Alum Creek. A lot of hikers don't care to share paths with mountain bikers who can sometimes go very fast or equestrians who can make trails muddy. This hike at Alum Creek State Park is on hiker-only trails, though I do recommend giving the bridle trails in the northern part of the park a try if you are looking for new terrain to hike, especially the Hunters Hollow Bridle Trail.

The trail system at this state park has continually evolved over the years as user groups have clamored for pathways. Over the past couple decades, mountain biking has been on the rise, and equestrians have always wanted paths for their horses. Hikers have been walking paths in Ohio state parks for as long as the parks have existed. Many of the trails here were built by the trail users themselves; for hikers, this means scout groups. The park is starting to look at the trail system as a comprehensive network rather than a hodgepodge of disparate paths. Part of the trail goal is to develop a path that will completely encircle Alum Creek Lake. Much of this lake loop is already done, especially in the northern half of the park.

Cattails and white pines grow alongside the park office pond.

In the future you will see the trail system continue to develop. For now, I recommend hiking from the park office and heading south on the Marina Trail, formerly known as the Hollenback Trail. It is in good shape and well-marked between the park office and the park marina. Beyond that the trail can diverge and become confusing. Hopefully, this will be corrected over time, for this section will certainly become part of the lake loop later on.

So, if you explore beyond the park marina, consider it an adventure. Otherwise, backtrack to the park office area, where a spider web of trails will take you to grand vistas of Alum Lake as well as more intimate nature experiences such as along the pond behind the park office. Oddly, it can be hard to get onto the Marina Trail from the web of paths near the park office, but once you do, the way is clear. First dip to bridge one of the seemingly innumerable tributaries of Alum Creek that now flow into the lake, forming wetlands where creek meets lake. These wetlands, which vary with lake levels and stream flows, are important to Ohio's flora and fauna. The trail next gently roller-coasters between hills and hollows, coming very near the park boundary, for one characteristic of this park is the limited strip of land between the lake and civilization, which has now virtually encircled Alum Creek Lake. Despite the sounds of cars and goings-on at nearby houses, you can enjoy the natural aspects of this trail.

Looking south across Alum Creek Lake.

Upon reaching Hollenback Road, the mown-grass path curves near houses and crosses the road. The trail then keeps south, passing a spur to Alum Creek's dog park and then the spur to the marina, finally reaching a park road turnaround. After backtracking to the park office, you will have nearly 3 miles of hiking under your belt. From there it is a matter of picking your routes in the park office hiking trail network. If you come here on a regular basis, you will see nearby residents who use these natural-surface trailways for daily exercise.

In this network, fine views of Alum Creek Lake can be had from multiple vantage points. You can also walk by the outflow of the small pond, walk around the pond itself, and explore small meadows that become prairie wildflower havens in late fall. Or discover deep evergreen thickets. Despite the potentially confusing interconnected nature of these trails, Alum Creek Lake and the adjacent roads will keep you from getting lost, even if you try.

What Is a Wetland?

The marshy areas where tributaries flow into Alum Creek Lake are wetlands vital to Ohio's natural health. When we hear the term "wetland," we are all likely to conjure up our own image of what exactly one is. You might imagine a swamp filled with snakes, with eerie trees hanging over dark waters. Or you might picture a large open body of water, with waterweeds growing on its surface and waterfowl grouped together. Or you may imagine somewhere like the Florida Everglades, a vast expanse of sawgrass, under which flows an inches-deep sheet of water.

Any one of these images is not entirely incorrect. According to the US Environmental Protection Agency, wetlands are "lands where saturation with water is the dominant factor determining the nature of soil development and the types of plant and animal communities living in the soil and on its surface." To translate the government garble, it means an ecosystem of which water is the key ingredient. Another part of the definition states that "wetlands generally include swamps, marshes, bogs and similar areas." So wetlands can take varied forms.

Wetlands don't have to be underwater or even wet year-round to be considered wetlands. Some plant communities in wetlands in fact depend on a cyclical flooding and drying out of their terrain. The Everglades is a prime example. So when you hike at Alum Creek State Park, look around and see what you define as wetlands.

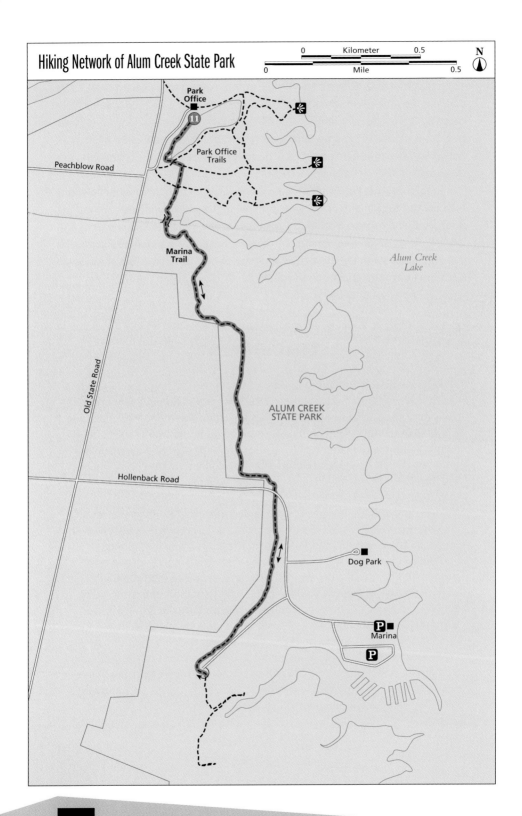

Hiking Network of Alum Creek State Park

0   Kilometer   0.5

0   Mile   0.5

N

Park Office

11

Park Office Trails

Peachblow Road

Marina Trail

Old State Road

Alum Creek Lake

ALUM CREEK STATE PARK

Hollenback Road

Dog Park

Marina

MILES AND DIRECTIONS

0.0 Start by walking along the pond back toward S. Old State Road. There is no trail here; simply walk along the grassy shoreline, bordered with cattails. To reach the Marina Trail, you have to walk easterly on one of the nature trails, then pick up the southbound Marina Trail. It is marked with blue blazes, or a blue dot on a plastic post.

0.2 Cross a tributary on a wooden bridge. Rise to a little bluff overlooking the small lake cove of the creek you just crossed. Resume southbound and keep undulating in woods, crossing a couple of other small creeks that may run dry during summer and fall. Enter an area of grass mixed with younger brush and small trees. The trail will be singletrack in woods and a wider mown track in open areas.

0.9 Cross Hollenback Road. You are now walking within sight of houses to your right.

1.1 A spur trail leads left to Alum Creek's dog park.

1.2 A spur trail leads left to the park marina.

1.4 Emerge on a park road turnaround. Beyond here the trail can be an adventure, as it diverges and becomes messy. Hopefully the network will be cleared up to the south beyond this point. For now, backtrack to the network of trails near the park office.

2.7 Reenter the park office trail network. Hiking mileage and directions will vary from this point on, depending upon the choice of trails you make between here and the trailhead at the office. If you hike every single park office trail, it adds up to about 2 miles of pathways.

Delaware State Park Loop

The shores of Delaware Reservoir are the setting for this woodsy trek. You will leave the busy park marina on the Mink Run Trail, hiking the valley of Mink Run, then begin a circuit that curves out to Delaware Reservoir, where you take in some fine lake vistas. Next, trace old pre-lake settlement roads, looking for evidence of the area's agricultural past, before leaving the now-wooded flatlands. Get a second look at Mink Run before returning to the trailhead. Elevation changes are minimal.

Start: Parking area near the state park marina
Distance: 4.2-mile loop
Hiking time: About 2.5 to 3.5 hours
Difficulty: Moderate
Trail surface: Natural surface
Best season: Sept through Apr
Other trail users: None
Canine compatibility: Leashed dogs permitted
Land status: Ohio state park

Fees and permits: None
Schedule: Open daily year-round
Maps: Delaware State Park; USGS Waldo
Trail contact: Delaware State Park, 5202 US 23 North, Delaware, OH 43015; (740) 548-4631 (Alum Creek SP office); (740) 363-4561 (Delaware SP camp office, open in warm season); www.dnr.state .ohio.us

Finding the trailhead: From exit 23 on I-270, north of downtown Columbus, take US 23 north for 20 miles to Delaware State Park on your right. (Do not turn right into the Army Corps of Engineers dam-area recreation facilities along the way.) Turn right into the state park, following signs to the park marina. Look for the Mink Run Trail entering the woods on the left just as you reach the large marina parking area. Trailhead GPS: N40 23.004' / W83 3.506'

THE HIKE

D elaware State Park is a large preserve with quality facilities set along the west shore of 1,300-acre Delaware Reservoir. Originally developed by the US Army Corps of Engineers and now run by the state of Ohio, the facilities here are top-notch. Despite being a water-oriented destination, the park's trail system is worth a hike. This trek cobbles together three different trails, maximizing the walking opportunity.

The park also features over 200 campsites, a well-developed marina with slips available for rent, swimming beaches, a nature center, picnic areas, disc golf, and volleyball. With all these other attractions, hikers are in the distinct minority, but that doesn't mean the park doesn't have good hiking. On the contrary, the trails are the best year-round attraction the park has to offer. Think about it—in winter the lake is too cold most of the time to utilize, the camping can be challenging, and picnickers aren't out, yet the trails offer something during every season. Be apprised late spring and early summer can be buggy, as the hike passes through flatwoods with vernal pools. Fall is ideal for deciduous tree color.

The hike starts off in second-growth woods, heading up the valley of Mink Run. At first you will be along the lake embayment. This section of the trail is heavily used by bank fishermen. The still water continues to narrow until you enter the

The morning sun tries to break through the fog on Delaware Reservoir.

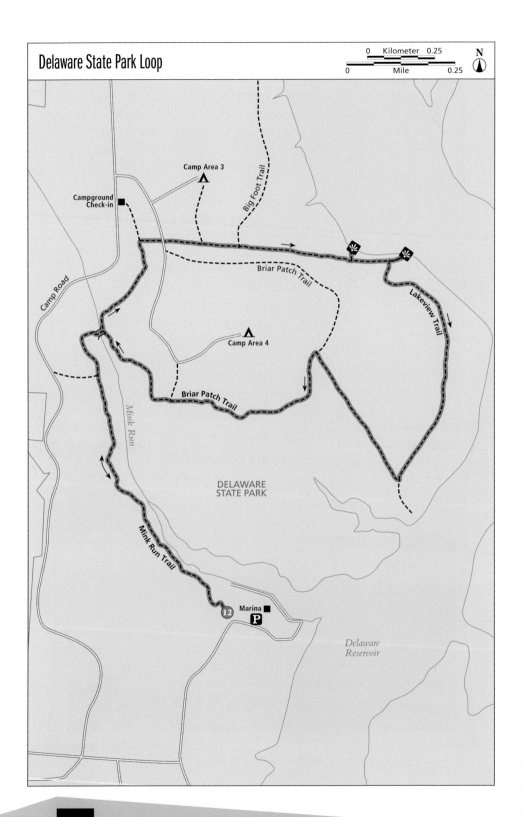

Delaware State Park Loop

Kilometer
0   0.25

Mile
0   0.25

N

Camp Area 3

Campground
Check-in

Big Foot Trail

Briar Patch Trail

Camp Area 4

Lakeview Trail

Camp Road

Briar Patch Trail

Mink Run

DELAWARE
STATE PARK

Mink Run Trail

12 Marina
P

Delaware
Reservoir

flowing stream part of Mink Run. After crossing the creek on a bridge, the loop part of the hike starts, continuing up Mink Run. Look for old-growth trees from pre-park days, scattered amid the younger forest.

The hike then picks up the Lakeview Trail and makes a beeline east for Delaware Reservoir, passing under tall cottonwood trees, their leaves whispering in the summer breeze. Views open from a bluff overlooking the reservoir. Note the foundation of an old structure here. Ahead, the Lakeview Trail travels to the shoreline, where a lone cottonwood stands on an otherwise grassy point. Here you get a real sense of the lake. Depending on the time of year, you may see the water full of boats under a strong sun or a forlorn, windswept, white-capped expanse ringed in snow. The path then leaves the shoreline and traces old roads abandoned after the Corps of Engineers condemned the land. Look for fence lines, old trees, road cuts, and other evidence that time, the elements, and nature are slowly erasing.

The trail turns back toward the campground in level forest. The hiking is easy as you reunite with the Briar Patch Trail, circling around the south side of Camp Area 4. Sites can be seen through the trees. Pass through flatwoods with small vernal pools and ponds. The Briar Patch Trail circles to the west side of Camp Area 4, coming alongside Mink Run, then meets the Mink Run Trail. From here it is a simple backtrack to the trailhead.

MILES AND DIRECTIONS

0.0   Start on the Mink Run Trail, located on the left side of the large marina parking area. Join a gravel track, immediately stepping over a couple of tributaries in sparse woods, and come near the embayment of Mink Run.

0.4   The embayment is but a stream's width to your right. A wetland borders the lake here, as the trail travels a low bluff. Blackberries line the path in summer.

0.7   Come to an intersection. Here a spur trail leads left to Camp Road. Keep straight with the Mink Run Trail, now in thicker riparian forest.

0.8   Cross Mink Run on a wooden footbridge. Meet the Briar Patch Trail and turn left, continuing up the valley of Mink Run.

1.1   Reach a T intersection and turn right, joining the Lakeview Trail. Immediately cross the Camp Area 4 access road. Keep straight, passing around a metal pole gate on a wide track. The Briar Patch Trail enters the woods to the right of the gate.

1.3   A spur trail heads left to Camp Area 3. Stay straight on the Lakeview Trail in hardwoods.

1.4   The Big Foot Trail leaves left for the north end of the park. Keep straight on the Lakeview Trail.

12

1.6 Look left for a wide track leading to a bluff overlooking Delaware Reservoir.

1.7 The Lakeview Trail splits right, but first keep straight on a spur that dead-ends at the impoundment with sweeping vistas of the water and land beyond it. Backtrack and continue on the Lakeview Trail.

2.4 The Lakeview Trail abruptly turns acutely right. A user-created trail heads left to the shore. Hike northwest in flatwoods.

2.7 Intersect the Briar Patch Trail. Turn sharply left, curving around the south side of Camp Area 4.

3.2 Keep straight as a connecter trail splits right to Camp Area 4.

3.4 Return to the Mink Run Trail and backtrack to the parking area.

4.2 Reach the marina parking area, completing the hike.

Listen to the Cottonwood Sing

Along this hike during the warm season, you may hear the sound of cotton-wood leaves fluttering in the breeze. Cottonwoods are large deciduous trees primarily found in wet soils along stream bottoms or moist woods. In the Plains and Southwest, they will grow in sheltered bottoms above treeless hills. Cottonwoods range from the plains of south-central Canada down to Texas, east to Georgia and north into Ohio, even up to Quebec.

The state's largest eastern cottonwood grows here in Delaware County, at nearby Alum Creek State Park. It is over 30 feet in circumference and 136 feet high! Cottonwoods are known for growing to great sizes, ultimately falling victim to wind or lightning strikes. The thick-barked tree is part of the willow family, and often grows with willows along streams or draws. The vertically fissured thick gray bark and triangular-shaped leaves make cottonwoods easy to identify.

In spring the cottonwood's downy seeds are released, giving the tree its name and another way to identify it. The wood of the fast-growing tree is used for pulp, plywood, boxes, and crates. Next time you are out this way, stop for a minute and listen to the cottonwoods sing.

Mount Gilead State Park Hike

This state park trek, located just outside the quaint town of Mount Gilead, presents a loop touring a variety of terrain, from lakeshore and creek bottom to hills and wetlands. Start the hike by cruising the shore of Mount Gilead Lake, then turn up Whetstone Creek. The excursion wanders amid a tight trail network before returning to Mount Gilead Lake. It then traverses scenic high bluffs above the impoundment and circles the upper drainage and wetlands of Sams Creek. The final leg of the hike leads through the park's campground and day-use facilities, along park roads, before returning to the trailhead. Consider bringing camping gear and make an overnighter of it, including a venture into town.

Start: Dam between upper and lower Mount Gilead Lake
Distance: 3-mile loop
Hiking time: About 1.5 to 2 hours
Difficulty: Moderate due to short distance, despite hills
Trail surface: Natural surface
Best season: Year-round
Other trail users: Equestrians and bicyclists in places
Canine compatibility: Leashed dogs permitted

Land status: Ohio state park
Fees and permits: None
Schedule: Open daily year-round
Maps: Mount Gilead State Park; USGS Mount Gilead
Trail contact: Mount Gilead State Park, 4119 OH 95, Mount Gilead, OH 43338; (740) 548-4631 (Alum Creek SP office); (419) 946-1961 (Mount Gilead SP camp office, open in warm season); www.dnr.state.ohio.us

Finding the trailhead: From exit 140 on I-71, take OH 61 north for 11.8 miles, then turn right on US 42. Follow US 42 for 0.6 mile to the town of Mount Gilead and OH 95. Turn right on OH 95 and follow it 1.1 miles to the state park. Turn left into the state park, then keep straight, passing the right turn into the campground. Follow the main road to its end after 0.5 mile near the upper dam on Mount Gilead Lake. Park here. Trailhead GPS: N40 32.932' / W82 48.786'

THE HIKE

Mount Gilead State Park is a fun destination bordering the town of Mount Gilead. The park is a little on the small side, yet offers a quality hike on a trail network that encompasses nearly the entire grounds of the 181-acre park. Upon completing the hike you will know the park, for it passes nearly every recreational opportunity that lies within its boundaries. And just as this park exudes a rural America atmosphere, so does the town. If you don't bring a picnic to enjoy in the state park, cruise into Mount Gilead and grab a bite.

The hike starts on the south shore of the two lakes. In essence, the state park has one lake but it is divided in the middle by a dam, so you have an upper lake and a lower lake. The trailhead is located near this dam. Simply start the hike by following the grassy shoreline. These lakes offer fishing opportunities for warm-water species such as bass, bluegill, and catfish. Canoes, kayaks, and small fishing boats are welcome, but only trolling motors are allowed on the 25-acre impoundment, keeping it quiet. The shore rises steeply from both sides of the lake, which is created by damming Sams Creek. Anglers may be set up along the banks on warm weekends.

Pass below the dam of the lower lake, and check out the spillway while hiking through the park's group campground. A bridge leads across Sams Creek. Follow

Looking down on the Sams Creek Trail.

Sams Creek to meet Whetstone Creek. The confluence of these two watercourses is an alluring spot and is a productive wildflower area in spring. The hike then takes you upstream along Whetstone Creek. Enjoy aquatic views while traveling through bottomland. Spur trails lead to favored streamside fishing holes. The sounds of town are never far away, as the pathway parallels the park's boundary here. During summer you will be tunneling through thick vegetation. The hike comes close to US 42 before passing a trailhead parking area accessed from the road.

A spider's nest of trails covers the north side of the park. Most of these paths are multiuse and open to bicycles and equestrians. Equestrians will use the trailhead off US 42 during their infrequent excursions. This particular hike visits the rolling hills back here, but also returns to the lake. The north shore of the impoundment is especially attractive, with its steep wooded bluffs rising high above the shoreline. Cross sharp, steep ravines en route to the wetlands at the head of the lake.

The steep terrain forces the trail to lake level and a marshy area with cattails and willows. The area around the upper Sams Creek bridge is one of the prettiest spots on the hike. From here you may smell smoke, as the campground is just ahead. The final part of the hike tours the developed facilities on park roads. A short footpath shortcuts you down to the parking area, completing the circuit.

The Harding Home

Less than 20 miles west of Mount Gilead stands the historic home of the twenty-ninth president of the United States, Ohio's own Warren G. Harding. Located in the town of Marion, and now on the National Register of Historic Places, the home is preserved and contains the original furniture and household items from the Harding family, who lived in the house for nearly thirty years before Harding became president.

Interestingly, the house factored in Harding's 1920 bid for the nation's top office. The Queen Anne–style home has an elaborate wide wraparound porch, and it was from this outdoor deck that the Ohio Republican spoke to supporters, leading to his presidential quest being dubbed the "Front Porch Campaign." The former newspaper editor, state senator, and US senator assumed office in 1921 but died suddenly in 1923, not finishing his only term. Vice president Calvin Coolidge assumed the office. Though Mrs. Harding returned to Marion, she didn't live in the house and passed away shortly after her husband.

Today you can tour the home and the adjacent museum building that served as campaign headquarters back in 1920. For more information, including seasonal tour hours, visit www.ohiohistory.org.

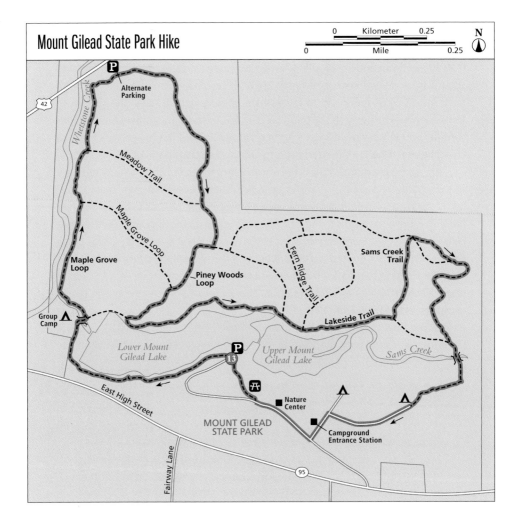

Mount Gilead State Park Hike

MILES AND DIRECTIONS

0.0 Start at the dead-end parking area by Mount Gilead Lake, near the dam dividing the upper lake from the lower lake. Head left, westerly, along the lakeshore, following the grassy bank. There is no defined trail, but you might see an occasional white blaze on a tree. You are now along the lower lake.

0.2 Reach the dam of the lower lake. Stay to the right of a nearby parking and fishing access. Drop down the hill below the lower dam, passing through the group camp. Look for trail signs entering the woods.

0.3 Cross a bridge over lower Sams Creek. Once across the bridge, turn left on the Maple Grove Loop. Here the Lakeside Trail leads right and continues circling the lower lake.

0.4 Reach the confluence of Sams Creek and Whetstone Creek. Stay right here, traveling upstream along Whetstone Creek.

0.6 Come to an intersection where the Maple Grove Loop leaves right. Stay straight, now on the Whetstone Trail.

0.7 The Meadow Trail leaves right. Keep straight, still on the Whetstone Trail. Curve right after coming near US 42.

1.0 Reach the alternate trailhead parking off US 42. Continue the loop by walking around a pole gate on a grassy track. Cruise over hills divided by small drainages.

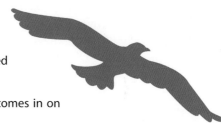

1.2 The other end of the Meadow Trail comes in on your right. Stay left.

1.3 Reach the Piney Woods Loop. Stay right and start descending sharply. The lake comes into view through the trees.

1.4 Stay straight as the Maple Grove Loop enters on your right.

1.5 Rejoin the Lakeside Trail. Turn left, briefly cruising along the shore before climbing hills above the water.

1.7 Stay straight as the Piney Woods Loop merges on your left.

1.8 Stay straight as the Fern Ridge Trail leaves left. At this point, very near the dam separating the upper lake from the lower lake, you can see the trailhead across the lake. Ahead, drop to lake level, crossing a perennial spring branch and wetlands.

2.0 Turn left on the Sams Creek Trail just after crossing a spring branch on a boardwalk. The Sams Creek Trail climbs steeply away from the lake.

2.1 Turn right with the Sams Creek Trail and return toward the lake.

2.5 Rejoin the Lakeside Trail. Turn left and pass through a riparian forest heavy with buckeye. Cross the footbridge over upper Sams Creek, then make the sharpest climb of the hike.

2.6 Reach the campground. Follow the campground road past the camp office and stay right on the main park road, passing the first picnic shelter, then the nature center on your right.

2.9 Pick up a footpath behind picnic shelter #2.

3.0 Complete the hike after following wood and earth steps to the lake.

This is an unusual hike. As its name implies, Dawes Arboretum is an interesting collection of trees, plants, and flowers—a place where roads and trails course through fascinating flora, allowing you to view the collection. Much of the terrain is open, however, and is not all dense forest. From the visitor center, explore the Japanese Garden, then climb Oak Hill. The hike next leads to Pershing Avenue, where trees memorialize war veterans. Pass Dawes Lake and climb a tower that gives a lay of the land. Your return route bisects the Deep Woods, a natural forest, before returning to the visitor center.

Start: Visitor center

Distance: 3.6-mile loop

Hiking time: About 2.5 to 3 hours

Difficulty: Moderate

Trail surface: Asphalt, gravel, grass, and natural surface

Best season: Spring through fall for botanical appreciation

Other trail users: None

Canine compatibility: Pets not allowed on trails

Land status: Privately owned arboretum

Fees and permits: None

Schedule: Open daily 7 a.m. to dusk except New Year's Day, Thanksgiving, and Christmas

Maps: Dawes Arboretum Visitor Map; USGS Thornville

Trail contact: Dawes Arboretum, 7770 Jacksontown Rd. SE, Newark, OH 43056; (740) 323-2355; www.dawesarb.org

Finding the trailhead: From exit 132 on I-70, east of downtown Columbus, take OH 13 north for 2.6 miles to the arboretum. Follow signs for the visitor center, then park in the lot south of the visitor center. Trailhead GPS: N39 58.799' / W82 24.809'

THE HIKE

Greater Columbus is better off having had Beman and Bertie Dawes in its midst. These two benefactors' love of trees and of nature in general led to the 1,800-acre arboretum we see today. The former country home and grounds of the couple, what is now the Dawes Arboretum includes over 15,000 living plants, 4,500 of them unique to their type. Here are some more numbers: 8 miles of trails and a 4-mile auto tour, all initially established in 1929. Today you can explore this impressive tract of land and gain a greater appreciation for some of the varied flora that grows upon planet Earth.

Start your Dawes Arboretum adventure in the visitor center. Here you can get oriented, grab a map and learn a few things from the nature displays, and even have a cup of coffee or a light meal. The Dawes Arboretum is a private facility and certainly appreciates membership or donations to keep the organization moving. The arboretum hosts school groups and presents nature programs and events. This destination has a lot to offer, not the least of which is the following enlightening hike.

Unlike your typical nature park, much of the grounds are landscaped and mown. Literally thousands of trees and shrubs are labeled and identified. If you read every one of these interpretive signs, it would literally take you days to walk this loop. Significant manpower is needed to keep up these grounds; you will likely

Hedges spell out Dawes Arboretum and can be seen by passing airplanes.

14

see arboretum employees plying their trade, whether it is clearing a path, sculpting the bushes, honing the Japanese Garden, or simply mowing a lawn. You'll undoubtedly appreciate all the work.

The trails are fairly well marked, but you do travel through open areas. Spur paths and walkways make the hike a little challenging direction-wise. You will follow the Oak Trail its entire length. Getting lost is an impossibility, as arboretum boundaries, the open terrain, and an auto tour road passing through the grounds will prevent this from happening.

The Japanese Garden is your first major destination. Take the concrete walkway around the pond, noting the sculpted bushes and trees and the small islands. The main loop continues through a mix of forest and field. As with most parts of Dawes Arboretum, this locale has a manicured look.

Pershing Avenue is a somber reminder of the wars we have fought to keep our nation free. The wide walking lane, lined with trees commonly used along city streets, memorializes those who have perished in previous wars. Beyond this locale you will come alongside Dawes Lake, which provides an aquatic complement to the gardens. A spur trail heads out to an island in the lake.

There are simply so many interesting trees. And since many of the trees are gathered in groupings, you can compare the different varieties of one species; for

The Japanese Garden pond reflects autumn colors.

example, magnolias or oaks. There's even a rare tree collection. This hike actually takes a short mini-loop to explore the oddest trees. Contemplation benches are situated throughout the hike, allowing you to relax and absorb the many scenes and settings.

A combination of hilly terrain and open vegetation reveals a surprising number of exciting views. Of course, the best view of them all may be from the observation tower, where you climb a series of steps and overlook the arboretum and points west. Take note of the gigantic hedge lettering that spells out Dawes Arboretum. It can be easily seen from an airplane, as well as the observation tower.

After seeing all these varieties of trees, you will enter what is known as the Deep Woods. Here a natural, thriving, mature hardwood forest, typical of central Ohio, flourishes. Within the Deep Woods you will visit a historic cemetery that even includes veterans of the Revolutionary War. Stop by a rustic log cabin that the Daweses used as a summer retreat. The Cypress Swamp is your final surprise. Traverse a boardwalk here through the eerie wetland trees, with their peculiar knees rising from the soil. After this hike you will have an added appreciation not only for the Daweses for establishing this retreat, but also for the vast vegetational variety found within its boundaries.

MILES AND DIRECTIONS

0.0 Start your hike at the visitor center, after getting an arboretum map. With the visitor center to your right, head left toward the parking lot, where you will see a post indicating the Oak Trail, Holly Trail, and Maple Trail. Take the Oak Trail, passing through mixed trees and grass, generally heading southwest.

0.1 The Maple Trail leads left at a post in open terrain. Continue toward the Japanese Garden, crossing the auto access road to the garden. Westerly views open.

0.3 Take the spur trail leading left around the pond at the Japanese Garden. Following a concrete path, complete the loop, then continue on a grassy trail. Drift in and out of woods as you climb toward Holly Hill.

0.9 Under a little arbor, the Holly Trail leaves left and shortcuts the loop. Turn right, still on the Oak Trail, heading toward Oak Hill. Myriad types of oak trees are on display here. Ahead, drift into the Beech & Buckeye Collection, down in a moist swale.

1.4 Cross the Auto Tour Road. Begin climbing a hill past many more identified trees. Unusual plants lure you away from the trail, and then you see another tree, identify it, and so on, finding yourself absorbed in the interpretive information.

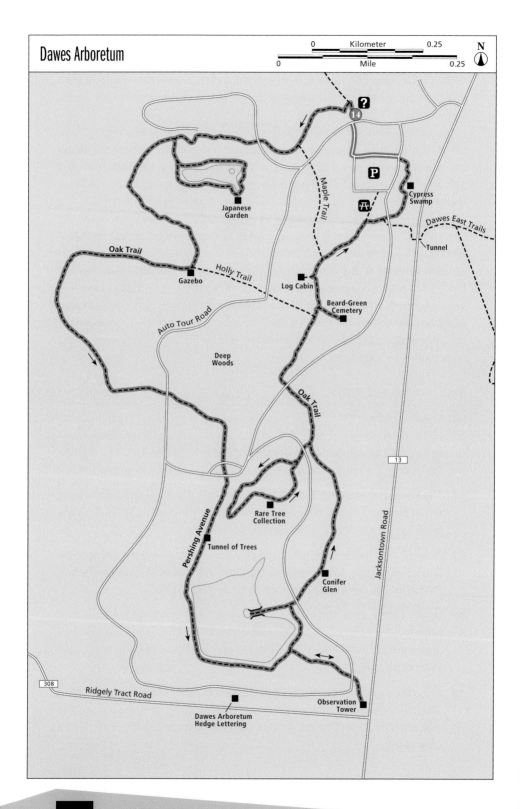

Dawes Arboretum

0 — Kilometer — 0.25

0 — Mile — 0.25

N

?

14

P

Japanese Garden

Maple Trail

Cypress Swamp

Dawes East Trails

Oak Trail

Holly Trail

Gazebo

Log Cabin

Tunnel

Beard-Green Cemetery

Auto Tour Road

Deep Woods

Oak Trail

13

Rare Tree Collection

Jacksontown Road

Pershing Avenue

Tunnel of Trees

Conifer Glen

308

Ridgely Tract Road

Observation Tower

Dawes Arboretum Hedge Lettering

1.6 Cross a small parking area on the Auto Tour Road, then cross part of the Auto Tour Road just before joining the main trail , here called Pershing Avenue.

1.7 Come alongside Dawes Lake. You will curve along its south shore. Note the hedge lettering just below you, spelling DAWES ARBORETUM.

2.0 Reach a trail junction. Turn right, following the trail to the park observation tower.

2.1 Climb the park observation tower, with view opening of the arboretum to the north and greater Columbus to the west. The hedge lettering below is especially notable. Backtrack to the Oak Trail.

2.2 Rejoin the Oak Trail. Curve around the east side of Dawes Lake and soon reach a spur trail leading left. Follow this trail out to the island in Dawes Lake, a relaxing setting. After enjoying the views, backtrack and cross the Auto Tour Road, heading east. Enter Conifer Glen and enjoy trekking through hundreds of species of evergreens. Ahead, wander through the magnolias.

2.7 Reach a trail intersection very near the Auto Tour Road. Cross the road west, then begin the loop trail working through the Rare Tree Collection. Stay right when the loop splits, heading counterclockwise. The circuit will come very near Pershing Avenue before returning.

3.0 Rejoin the Oak Trail after completing the loop through the Rare Tree Collection. Enter natural forest in what is known as the Deep Woods.

3.1 Cross the Auto Tour Road and continue in mature hardwoods.

3.3 The Holly Trail comes in from your left; stay straight on the Oak Trail. In just a few feet, a spur trail leads right to the Beard-Green Cemetery, the resting place of Revolutionary War veterans who resettled in Ohio.

3.4 A short spur leads left to the Dawes log cabin, built as a cool woodland retreat from the oppressive summers of pre-air-conditioning days. It is now a sugar shack, where maple sap is turned into syrup.

3.5 Come near the picnic shelter on the south end of the visitor parking area. Stay right here, then head left, toward the Cypress Swamp.

3.6 Walk through the boardwalk of the Cypress Swamp, noting the unusual "knees" below the main trunks. Emerge onto the parking area, finishing the hike.

Dawes Arboretum East

This hike explores the lesser visited, lesser developed, natural side of Dawes Arboretum. Located east of OH 13, this wild-area hike makes a loop, first climbing to the site of an Indian mound and then traveling east through tall mature woods to the gorge of Quarry Run. You will then backtrack and resume the circuit, passing a few meadows before coming to serene Scout Pond. Relax beside this watery escape before returning to the main arboretum grounds.

Start: Picnic shelter just south of visitor parking lot
Distance: 3.1-mile loop with out-and-back
Hiking time: About 1.5 to 2 hours
Difficulty: Easy to moderate
Trail surface: Natural surface
Best season: Year-round; fall for leaf color
Other trail users: None
Canine compatibility: Pets not allowed on trails
Land status: Privately owned arboretum

Fees and permits: Day-hiking permit required for hiking east of OH 13 (available at visitor center)
Schedule: Open daily 7 a.m. to dusk except New Year's Day, Thanksgiving, and Christmas
Maps: Arboretum East Trails; USGS Thornville
Trail contact: Dawes Arboretum, 7770 Jacksontown Rd. SE, Newark, OH 43056; (740) 323-2355; www.dawesarb.org

Finding the trailhead: From exit 132 on I-70, east of downtown Columbus, take OH 13 north for 2.6 miles to the arboretum. Follow signs for the visitor center, then park in the lot south of the visitor center. Trailhead GPS: N39 58.695' / W82 24.775'

THE HIKE

Dawes Arboretum is best known for its collection of trees and plants and the trails and roads that run through them. When people think of this private outdoor destination, they think of the visitor center, the Japanese Garden, and the Daweswood House and Gardens, where Beman and Bertie Dawes had a home that was to become the 1,800-acre arboretum we know and love. However, there is another side to Dawes Arboretum, literally, for on the east side of OH 13 lies an additional tract of land managed by the arboretum. Primarily kept in its natural state, a set of trails meanders through alluring woods. You can explore these trails for yourself and include a tour of the main grounds if you want. However, if you do hike the east-side trails, make sure to sign in at the visitor center. Currently park personnel want hikers who trek what is known as Arboretum East to register, so no

The smooth gray trunk of this beech contrasts freshly fallen leaves.

one will get lost or otherwise discombobulated. The rules may change on this in the future, but you need to go to the visitor center first anyway to get a trail map and enjoy the exhibits located therein.

It is amazing how few people come over to this part of the preserve. The main arboretum can be swamped with visitors, but this part will be as lonely as the Lake Erie shore in January. Finding the crossing to the Arboretum East trails may be the hardest part of the hike. But once across OH 13, you will enter a meadow and then begin the primary loop. Here the Mound Loop leads right and uphill to the arboretum's high point and the site of an ancient Indian mound. which verifies that this swath of central Ohio has been revered for hundreds of years. The mound is now cloaked in trees, with woods rising all around, but it is in a protected area, which is good. Aboriginal Ohioans lived here between 1000 BC and AD 100, primarily in small agricultural villages. They used these mounds to bury important members of their clan. Interestingly, this particular mound has never been scientifically excavated, though amateur diggings are evident.

The Mound Loop drops off the high point, wandering through tall hardwoods of cherry, beech, and walnut. The trail system here is as well-maintained as the gardens of the arboretum are on the far side of OH 13. But the paths over here are virtually unused, thus you'll experience solitude on your trek.

This quiet pond presents an opportunity for natural reflection.

Stay in deep forest beyond the Main Trail, after picking up the Gorge Spur. Watch for dug holes to your left, part of an old quarry, and enjoy a classic "big woods" walk. After resuming the Main Trail, you will travel the nexus of field and forest, an edge also known as an "ecotone overlap." These areas make for productive wildlife viewing. Deer trails will be evident to the cagey hiker, even if you don't see a deer yourself.

The Scout Pond adds another environment to the mix. Listen to frogs croak on the edge of the dark pool, and look for fish in the water. Bugs and birds will be attracted to the small impoundment. This was probably once a pond for livestock, but now adds to the Arboretum East experience. Beyond the pond, the Main Trail takes you back to OH 13 and the primary grounds of Dawes Arboretum.

MILES AND DIRECTIONS

0.0 Start your hike at the picnic shelter located just south of the main parking lot. Make sure to sign in at the visitor center and get an Arboretum East trail map. With your back to the parking lot and visitor center, walk past the picnic shelter, then immediately turn left and come to a trail junction. Here the Oak Trail leaves left but you keep straight, heading easterly toward OH 13. Look for a sign stating ACCESS EAST SIDE NATURAL AREA. As you near OH 13, come to a concrete walkway leading to a low tunnel that passes under OH 13.

0.2 Pass a kiosk, then come to a trail junction in an open grassy area. OH 13 is just west. Grassy trails go straight and right. Head right, uphill, on the Mound Loop. Pass through meadowland that will be flowering colorfully in fall.

0.3 Enter a full-blown hardwood forest of hickory and maple.

0.4 Top out at the Indian mound. The Mound Loop turns easterly and descends from the mound to meet the Main Trail.

0.6 Turn right at the intersection, joining the Main Trail, a seldom-trod double-track path. Watch for big beech trees along this stretch of trail. Other mature hardwoods shade the path as it travels through rolling country.

0.9 Come to a trail junction. Continue straight on the wide Gorge Spur, as the Main Trail turns left. You will return to this intersection later. Step over small drainages flowing toward Quarry Run.

1.4 The official trail ends at a bluff overlooking Quarry Run, its gorge cut during glacial runoff thousands of years ago. Backtrack to the Main Trail.

1.9 Return to the Main Trail and turn right, northbound. Descend through big woods.

Dawes Arboretum East

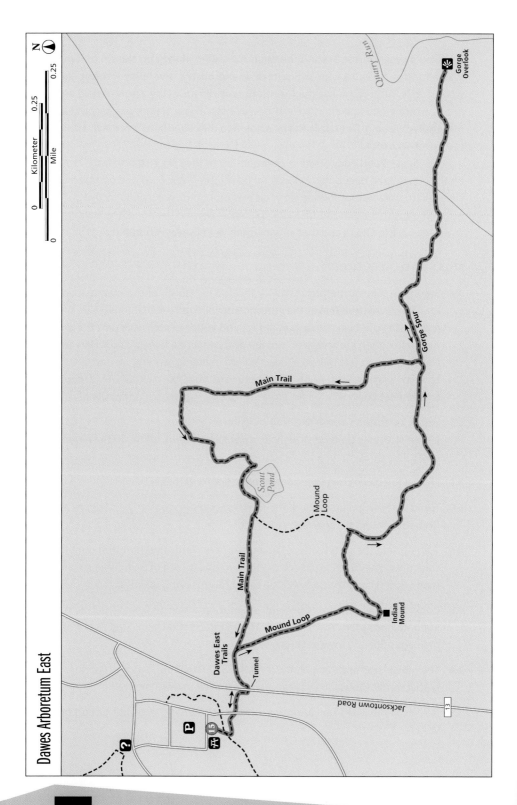

Gorge Overlook

Quarry Run

Gorge Spur

Main Trail

Scout Pond

Mound Loop

Main Trail

Mound Loop

Indian Mound

Dawes East Trails

Tunnel

Jacksontown Road

13

N

Kilometer
0   0.25

Mile
0   0.25

2.0 Curve past the edge of a field. Continue hiking along the margin of forest and meadow. Look for deer trails connecting the clearings to the woods.

2.3 The path turns abruptly west, then south, aiming for Scout Pond.

2.6 Open onto Scout Pond. A mown strip borders the upper pond and makes for a fine contemplation area. Hike past its lower end, along the small dam.

2.7 The Mound Loop leaves left for the high mound atop the hill. This hike keeps straight on the Main Trail, bisecting open grasses.

2.9 Complete the Main Trail loop. Backtrack through the tunnel under OH 13.

3.1 Reach the picnic shelter by the visitor parking area, finishing the hike. Let the folks at the visitor center know you have returned from the Arboretum East.

About Beech Trees

Beech trees are common on this hike, especially on the north-facing slope beyond the Indian mound. The gray-trunked tree ranges throughout the Buckeye State. Beech trees are among the easiest trees to identify in northern hardwood forests, such as here at Dawes. First, the smooth gray trunk makes it stand out in the forest, as the carvings common to this tree testify. Many woodland walkers simply can't resist the flat surface of the beech—it seems a tablet for a handy pocketknife. The smooth trunks contrast vividly with the knobby and fissured oaks that thrive in this region.

Pick up a beech leaf from the forest floor. The sunlight-absorbing leaves are generally 2 to 4 inches long. Note the sharply toothed edges of the leaves. They are a dark green on top and lighter underneath. In fall they turn a yellowish golden brown. Under ideal conditions, beech trees can reach 120 feet in height. However, the average mature trees, like those you will see along the trail, stretch 60 to 80 feet from the ground.

After the leaves fall from the beech, you will notice the buds of next year's leaves. They are just a half-inch in length but resemble a mini-cigar. Come spring, these buds will unfurl to once again convert sunlight for the tree as it resumes growing during the warm season.

Beechnuts are about the size of your thumbnail. They are an important food for wildlife, from mice to deer, and for birds, from ducks to blue jays. Critters break apart the burr-covered shell to reach the nutrient-rich treat. Humans use the wood of beech trees for everything from flooring to railroad ties to charcoal. And, of course, many people think of it as a carving tablet.

Flint Ridge State Memorial

This historic hike heads to an important resource for aboriginal Ohioans and beyond who came to to quarry for the ideal stone with which to create points for arrows, spears, and other tools. Here you will hike past former quarry pits and along flint outcrops. The Creek Trail leads to big trees and impressive woods below the main quarry site. Visit the museum in season. A second nature trail explores other flint quarries north of the main grounds.

Start: Flint Ridge State Memorial picnic area
Distance: 2.1 miles with multiple loops
Hiking time: About 2 to 2.5 hours
Difficulty: Easy
Trail surface: Natural surface and a little asphalt
Best season: Year-round
Other trail users: None
Canine compatibility: Leashed dogs permitted

Land status: State memorial
Fees and permits: None required for hike; fee required for museum
Schedule: Open daily year-round; museum open May through Oct, Sat 9 a.m. to 5 p.m. and Sun 10 a.m. to 5 p.m.
Map: USGS Glenford
Trail contact: Flint Ridge State Memorial, 15300 Flint Ridge Rd., Glenford, OH 43739; (800) 283-8707; www.ohiohistory.org

Finding the trailhead: From exit 141, Brownsville/Gratiot, on I-70 east of downtown Columbus, follow OH 668 north for 0.7 mile. Jog left on US 40 in the hamlet of Brownsville, then turn right and take Brownsville Road north for 3.1 miles to Flint Ridge Road. Turn right on Flint Ridge Road, then immediately turn right again into the state memorial. Drive to the parking area near the picnic shelter and pick up the trails there. Trailhead GPS: N39 59.326' / W82 15.669'

THE HIKE

The Ohio Historical Society Marker about this site sums it up well:

> For more than 10,000 years, Flint Ridge was one of the most impor-
> tant flint quarries in eastern North America. The flint formed at
> the bottom of the shallow ocean 300 million years ago. The softer
> rock surrounding the flint has washed away, leaving the hard flint
> exposed near the surface. Prehistoric people came here to quarry
> the flint, which they crafted into a variety of stone tools. Hundreds
> of quarry pits and workshops are scattered for miles along this
> ridge. The beautiful rainbow-colored flint was especially prized
> by the Hopewell culture that built the nearby Newark Earthworks.
> Artifacts crafted from Flint Ridge flint may be found throughout
> eastern North America.

That's a good summary of the importance of this special slice of Ohio to aboriginals from throughout the continent. Their tools, their weapons, and their means of hunting, defending themselves, and improving their everyday lives all came back to this 9-by-3-mile ridge. Flint Ridge Memorial encompasses but a sliver of Flint Ridge, yet it preserves exemplary quarry sites and leaves the terrain as the early miners might have found it. They not only mined here, but also camped and hunted while extracting the stone. At the museum you can learn about how they mined for flint as well as knapped it. It's fascinating to contemplate all the people that came to Licking County here in central Ohio to get some of this special flint. In the early 1900s the area preserved today was extensively researched by archaeologists. They convinced the state of Ohio of the historical value of the area, and Flint Ridge was made a state memorial in 1934.

The Quarry Trail leads you away from the picnic area and into a forest of maple, ash, and oak. Interestingly, even today flint outcrops border the trail. You will soon join the Creek Trail, where huge white oaks and tulip trees shade the path. A spur trail leads uphill to a flint outcrop that was mined. Notice all the chipped rock as you scale the hill to a line of outcrops. See where these outcrops have been broken—the rock looks cleaner and brighter. Rubble is strewn about. Imagine aboriginals working this rock, despite the weather, while camping in the hollow below. To this day a spring provides year-round water, which was undoubtedly utilized back then, for mining is hard work, especially with the limited tools of that time.

However, miners often just carted off chunks of this Ohio flint, for trading and for their own use. This flint was of such quality that, when needed, a skilled hunter could simply knock off a piece from the greater slab and work it into a point as sharp as that of a modern knife. But flint was also fashioned into everyday tools for scraping hides, preparing food, and making hatchets. It was this multipurpose rock that increased the efficiency of everyday early Ohioans. True, various flints can be found in most parts of the United States, but the flint here, known as Van Port flint, was of superior quality that made it easy to work, and thus increased its value. In addition to its mineral qualities, the flint—brownish gold, mixed with reds and other hues—is simply aesthetically attractive, too, which further increased the demand for it.

The Creek Trail takes you into a gently sloping hollow and big woods. A pair of streams cuts down the valley, adding an aquatic contrast to the tall trees. The rocky watercourses may or may not be flowing. Look for flint outcrops in the woods as you hike. Don't be surprised to see deer and especially squirrels in this refuge.

The Creek Trail takes you back up to the main facilities and mining areas. Here the Quarry Trail leads to the open pit mines. Irregular depressions among the trees indicate where flint was mined from the site. Ironically, as these pits have filled, they have become vernal pools, important for amphibian life. After noticing the number of these holes—and there are upwards of 1,000 pit mines on the entire length of Flint Ridge—ponder the labor that went into digging them.

You will eventually end up at the Flint Ridge State Memorial Museum. It is open on warm-weather weekends and can enhance your understanding of what went on here in Licking County for thousands of years. Beyond the museum, take the asphalt nature trail past more mines. Enjoy the interpretive information before completing the first hike.

The second hike lies north across Flint Ridge Road. This other trail is simply called the "Nature Trail," but it actually visits an incredible number of pit mines nestled in the woods, bordered by dirt mounds that have slowly eroded over time. It then curves along a wildflower-filled ravine before making a little loop back to the ravine's edge. Look—and listen—for quaking aspen trees along the way. After completing this mini-loop, you simply backtrack to the state memorial entrance. This bonus trail adds a little mileage and enhances your appreciation of the size of Flint Ridge and the mining that went on throughout the ridge. By the way, flint is the official gemstone of the state of Ohio, recognition of the significance of Flint Ridge.

> **Green Tip:**
> *After rains, trails can often be muddy. Avoid sidestepping around muddy areas, as this eventually widens the path and tramples adjacent vegetation.*

Not only is this flint valuable for toolmaking, it is also colorful.

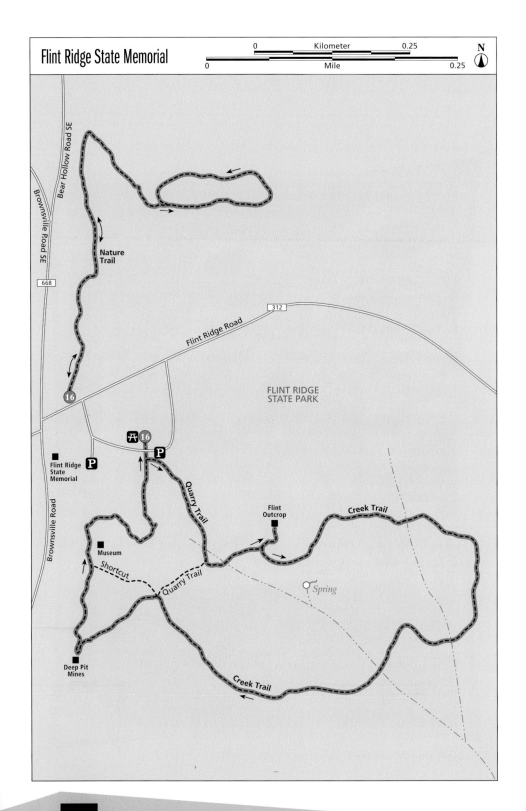

Flint Ridge State Memorial

0   Kilometer   0.25
0   Mile   0.25

N

Bear Hollow Road SE

Brownsville Road SE

Nature Trail

668

Flint Ridge Road

312

FLINT RIDGE
STATE PARK

16

16

P

Flint Ridge
State
Memorial

P

Quarry Trail

Flint
Outcrop

Creek Trail

Brownsville Road

Museum

Shortcut

Quarry Trail

Spring

Deep Pit
Mines

Creek Trail

MILES AND DIRECTIONS

0.0 Start near the picnic shelter. With your back to the shelter, facing south, pick up the Quarry Trail. Do not take the asphalt Nature Trail—that will be your return route. The natural-surface Quarry Trail leads away from the picnic area and into forest. Descend a bit.

0.1 Intersect the Creek Trail in the shade of a massive tulip tree. Turn left here.

0.2 Take the spur trail on the left leading up to a flint outcrop that was mined. Resume the Creek Trail after backtracking from the flint outcrop. The mature woods are favorable for spring wildflowers.

0.4 Bridge an intermittent streambed.

0.6 Bridge the streambed again.

0.7 Bridge the main stream of the hollow and begin angling back uphill.

1.0 Intersect the Quarry Trail. Turn left here and soon pass a shortcut.

1.1 Reach the state memorial museum. There is an entry fee for the museum, but it is worth it. Beyond the museum, look right for the asphalt Nature Trail. Join it, passing more mine sites.

1.2 Complete the first hike, returning to the trailhead and picnic area. Walk toward Flint Ridge Road, and just across from the entry to the state memorial, look for a sign indicating Nature Trail. Enter rich woods and immediately pass scores of pit mines, now mere depressions in the forest, bordered by leaf-covered dirt banks. In spring the pits will be water-filled. You will come alongside a steep wooded ravine—the moist hollow is prime wildflower habitat. Look for flint outcrops along the edge of the ravine.

1.6 Reach the loop portion of the Nature Trail. Stay right, still in flatwoods.

1.7 Finish the loop, returning to the edge of the ravine. Backtrack toward Flint Ridge Road.

2.1 Return to Flint Ridge Road, completing the hike.

17

Blackhand Gorge State Nature Preserve

This is one beautiful hike, a must-do for all central Ohioans. Take the Blackhand Trail into a deepening gorge along the Licking River, and enjoy bluffs towering over the river while traversing a user-friendly paved path. Take the Chestnut Trail, climbing along the gorge rim. Backtrack toward the trailhead, then take the Quarry Rim Trail to explore water-filled sandstone quarries that offer contrasting beauty. If the distance is too much, you can tailor the hike to suit your desires.

Start: Toboso trailhead at Blackhand Gorge Nature Preserve
Distance: 7.2 miles out and back
Hiking time: About 3.5 to 5 hours
Difficulty: Moderate to difficult due to distance
Trail surface: Asphalt and natural surface
Best seasons: Spring for wildflowers, winter for viewing rock features
Other trail users: Bicyclists and joggers on paved Blackhand Trail
Canine compatibility: Dogs not permitted in nature preserve
Land status: State nature preserve
Fees and permits: None
Schedule: Open daily year-round
Maps: Blackhand Gorge State Nature Preserve; USGS Toboso, Hanover
Trail contact: Ohio Department of Natural Resources, 2045 Morse Rd., Building C-3, Columbus, OH 43229-6693; (614) 265-6453; www.dnr.state.oh.us

Finding the trailhead: From the intersection of OH 13 and OH 16 in downtown Newark, east of downtown Columbus, take OH 16 east for 9.7 miles and get off at the Hanover/Zanesville/OH 146 exit. Join OH 146 east for 0.2 mile to Toboso Road. Turn right on Toboso Road and follow it 1.7 miles, then turn right into the Blackhand Gorge State Nature Preserve parking area on a one-way road, shortly after bridging the Licking River. Trailhead GPS: N40 3.368'/W82 13.106'

THE HIKE

Blackhand Gorge is one of those special places that make the case for state nature preserves. Coming in a little under 1,000 acres, the parcel of land protects a sandstone gorge cut by the Licking River. Not only is the place rich in geological features—cliffs, rock overhangs, and boulder fields—it is also rich in vegetation such as wildflowers and diverse woodlands from xeric oak stands to bottomland hardwoods. And don't forget the Licking River, a scenic waterway flowing through the heart of the gorge.

Additionally you have the human history of the preserve. At one time a petroglyph of a hand, outlined in black, purportedly overlooked the Licking River. Unfortunately the Blackhand petroglyph was blasted away when the Licking River was widened during the construction of the Ohio-Erie Canal back in the 1820s. The keen eye will spot leftover relics of canal locks along the waterway. A separate short path, the Canal Lock Trail, explores one of these necessary structures created to solve the canal's elevation changes. The Canal Lock Trail can be found on the west side of the Licking River near the Toboso trailhead, where you start your hike.

Later, a railroad would pass through the gorge. The bed of this former rail line is what forms the primary trail cutting east–west through this scenic vale. The dam-

Water-filled quarries lie silent long after the marble extractors have left.

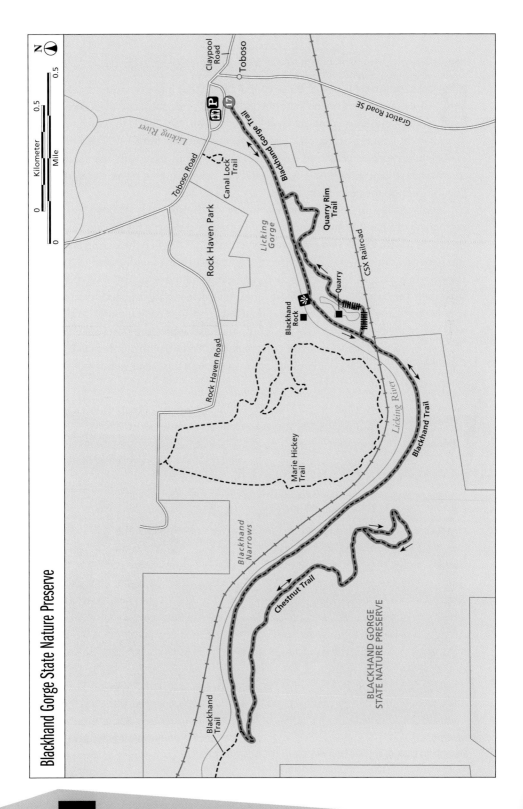

Blackhand Gorge State Nature Preserve

ming of Dillon Lake downstream forced the line to be moved to the present one that passes through the gorge.

Blackhand sandstone is a prized building block found in central Ohio, and its name originated here. Check out mining history on the trek. The sandstone was quarried along the south rim of Blackhand Gorge. A trail takes you amid these water-filled pits that add an unnatural yet alluring land/waterscape to the entire experience.

Nowadays hikers and bicyclists follow the Blackhand Trail along the Licking River. Interestingly, the paved Blackhand Trail is the only bicycle path in the entire state nature preserve system. Joggers also use the paved trail, which extends over 4 miles one-way from Toboso to CR 668 near the hamlet of Claylick. Bicyclists are not allowed on the other trails in the preserve.

The hike leaves Toboso on a level asphalt track. Note the old millstones and the trailhead wall made from Blackhand sandstone. Casual strollers will be found near the trailhead. You will soon saddle alongside the Licking River, where tall cotton-wood, ash, and sycamore trees grow over the boulder-strewn watercourse, shading gravel bars. It isn't long before you walk under sheer sandstone bluffs, where hemlocks rise in thick ranks. Look for yellow birch in the cooler north-facing parts of the gorge. This is near the southern end of their range in Ohio. They are more commonly found in the northeastern section of the state and in north-facing hollows in the Appalachian foothills. Their shiny yellow peeling bark gives them away.

Continue following the curves of the river. Short paths lead down to the water's edge, where anglers and water lovers access the Licking. The main trail passes under the CSX railroad and continues up the gorge, where rocky drainages filled with rainwater flow from the hills above. Elevation changes are negligible until you leave the Blackhand Trail and pick up the singletrack Chestnut Trail.

The natural-surface Chestnut Trail leads above the river to enjoy some top-down views of the Licking before climbing still higher in the oaks. The trail travels mid-slope in the gorge, delivering a greater perspective of just how big Blackhand Gorge is. Eventually the path turns into a tributary valley and then makes a small loop. Look for more rock features amid the sloped woods before backtracking, first on the Chestnut Trail, then on the Blackhand Trail. You may also see new trails under development that spur off the Chestnut Trail. Local residents have been teaming up with Blackhand Gorge management to expand the trail system on both the north and south sides of the Licking River. Stay tuned as the trail system evolves for the better.

On your return, join the Quarry Rim Trail, another singletrack trail, and take a trip into mining history. Here you will see remaining concrete structures, tailings, and deep pits where sandstone was removed and became building material. Visitors are asked to stay out of the pits and the nearby active rail line for safety reasons. However, you can enjoy good views as the path swings by the edges of quarries. Some final hilltop meanderings lead back to the Blackhand Trail and a short backtrack to the trailhead.

MILES AND DIRECTIONS

0.0   Start at Toboso trailhead of Blackhand Gorge Nature Preserve, The nearby signed parking lot has several parking spaces, an informational kiosk, and a restroom. Join an asphalt path with a few houses on your left and the Licking River flowing out of sight to your right.

0.3   The Quarry Rim Trail leaves left as a singletrack path. You will emerge here on your return trip. For now, continue along the Blackhand Gorge Trail. Sandstone bluffs rise from the trail.

0.5   The trail is squeezed in by sandstone bluffs on one side and the Licking River on the other. Tulip trees grow straight and thick here. In winter you will see impressive bluffs on the far side of the river.

0.7   A short spur trail leads right to the Licking River. Across the river you can see the sandstone bluffs where the Blackhand petroglyph purportedly once was. Ahead, the main trail cuts through blasted rock, flanking both sides of the path, cleared for the railroad right-of-way upon which the trail lies.

0.9   Reach the other end of the Quarry Rim Trail. On your return trip this is where you will pick it up. Ahead, walk under the CSX railroad line that bridges the Licking River and then runs along the north bank.

2.0   Watch for a pair of trailside rock houses on the left.

2.3   Turn left on the Chestnut Trail. The singletrack path cuts into a tributary drainage and climbs past some rock bluffs before ascending further into the wooded and sloped upper part of the gorge.

3.3   The Chestnut Trail bridges a ravine in a tributary valley, then comes to a trail intersection. Here the path begins a small loop up a still-smaller valley. Head left up the mini-loop on a sometimes faint path.

3.8   Complete the mini-loop of the Chestnut Trail. Backtrack to the Blackhand Trail and the Licking River.

4.8   Return to the Blackhand Trail and turn right. The Licking River is now to your left. Retrace your steps down Blackhand Gorge.

6.2   Turn right on the Quarry Rim Trail and begin meandering through mining history. Pass a concrete structure, then span a wet area on a bridge. Ahead, a view opens of a watery quarry pit to your left. Traverse a narrow ridge between two quarries.

6.5 The trail narrows to a slender land bridge with wooden steps. Beyond here, cruise in sassafras, oak, and hickory woods above the Licking River. Climb a wooded knob before dropping to the river.

6.9 Return to the Blackhand Gorge Trail. Turn right and resume backtracking toward the trailhead.

7.2 Arrive back at the Toboso trailhead, completing the hike.

The Licking River flows alongside the trail, adding an aquatic component to the hike.

Marie Hickey Loop at Blackhand Gorge

This is the forgotten hike of Blackhand Gorge, the one passed over by most visitors to this state nature preserve. Don't make the same mistake. This circuit oozes solitude and the back of beyond. Hike through deep and hilly woods, then come along the north rim of Blackhand Gorge, where views await. From there the hike visits a smaller tributary, investigating a deep and dark hemlock copse through which a stream cuts a mini-gorge, complete with waterfalls. Pass more geological features before completing your loop, adding the short Oak Knob Trail, likely without seeing another soul along the way.

Start: Blackhand Gorge North Parking Lot

Distance: 2.4-mile loop

Hiking time: About 1.5 to 2 hours

Difficulty: Moderate

Trail surface: Natural surface

Best seasons: Spring for wildflowers, winter for viewing rock features

Other trail users: None

Canine compatibility: Dogs not permitted in nature preserve

Land status: State nature preserve

Fees and permits: None

Schedule: Open daily year-round

Maps: Blackhand Gorge State Nature Preserve; USGS Toboso, Hanover

Trail contact: Ohio Department of Natural Resources, 2045 Morse Rd., Building C-3, Columbus, OH 43229-6693; (614) 265-6453; www.dnr.state.oh.us

Finding the trailhead: From the intersection of OH 13 and OH 16 in downtown Newark, east of downtown Columbus, take OH 16 east for 9.7 miles and get off at the Hanover / Zanesville / OH 146 exit. Join OH 146 east for 0.2 mile to Toboso Road. Turn right on Toboso Road and follow it 1.3 miles, then turn right onto Rock Haven Road (if you cross the Licking River, you have gone too far). Follow Rock Haven Road for 1 mile to the trailhead, an asphalt parking area, on your left. Trailhead GPS: N40 3.518'/W82 14.300'

THE HIKE

The vast majority of hikers who walk Blackhand Gorge travel all or a portion of the Blackhand Trail, which runs east–west through the entire length of the gorge, south of the Licking River. And that 4-plus-mile segment of trail is well worth your time. However, there is another side of the gorge—the north side. It is on the north side where you can find solitude. You can also find deep woods, groves of aspen trees, and a mini-gorge in a quiet parcel of this state nature preserve.

Even the trailhead is understated here on the north rim. Two trails and a road-bed emanate from the parking area. The roadbed (not shown on our map) accesses some oil platforms on the property. The trail leading left is your return route. You will take the singletrack path leading right and uphill, the Marie Hickey Trail. The hike scales a knob and then works its way downhill, southbound, toward the Licking River and the base of Blackhand Gorge. Down here a moister forest of quaking aspen, cherry, maple, and hackberry shades the path. The trail levels off and you curve with the curves of the river. Enter a thicket of scrub pines and cedars; other evergreens include hemlock and planted spruce. A wide flat extends to your left.

You think the highlights may be over when you leave the Licking River, but this is when you turn up a tributary gorge with its own intimate beauty. Here rock

This water-carved mini-gorge lies hidden by hemlocks.

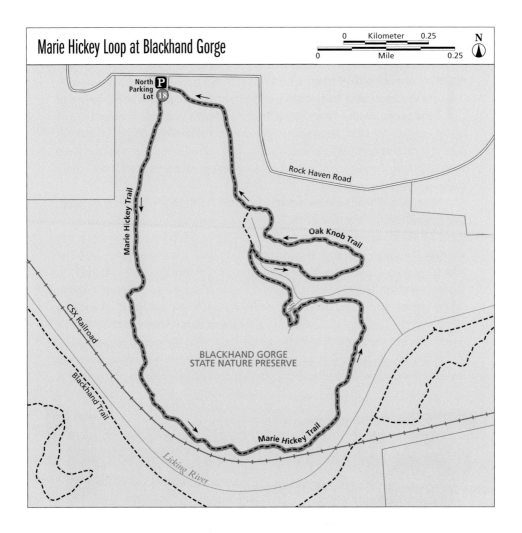

0   Kilometer   0.25

0   Mile   0.25

N

North Parking Lot 18

Rock Haven Road

Marie Hickey Trail

Oak Knob Trail

CSX Railroad

Blackhand Trail

BLACKHAND GORGE
STATE NATURE PRESERVE

Marie Hickey Trail

Licking River

walls form a semicircular cathedral where two streams come together, making a pair of low-flow waterfalls. The trail soon curves around the other side of this tight-knit mini-gorge, a pocket parcel of superlative beauty that makes the entire hike worthwhile.

The path then takes you around the edge of a larger, slightly less spectacular gorge, which also displays sandstone walls. The Oak Knob Trail leads into a tributary gorge before climbing a wooded hill. Watch for big tulip trees and oaks. Soon you will rejoin the Marie Hickey Trail and hike through young woods overtaking a former level field. The trail closes the loop after bridging a wet-weather tributary.

MILES AND DIRECTIONS

0.0 Start at the North Parking Lot. As you face the gated roadbed at the upper end of the parking area, look right for a singletrack path leading right and uphill on the Marie Hickey Trail, away from the trailhead kiosk.

0.2 Reach an oil platform access road and briefly follow it, then turn back onto singletrack path. Watch for large sassafras trees on the wooded ridge you travel. Oaks are prevalent as well.

0.6 Level off and come alongside the edge of the gorge. The CSX railroad track lies between you and the river.

0.9 Take in unobscured views of the gorge below. You can see the CSX railroad bridge crossing over to the south side of the Licking River. The Marie Hickey Trail continues along the edge of the gorge in pines, with other views occasionally opening of the river below.

1.2 Enjoy a last rim view of the Licking River. This one extends easterly, straight down the river valley.

1.4 Enter a dark-as-night hemlock copse bordering the edge of the tributary gorge. Listen for wet-weather waterfalls as you circle almost completely around this mini-gorge, cut in sheer sandstone walls.

1.6 Turn right, joining the Oak Knob Trail, and soon bridge a streamlet slicing a valley toward the Licking River. Look for the concrete foundations of a forgotten structure in the hollow below.

2.1 The Oak Knob Trail ends. Turn right, rejoining the Marie Hickey Trail, and begin hiking through successional fields, now more forest than field.

2.4 Arrive back at the North Parking Lot, finishing the hike.

> 🌿 **Green Tip:**
> *When choosing trail snacks, consider making healthy homemade goodies like granola bars. Or simply bring fruit—it tastes great with no preparation.*

More Trails to History in Blackhand Gorge

Blackhand Gorge was explored and traveled by aboriginal Ohioans at least since 1000 BC. During this time they painted on the gorge walls, leaving petroglyphs, the most famous of which was the black hand, around which many legends have sprung. One states that the hand, destroyed during the widening of the Licking River during construction of the Ohio-Erie Canal, pointed toward a sacred Indian burial mound. Another claims a shunned suitor of a native princess cut off his own hand and threw it into the gorge, the hand leaving a print on the gorge wall. Still another has the shunned suitor having his hand cut off by the man who won the princess.

In the 1820s, as the state became settled, the Ohio-Erie Canal project was undertaken. Canals were thought to be the future of American transportation, despite being labor-heavy projects that required lots of maintenance and infrastructure such as locks. But this canal would connect the Ohio River with Lake Erie, thus greatly enhancing the ability of farmers and manufacturers to transport their food and goods. They had to get through Blackhand Gorge and so built the dam to keep the Licking River at a reliable depth.

The canal worked during its time, but was eventually displaced by rail-roads after a long, slow decline. The infrastructure was then destroyed by a great flood in 1913. You can still see evidence of the Erie-Ohio Canal on the Canal Lock Trail, located near the Toboso Road bridge over the Licking River.

When railroads spread across the land, the Central Ohio Railroad used the gorge as a convenient east–west travel corridor. By 1851 they had bisected the sandstone and laid track through the south side of the gorge. This was an active line until the mid-1950s, when the US Army Corps of Engineers dammed the Licking River downstream of the gorge, necessitating a rerouting of the rail line.

It wasn't only barges and railroads that passed through Blackhand Gorge. In the late 1800s an electric trolley line was developed to connect Newark in the west to Zanesville in the east. This line ran along the north bank of the Licking River and included a 300-foot tunnel that was blasted through the sandstone. However, the timing of the electric trolley line was bad. Automobiles soon grew in popularity, and the electric line was abandoned.

And that's where the story becomes interesting today. A movement arose to open more of Blackhand Gorge. The north side of the gorge, the route of the electric trolley line, is a right-of-way owned by the state of Ohio and is being used as another trail corridor through the gorge. This trail also travels by Council Rock, the spot that some people argue contained the actual black hand petroglyph that gave the gorge its name, further muddling that issue. The new trail extends along the river beyond the Canal Lock Trail through the Interurban Tunnel and astride Council Rock. So, on your next trip to Blackhand Gorge State Nature Preserve, you will have more trails to explore on the north side of the Licking River.

Southeast Hikes

A glacial erratic stands stark on an open meadow (hike 23).

A sizable number of hikes in this guide are situated in the southeastern quadrant of greater Columbus. This is no accident. It is simply a reflection of what most Columbians regard as the best topography for walking in central Ohio (think Hocking Hills). Near Columbus the terrain is more level, yet offers worthy walks in southeastern Franklin County and Pickaway County. Then you enter the Appalachian foothills, full of geographical and geological wonders, in Fairfield County, Hocking County, and rugged Ross County.

The Metro Parks form a fine starting point. Explore land and waterscapes at Three Creeks Metro Park. Blacklick Woods is the oldest park in the Columbus Metro Parks system. Wander through this gem to enter Tucker State Nature Preserve, a special place featuring big trees, wetland woods, and incredible spring wildflowers. Pickerington Ponds Metro Park harbors wetlands galore—ponds, marshes, and creeks—among its 1,600 acres. A collection of trails take you through them.

Chestnut Ridge Metro Park contains the first Appalachian mountain rising southeast of Columbus. Hike past springs, a rock quarry, and wooded slopes to a view of downtown Columbus. Slate Run Metro Park has a living-history farm, where you can see central Ohio lifeways from days gone by. Hike along clear creeks cutting steep hills to grab a first-rate view from a ridge, down into wetlands where trails roam. Save energy to tour the farm, too.

Stages Pond State Nature Preserve turns the argument on its head that Ohio's flatlands offer little for the nature enthusiast. Walk to a glacially created lake, wetlands, and woods, with ample opportunities for birders and other wildlife enthusiasts. Hike a loop around the lake at A. W. Marion State Park, affirming your belief that the flatlands aren't boring lands.

Shallenberger State Nature Preserve, a great spring wildflower destination near Lancaster, takes you atop Allen Knob, which rises 240 feet above the surrounding terrain. Alley Park, also in Fairfield County, has extremely hilly and wooded terrain centered by a small lake. Its geological features will surprise you.

At 5,300 acres, 4,769 of which are designated state nature preserve, Clear Creek Metro Park is a Columbus hiking classic. The largest nature preserve in Ohio, it presents creekside and ridgetop trekking. Another area superlative is Rockbridge State Nature Preserve, which contains the largest natural bridge in the Buckeye State. Hike to the span, then make a side trip to the nearby Hocking River. Finally, visit a rock house and low-flow waterfall.

What can you say about Cantwell Cliffs except "go there"? Cruise the sandstone canyon's bluffs, then explore its interior, where a large rock house and waterfalls await, and escape through "Fat Woman's Squeeze." Conkles Hollow makes a geologically mind-blowing trek in a state nature preserve. First, climb the rim above Conkles Hollow, where rock outcrops provide inspiring views across a deep gorge, then find a waterfall in the innermost depths of the gorge before backtracking out.

Tar Hollow State Park and Forest is a big preserve. It has two of the longest hikes in this guide, both along the wild and wandering Logan Trail. The Ross Hollow Loop Hike presents a shorter option. Tar Hollow State Park comes in at a modest 600 acres; however, it is completely encircled by the 16,000-plus-acre Tar Hollow State Forest, which effectively enlarges the wild area of steep wooded hills divided by wildflower-filled "streamsheds." Hiking here is a must for central Ohioans. Finally, Great Seal State Park also presents rugged Appalachian foothill terrain that will challenge a hiker's stamina while revealing abundant splendor.

19

Three Creeks Hike

This multi-loop trek combines several trails and habitats at Three Creeks Metro Park, exploring the land and waters contained within. Leave the Confluence Area on the wildflower-rich Bluebell Trail, visiting the point where Alum Creek, Big Walnut Creek, and Blacklick Creek flow together, a place where big trees grow streamside. Enjoy more natural-surface pathway up Alum Creek on the Confluence Trail, then join the Alum Creek Greenway to eventually make a loop at Sycamore Fields. From there backtrack to make a final circuit around Turtle Pond, topping off your tour of the varied land and waterscapes at this park.

Start: Confluence Trails trailhead

Distance: 6.6-mile multiple loops

Hiking time: About 4 to 5.5 hours

Difficulty: Moderate; trails are mostly level

Trail surface: Natural surface and asphalt

Best season: Year-round

Other trail users: Joggers and bicyclists

Canine compatibility: Leashed dogs permitted

Land status: Metro Parks

Fees and permits: None

Schedule: Open daily year-round

Maps: Three Creeks Metro Park; USGS Southeast Columbus

Trail contact: Metro Parks, 1069 W. Main St., Westerville, OH 43081; (614) 891-0700; www .metroparks.net

Finding the trailhead: From exit 46 on I-270, southeast of downtown Columbus, take US 33 east toward Lancaster and drive 0.7 mile to the Hamilton Road/OH 317 exit. Join Hamilton Road right and follow it 1.1 miles toward the Confluence Trails and Bixby Road (do not turn right on Williams Road to the middle section of Three Rivers Park). Turn right on Bixby Road and follow it 0.7 mile, then turn right into the main entrance to Three Rivers Park. Follow the entrance road to the dead end at the parking area. Trailhead GPS: N39 52.841'/W82 54.185'

THE HIKE

The Columbus Metro Parks system improves the hiking possibilities in the greater capital area. Most parks have plenty of trails and plenty to see from the interconnected paths lying within their boundaries. Three Creeks Park demonstrates this with its multiplicity of paths, from the long Alum Creek Greenway to the natural-surface Bluebell Trail to the mini-loop encircling Turtle Pond. The hike detailed here stretches 6-plus miles and visits streams, bottomland, forests, ponds, and meadows. Hikers can always alter and adapt their hike depending on time, mood, and company. That is the advantage of such a trail network.

This trek starts at the Confluence Area, where paths spur in all directions. You will join the Bluebird Trail, a lesser-used natural-surface path that heads for the banks of Blacklick Creek and then follows it downstream past some big trees to reach the confluence of three streams. This low-lying bottomland is subject to flooding in spring but also offers a wildflower haven, including its namesake—Virginia bluebells. In summer the bottoms will be replete with stinging nettle shaded by huge sycamores and cottonwoods. Blacklick Creek gurgles downstream over gravel bars, sandbars, and rocks. The path can be muddy following heavy rains. It

A trail runner crosses the bridge over Big Walnut Creek.

reaches the unusual confluence of three fairly big streams, of which Alum Creek is the largest. See if you can detect different colorations in the streams. One or more may be dingy depending on localized rain, especially when sporadic summer thunderstorms strike.

The hike then joins the paved Alum Creek Greenway. This path attracts trail runners, bicyclists, and daily exercisers, many with determined looks on their faces. The greenway spans Alum Creek on a high bridge, delivering a different perspective on the stream below. Soon you are off the greenway and on the Confluence Trail. This natural-surface path heads upstream along Alum Creek, reaching the three-creek confluence from the west bank of Alum. You can clearly see where you were earlier. From there cruise up Alum Creek, looking for more wildflowers in season under more big cottonwood trees. This is favorable deer habitat.

Rejoin the Alum Creek Greenway just before it passes under I-270. Continue up the paved path, passing alternate parking at Madison Mills. The walking has been easy thus far and the trend continues, with little elevation change. The Heron Pond area presents alternate parking and a spur loop that circles the pond. The hike continues north to reach the Sycamore Fields Trail. Take this asphalt path to circle a meadow after bridging Alum Creek. You then backtrack, staying with the greenway past its intersection with the Confluence Trail. Travel beneath big cottonwoods and beside small ponds. Cross Alum Creek one last time, returning almost to the trailhead before spurring off to circle around one last aquatic feature—Turtle Pond. Rejoin the greenway and end your hiking adventure.

MILES AND DIRECTIONS

0.0 Start at the Confluence Trails parking area. Follow a path northbound a short distance to meet an asphalt greenway. Here the Blacklick Creek Greenway leaves right and the Alum Creek Greenway leaves left. Cross the asphalt and a small grassy area, picking up the natural-surface Bluebell Trail as it enters forest, descending. Come alongside Blacklick Creek, heading downstream.

0.3 Reach the confluence of Blacklick Creek, Big Walnut Creek, and Alum Creek. Continue downstream along now-bigger Alum Creek.

0.6 Join the Alum Creek Greenway and turn right, passing walnut trees, then bridge Alum Creek. The greenway next descends back to bottomland.

0.8 Turn right onto the Confluence Trail and hike up the west bank of Alum Creek under planted white pines. Shortly reach the confluence of the three creeks, then continue up Alum Creek.

1.6 Rejoin the Alum Creek Greenway. Turn right and immediately pass under I-270.

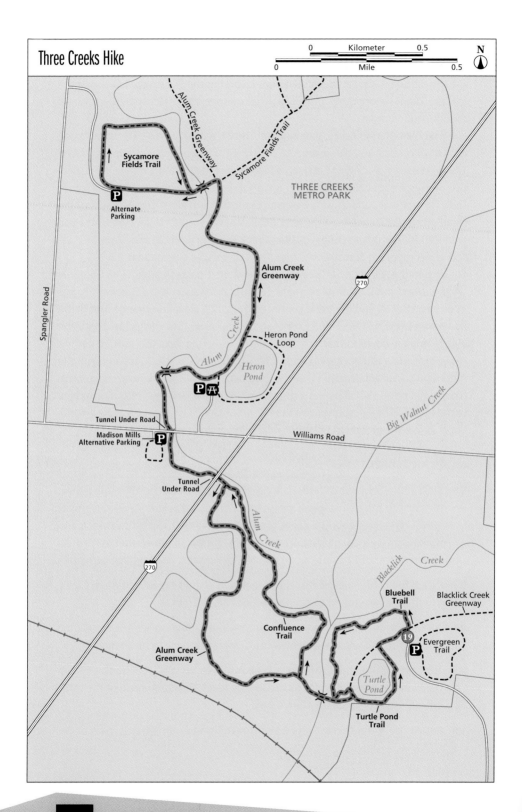

Three Creeks Hike

1.8 Pass the Madison Mills parking area on your left, then go under Williams Road. The parking area offers restrooms during the warm season.

2.0 Cross Alum Creek on an iron bridge. Continue upstream on the right bank.

2.1 Pass the Heron Pond area on your right and the lower end of the Heron Pond Loop.

2.3 Pass the upper end of the Heron Pond Loop. Keep northbound with Alum Creek to your left, now hiking through meadowland.

2.8 Reach a four-way asphalt intersection. Turn left on the Sycamore Fields Trail, soon bridging Alum Creek again.

2.9 The paved path splits. Stay straight and begin the loop part of the Sycamore Fields Trail. Pass by a parking area, a picnic area, and ball fields.

3.7 Complete the Sycamore Fields Loop. Backtrack across Alum Creek, then continue backtracking on the Alum Creek Greenway, passing the Heron Pond Area.

4.5 Bridge Alum Creek; you are now on the right bank, continuing downstream. Go through the tunnel under Williams Road and pass the Madison Mills Area.

5.0 Reach the intersection of the Confluence Trail and Alum Creek Greenway just after passing under I-270. Stay to the right with the Alum Creek Greenway, picking up new trail, and pass near a pair of ponds.

6.0 The Alum Creek Greenway bridges Alum Creek a final time and is the bridge you crossed earlier.

6.1 Turn right onto the gravel Turtle Pond Trail. Circle the pond, then return to the Alum Creek Greenway. Turn right and head down the home stretch.

6.6 Complete the hike at the Confluence Trails parking area.

🐢 Green Tip:
Be a happy land steward. Pick up after others who have left trash behind so that those who come after you will enjoy a more natural hiking experience.

Admiring the Sycamore

Along this hike's three creeks—Blacklick, Big Walnut, and Alum—you will see many large sycamores, a few certainly hundreds of years old. Sycamores thrive in Ohio's bottomlands and prefer deep, rich, moist soil such as that found here. There's even a Sycamore State Park in the Buckeye State. It is in the Wolf Creek Valley of western Ohio, and has trails aplenty. But you don't have to go to Sycamore State Park to find this tree. It is found throughout the state and is generally accorded kudos for being the most massive tree in Ohio—not necessarily the tallest, but literally having more mass on an old-growth giant than any other tree in Ohio. Eastern cottonwoods, also a bottomland tree, are the only serious challenger to the sycamore in terms of size and mass.

Even the most novice student of trees can identify the sycamore. Its bark is unlike any other tree. On older specimens the bark will be plated like other trees, but higher up the mottled white bark is a dead giveaway. Sometimes the bark looks like it is peeling, hence the saying to help you remember the name: "Sycamores look sick." The leaves of the tree are large and have three to five points. In fall they turn a golden brown.

The sycamore ranges far and wide in the eastern half of the United States, from eastern Texas north to Michigan, east to the Atlantic Ocean and south to Florida. On your hike at Three Creeks, look for sycamores young and old.

Green Tip:
Load PDFs of park trail maps onto your smart phone or handheld device, eliminating the necessity of paper maps. If you do use paper maps, please return them to where they were originally obtained so they can be reused by other hikers. This saves trees and taxpayer dollars.

Blacklick Woods Hike

Enjoy a multi-mile, multi-environment, multi-loop trek through the oldest park in the Columbus Metro Parks system, and visit one of Metro Parks' oldest structures. Head south to enter Tucker State Nature Preserve, a special slice of this park featuring big trees, wetland woods, and incredible spring wildflowers. Stop by the nature center, then make a large loop through field and forest on a portion of the Multipurpose Trail. Your return trip takes you back into the state nature preserve, where more beauty can be seen. A meal in one of the host of picnic areas with shelters will complement your hike.

Start: Ash Grove Picnic Area

Distance: 3.9-mile multiple loops

Hiking time: About 2.5 to 3 hours

Difficulty: Moderate; trails are mostly level

Trail surface: Asphalt and gravel

Best season: Year-round

Other trail users: Joggers and bicyclists on Multipurpose Trail

Canine compatibility: Leashed dogs permitted, except in nature preserve

Land status: Metro Parks

Fees and permits: None

Schedule: Open daily year-round

Maps: Blacklick Woods Metro Park; USGS Reynoldsburg

Trail contact: Blacklick Woods Metro Park, 6975 E. Livingston Ave., Reynoldsburg, OH 43068; (614) 891-0700; www.metroparks.net

Finding the trailhead: From exit 110B, Brice Road North / Reynoldsburg, on I-70 east of downtown Columbus, take Brice Road north 0.6 mile to a traffic light and Livingston Avenue. Turn right on Livingston Avenue and follow it east 1.1 miles into Blacklick Woods. Drive for 0.3 mile, then turn left into the Ash Grove Picnic Area. Trailhead GPS: N39 40.916' / W82 34.560'

THE HIKE

We take the greater Columbus Metro Parks system for granted nowadays—it is simply integrated into the heart of Ohio. And to think that Blacklick Woods was the first Metro Park, established back in 1948. Things looked different around these parts back in those days. For starters, there was no I-70 to zoom you to this part of town. Come to think of it, this area wasn't even considered "part of town"... Livingston Avenue, your access road, was simply a two-lane dirt track heading east through the countryside. And much of Blacklick Woods wasn't even woods, but rather open fields planted with trees after the park was established. Today Blacklick Woods is encircled by suburbia and its 643 acres harbors forest, meadows, a nature preserve, a nature center, and even a golf course. It also has picnic areas aplenty, remaining a refuge of nature for present-day Columbians, as it has been for the past seven decades.

The multitude of walkways and trails can make it seem challenging to start your hike. However, simply find the Old Trading Post and you are ready to go. This building is one of the oldest in the Metro Parks system, and is now being preserved as such. In the early days of the park, the Old Trading Post was a sort of park store where visitors could buy cold drinks and souvenirs. Eventually, the small structure became the ranger station for Blacklick Woods and later a nature center. Today the

Hikers young and old can enjoy Metro Parks trails.

shaded structure serves as a reminder of days gone by and how things always keep changing, even Blacklick Woods.

After reflecting on the Old Trading Post, your hike heads east on the Beech Trail. It wanders flatwoods past the Beech Maple Lodge before turning south to meet the Maple Loop. As you might expect, beech and sugar maple are the dominant trees in this hardwood forest. The Maple Loop takes you into Tucker State Nature Preserve. Its special qualities include mature beech and sugar maple trees, seasonal ponds rich with amphibians, and swamps that also harbor water-loving wildlife often lost in the growth of large urban areas. The preserve was named for Walter A. Tucker, the founding director of Metro Parks as well as one of the forces who pushed the state of Ohio to establish a nature preserve system. With that in mind, it could hardly be more fitting to have the Tucker Nature Preserve located within a Columbus Metro Park. By the way, Tucker Nature Preserve is a registered National Natural Landmark, an added distinction validating its qualities.

A high-canopied forest towers above wildflowers and wet flatwoods. The farther south into the preserve, the wetter the forest, until you are walking boardwalks part of the time, especially along the Buttonbush Trail. Learn more about the preserve and park by stopping at the Blacklick Nature Center. Not only can you ask questions of naturalists and read informative displays, but you can also participate in programs as they are offered. That could be a real highlight if you time your hike with a nature program! Otherwise, leave from the nature center south, passing through a large parking area to join the asphalt Multipurpose Trail. This is an exercise-oriented path that winds through the park and connects to the Blacklick Creek Greenway Trail, which in turn connects to other greenways as they expand throughout greater Columbus.

Our hike takes us easterly on a loop through field and forest. The Multipurpose Trail comes near enough to Blacklick Creek to present glimpses of this large watercourse. The path also comes close enough to I-70 that auto noise reverberates. Alas, such is a modern life that park-goers at Blacklick did not experience in the 1950s.

Make a loop on the Multipurpose Trail, and look for short spur trails leading to Blacklick Creek, flowing unseen to the east. Despite the proximity to the interstate, this can be a promising wildlife-viewing area in the morning and evening. The interstate noise provides auditory cover, allowing you to see critters such as deer or coyotes without being heard first.

A little backtracking past the nature center returns you to the Tucker Nature Preserve and swampy woods on the Buttonbush Trail. Stride a long boardwalk, enjoying this watery woodland dry-footed. Next, rejoin the Maple Loop. This particular area can be a wildflower bonanza. Look for trillium, jack-in-the-pulpit, and a cornucopia of colorful groundcover. The final part of the trek leaves the preserve and leads back to the Ash Grove Picnic Area and the hike's end.

Blacklick Woods Hike

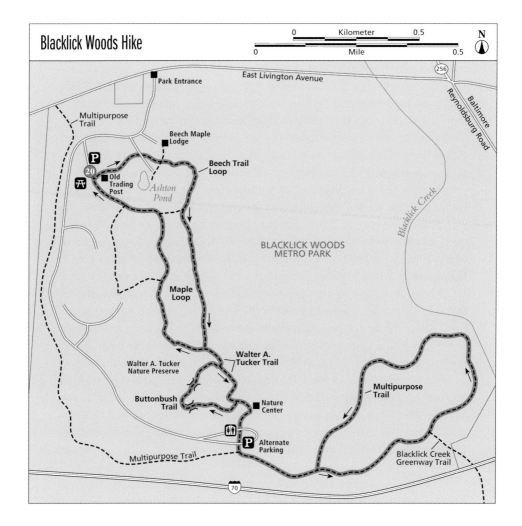

0 | Kilometer | 0.5
0 | Mile | 0.5

N

Park Entrance

East Livington Avenue

256

Reynoldsburg Road

Baltimore

Multipurpose Trail

Beech Maple Lodge

Beech Trail Loop

P

20

Old Trading Post

Ashton Pond

Blacklick Creek

BLACKLICK WOODS METRO PARK

Maple Loop

Walter A. Tucker Trail

Walter A. Tucker Nature Preserve

Multipurpose Trail

Buttonbush Trail

Nature Center

Alternate Parking

Multipurpose Trail

Blacklick Creek Greenway Trail

70

MILES AND DIRECTIONS

0.0 Start by finding the Old Trading Post, located at the south end of the parking lot for the Ash Grove Picnic Area. Facing the Old Trading Post, walk left on an asphalt path heading easterly. Stroll by numerous picnic facilities. Upon entering full-blown woods, you will see a sign for the Beech Trail.

0.1 Cross the entrance road to the Beech Maple Lodge and Ashton Pond. Here the trail turns to gravel. Ahead, pass spur trails connecting to the lodge and pond. The path soon turns south.

0.4 Reach a trail intersection. Turn left onto the Maple Loop and enter the Walter A. Tucker Nature Preserve.

0.7 Come to another intersection. Stay left, joining the Walter A. Tucker Trail. Traverse a boardwalk through flatwoods.

0.8 Stay left at the next intersection, joining the Buttonbush Trail. Buttonbushes grow in Ohio's swampy flatwoods.

0.9 Reach a trail intersection. Here the Buttonbush Trail curves right, but for now stay straight, heading for the nature center.

1.0 Reach the nature center (check ahead of time for posted hours). Turn right here, following a cobblestone trail to the nature center parking area. Cross the parking area and join the Multipurpose Trail, heading left, easterly. I-70 roars beyond the trees.

1.3 Stay right as you reach the loop portion of the Multipurpose Trail. Note the water fountain here. The asphalt path takes you through a mix of forest and open terrain.

1.6 Stay left as the Blacklick Creek Greenway Trail leaves right and passes under I-70. Cedar trees border the trail.

1.9 Come very near Blacklick Creek, and look for spur trails leading to the water's edge. The stream can flow clear but does show adverse effects of being a suburban waterway.

2.5 Complete the loop portion of the Multipurpose Trail. Begin backtracking toward the nature center by turning right.

2.8 Pass the nature center. Ahead, stay left and join a boardwalk on the Buttonbush Trail. Walk beneath impressive hardwoods.

3.2 Stay left again, rejoining the Walter A. Tucker Trail.

3.3 Stay left yet again, rejoining the Maple Loop. The next stretch of path features impressive spring wildflowers.

3.5 A spur trail leads left to the Buttonbush Picnic Area. Stay straight on the Maple Loop, passing through swampy woods.

3.7 Reach a trail intersection. Turn left onto the Beech Trail, making your final loop.

3.8 Come to another intersection. Here an asphalt path leads left for the Buttonbush Picnic Area. Stay straight, on an asphalt path that returns to the Ash Grove Picnic Area.

3.9 Arrive back at the Old Trading Post, completing your hike.

Hikes of Pickerington Ponds Metro Park

Pickerington Ponds Metro Park is an aggregation of wetlands—ponds, marshes, and creeks. It also has a collection of mostly unconnected trails that explore the wetlands. To best enjoy the 1,600-acre park, one of Franklin County's largest remaining wetlands, you should take these three trails, each exploring the natural glacially created wetland. Though the trails are not connected, the distance between the trailheads is less than a mile, so you can keep your feet mostly on the ground instead of pushing the gas pedal.

Start: Glacier Knoll Picnic Area
Distance: 5.2 miles on 3 separate but nearby trails
Hiking time: About 3.5 to 4 hours
Difficulty: Moderate due to distance only
Trail surface: Gravel and natural surface
Best season: Year-round
Other trail users: Joggers
Canine compatibility: No pets allowed

Land status: Metro Parks
Fees and permits: None
Schedule: Open daily year-round, 6:30 a.m. to dark
Maps: Pickerington Ponds Metro Park; USGS Reynoldsburg
Trail contact: Metro Parks, 1069 W. Main St., Westerville, OH 43081; (614) 891-0700; www.metroparks.net

Finding the trailhead: From exit 46 on I-270, southeast of downtown Columbus, take US 33 east for 4.7 miles to the Canal/Winchester/OH 674 exit. Turn left on Gender Road and follow it for 2.1 miles, then turn right on Wright Road. Follow Wright Road for 1 mile to T intersection and turn left on Bowen Road. Follow Bowen Road for 0.4 mile, then turn left into the Glacier Knoll Picnic Area. The Arrowhead Trail starts here. Trailhead GPS: N39 53.634' / W82 48.412'

THE HIKE

Pickerington Ponds Metro Park is not only a recreation destination, but also an important preservation park for glacial wetlands in the greater Columbus area. When the last glaciers retreated from Ohio, immense pieces of ice broke away from these gigantic receding ice sheets. The great ice hunks embedded themselves in the land and later melted. This melting created what are known as glacial kettle lakes, which aren't always classic ponds but are also marshy, grassy wetlands that add biodiversity for both flora and fauna. Early Ohio farmers saw these wetlands as fertile farming places and drained some of them for crops. However, after being purchased by the Metro Parks system, over 750 acres of Pickerington Ponds have been restored to their original wetland state. This allows animal and plant communities to thrive in an increasingly rare environment for central Ohio.

The trail system laid out by Metro Parks allows us to explore and enjoy this agglomeration of creeks, ponds, and intermittent wetlands. The trails are mostly level and make for easy hiking. However, be prepared to walk in the open sun, hat on your head and sunscreen in your hand. The trails here are often trod by bird enthusiasts. The avian set includes both waterfowl and more typical songbirds,

This observation deck overlooks Arrowhead Marsh.

and the ponds and adjacent woods also attract migratory birds moving north and south with the seasons. You may also see land critters such as deer, coyotes, or foxes. Wildlife aside, the mosaic of land and water makes for an attractive spot in any season.

First take the Arrowhead Trail. The trailhead has restrooms and a covered picnic area. At the beginning of your hike, make sure to enjoy the observation deck overlooking Arrowhead Marsh. The hike then traverses a mix of successional meadows full of wildflowers and young trees before coming to Georges Creek. Here the trail travels along this perennial stream, offering a contrast to the still waters of the marshes and ponds in the park. The trail works into a successional meadow, where prairie grasses compete with young trees for supremacy. You then come alongside Georges Creek, shortly crossing it on a little footbridge. The small waterway is normally clear. The Arrowhead Trail then loops through woods and open terrain, coming back alongside Georges Creek. After backtracking, you will have completed your first trail.

It is but a short drive to the Killdeer Trail trailhead and your next hike. You will first circle along Blue Wing Pond, coming very near Bowen Road. Step over the outflow of Blue Wing Pond before turning easterly in tallgrass prairie. After passing through tall woods, you eventually reach an observation deck overlooking Pintail Marsh, a grassy wetland that rises and falls with the seasons. During the right time of year, hikers are rewarded with bird sightings to add to their life list. Even if you aren't a birder, the wooden bench at the observation deck makes for a relaxing locale. If you missed something along the way, look for it on the backtrack to the trailhead.

After completing the Killdeer Trail, continue south on Bowen Road, passing Wright Road both westbound and eastbound. Come to the turn into the Ellis Pond parking area on your left and the Meadow Lark Trail. It has restrooms. Before hitting the Meadow Lark Trail, make the short walk to the observation deck overlooking Ellis Pond. Spot waterfowl using the mounted telescope overlooking the glacially created body of water.

The Meadow Lark Trail explores prairie and woods, but is mostly in open terrain. The main loop is one of the few trails here that doesn't visit a pond, though the path does go along Georges Creek South. The short, level track makes for a quick walk back to the trailhead.

Be apprised this isn't all of the trails at Pickerington Ponds Metro Park. The paved Blacklick Creek Greenway Trail, popular with bicyclists, leaves north from the park, then travels east and west along Blacklick Creek. It has several branches that spur off the main track. Consider bringing your bike along for the full Pickerington Ponds experience.

Metro Parks' Wetlands

Pickerington Ponds is but one of many wetlands preserved by the Metro Parks system. Over 1,000 acres of wetlands are protected within the system. Park personnel have done more than simply put a fence around a low spot. The system has purchased additional lands to include a more complete ecosystem, replanted wetland vegetation, and filled in drainage ditches.

Nearby, Battelle Darby and Slate Run parks also have wetlands you can enjoy. Other Metro Parks with wetlands include Highbanks, Prairie Oaks, Chestnut Ridge, Glacier Ridge, and Three Creeks. So no matter where you are in greater Columbus, there is a protected wetland to visit near you.

MILES AND DIRECTIONS

0.0 Start at the Glacier Knoll Picnic Area. Join the Arrowhead Trail, then quickly bear left and climb to the observation platform overlooking Arrowhead Marsh. Return to the Arrowhead Trail, turning right, away from the parking area, and soon pass another short spur trail leading left up a hill. This spur presents another elevated view.

0.4 The Arrowhead Trail splits. Stay right, curving alongside Georges Creek on a wide grassy track.

0.7 The Arrowhead Trail comes back together. Turn right, crossing a small wooden bridge over Georges Creek. Once across the bridge, turn right again, heading north on a separate loop.

0.9 A short spur leads right to the Blacklick Creek Greenway Trail. Stay left and soon turn south on a wide grassy track. This is favorable deer habitat—watch for deer paths crossing the main trail.

1.4 Complete the loop. Bridge Georges Creek again, then stay right on new path. Round out the eastern loop of the Arrowhead Trail, then backtrack to the trailhead.

2.1 Complete the first hike. Drive south a short distance to the Wood Duck Picnic Area. Note the small cemetery beside the parking area. Join the Killdeer Trail on a pea-gravel track.

2.3 The Killdeer Trail turns easterly, away from Bowen Road. Skirt between Blue Wing Pond to your left and Georges Creek South to your right.

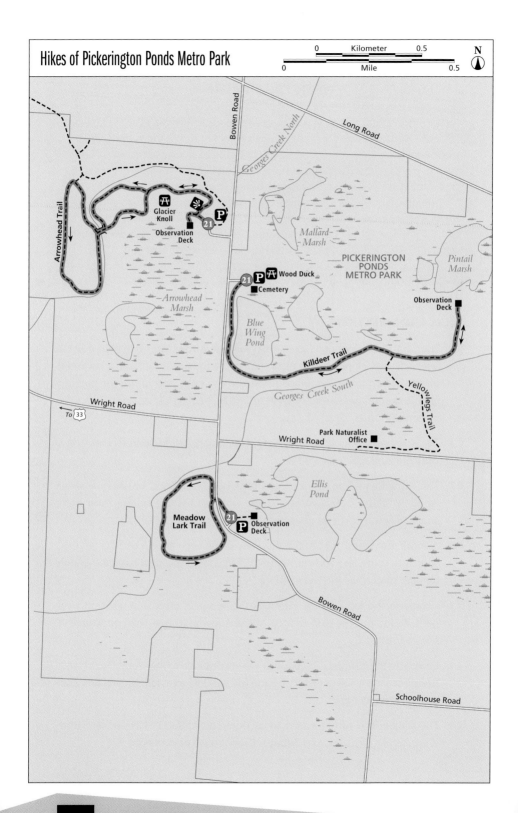

0   Kilometer   0.5

0   Mile   0.5

N

Bowen Road

Long Road

Georges Creek North

Arrowhead Trail

Glacier Knoll

Observation Deck

21 P

Mallard Marsh

PICKERINGTON PONDS METRO PARK

Pintail Marsh

21 P Wood Duck

Cemetery

Arrowhead Marsh

Blue Wing Pond

Observation Deck

Killdeer Trail

Georges Creek South

Wright Road

To 33

Yellowlegs Trail

Park Naturalist Office

Wright Road

Ellis Pond

Meadow Lark Trail

21 Observation Deck
P

Bowen Road

Schoolhouse Road

2.9 The Yellowlegs Trail leads right to bridge Georges Creek South and continue past the park naturalist office after skirting yet another pond. Stay straight on the Killdeer Trail.

3.2 Come to an observation deck and the end of the Killdeer Trail. North views open of Pintail Marsh and lands beyond the park boundary at Long Road. Turn around and backtrack to the Wood Duck Picnic Area.

4.3 Return to the Wood Duck Picnic Area, then drive 0.7 mile south on Bowen Road to Ellis Pond and the Meadow Lark Trail trailhead. Join the Meadow Lark Trail after visiting Ellis Pond.

4.4 The Meadow Lark Trail crosses over to the west side of Bowen Road. Begin the loop portion of this trail by turning right. Come near unseen Georges Creek South as it flows under tree cover, and continue along the stream.

5.1 Complete the loop portion of the Meadow Lark Trail. Cross back over to the east side of Bowen Road.

5.2 Arrive back at the Ellis Pond parking area, finishing the last of the three trails on this hike. To return to US 33 from Ellis Pond, drive north on Bowen Road, then turn left at the second intersection with Wright Road, backtracking to Gender Road.

Asters brighten the prairie.

Chestnut Ridge Hike

Purportedly the first Appalachian mountain rising southeast of Columbus, Chestnut Ridge presents a circuit hike past springs, a rock quarry, and wooded slopes, and atop a high ridge where views await. Continue along the ridge, with its slopes dropping steeply off either side of you. Descend the mount to bridge a stream pouring off the ridge. Toward the end a side trek takes you to the gardens and remains of a formerly fancy homestead. The climb up Chestnut Ridge is under 200 feet, making it doable by almost all hikers, especially when you consider the relatively short distance of the overall hike.

Start: Ridge Trail trailhead
Distance: 2.3-mile loop with out-and-back
Hiking time: About 1.5 to 2 hours
Difficulty: Moderate
Trail surface: Gravel and natural surface
Best seasons: Fall, winter, and spring for the best views
Other trail users: Trail runners and cross-country skiers
Canine compatibility: No pets allowed on trails

Land status: Metro Parks
Fees and permits: None
Schedule: Open daily year-round, 6:30 a.m. to dark
Maps: Chestnut Ridge Metro Park; USGS Canal Winchester
Trail contact: Metro Parks, 1069 W. Main St., Westerville, OH 43081; (614) 891-0700; www .metroparks.net

Finding the trailhead: From exit 46 on I-270, southeast of downtown Columbus, take US 33 east for 12.7 miles to Winchester Road. Turn right on Winchester Road and follow it for 2.7 miles, then turn left into Chestnut Ridge Park. Continue past the wetland-viewing deck and turn right into a parking area after 0.1 mile. The connector to the Ridge Trail starts at the parking area's upper end. Trailhead GPS: N39 48.421' / W82 45.349'

THE HIKE

Chestnut Ridge Metro Park's claim to fame is being the first true ridge representing the Appalachian Mountains, rising southeast of Columbus. And when you stand atop Chestnut Ridge, almost 1,100 feet in elevation, a viewing platform reveals the downtown Columbus skyline in the distance. You will also get a southeast view from the homesite and gardens of a country squire, but this panorama is more intimate, taking in the wooded hills bordering the park.

The park makes the most of its varied terrain and history. You will see not only the old homesite, but also other features. The developed area of the park has picnic tables, picnic shelters, a playground, a couple of small ponds—one of which is open to children's fishing—and a wetland-viewing area, so it is a kid-friendly place. See if you can drag the young ones on the hike with the promise of all the play in addition to the trail trekking.

Leave the developed park facilities on the Ridge Trail. The wide gravel path immediately enters woods and turns north up the east slope of Chestnut Ridge. Tall trees shade the path, and the steep hillside to your left delivers solid evidence that you are truly astride an Appalachian ridge. The path angles uphill beneath maple, beech, northern red oak, and other hardwood trees.

You will come to a boardwalk that rises above sandstone outcroppings on an incredibly sharp slope. Resting benches allow you to relax among the trees. Eventually come to an old quarry, better seen in the winter when the leaves are

Autumn colors peak at Chestnut Ridge Metro Park.

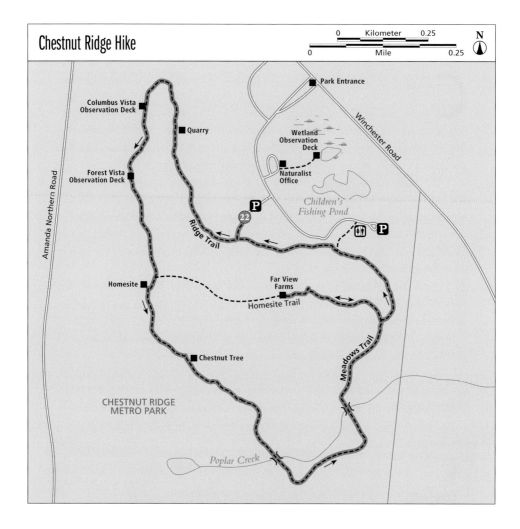

0   Kilometer   0.25

0   Mile   0.25

N

Columbus Vista
Observation Deck

Quarry

Park Entrance

Winchester Road

Wetland
Observation
Deck

Forest Vista
Observation Deck

Naturalist
Office

Amanda Northern Road

Ridge Trail

22

P

Children's
Fishing Pond

P

Homesite

Far View
Farms

Homesite Trail

Chestnut Tree

Meadows Trail

CHESTNUT RIDGE
METRO PARK

Poplar Creek

off the trees. This pit was dug to extract valued Blackhand sandstone, used in construction. The boardwalk continues and is quite long. It serves to both protect the seeps flowing off the mountain and allow hikers a better view of adjacent trees, and keeps them from heading down the steep slope to explore the quarry. The sometimes-slippery wooden walkway extends for nearly 0.2 mile!

The path leads to the crest of Chestnut Ridge, then turns south. It isn't long before you come to a major highlight—the cleared view of downtown Columbus. The hike runs atop the ridge and comes to a second viewpoint, but this one is different. It extends into thick forest, giving you a bird's-eye view of life in the trees of an Appalachian ridge.

Ahead, pass your first homesite. The clues are not obvious: Look for a peach tree, a line of trees indicating an old fence line, and a few cut stones. The hike then drops off the ridgeline on the Meadows Trail. It leads down to Poplar Creek and passes through some openings before curving back toward the main park facilities. However, before completing the loop, take the Homesite Trail up a hill to the gardens and foundation of a fancy home that had a fantastic view. In 1936 Dr. Edward E. Campbell built what he named Far View Farms. This was no hardscrabble subsistence farm, but rather a showplace on a hill in a scenic setting. You can walk around the gardens; check out the grape arbor and numerous species of trees. Perhaps Dr. Campbell would relish knowing his country destination has since become a park to be enjoyed by all.

The final part of the hike takes you along the base of Chestnut Ridge. Enjoy the tall forest before returning to the developed area of the park. Be sure to take advantage of the other facilities while you are here.

MILES AND DIRECTIONS

0.0 Start at the parking area closest to Chestnut Ridge, rising to the west. Enter woods on an asphalt track and walk a few feet to reach the actual Ridge Trail. Turn right here, heading northwest, making a counterclockwise loop.

0.2 Come to a surprising mountainside boardwalk that traverses sidelong on a steep slope. Look for the sandstone quarry below.

0.4 Reach the top of Chestnut Ridge and pass through a small meadow. Turn south and quickly come to a wooden deck. Here you can step out and enjoy a cleared view of downtown Columbus to the northwest. Resume southbound on Chestnut Ridge, ascending slightly.

0.5 Come to a second observation deck. This one is more of a woodland view. A plaque details a book by David Rains Wallace titled *Idle Weeds: The Life of an Ohio Sandstone Ridge,* which describes the life forms found on Chestnut Ridge.

0.7 The Homesite Trail leads left. Keep straight, joining the Meadows Trail, and pass an old homesite on your right.

0.9 Pass a planted chestnut tree near some wooden benches overlooking a meadow.

1.0 Stay right at an intersection, still on the Meadows Trail. A roadbed leaves left to a meadow.

1.2 The Meadows Trail descends through successional meadows and bridges Poplar Creek. Turn left after crossing the stream.

1.4 Cross Poplar Creek a second time.

1.6 Intersect the Homesite Trail a second time. Note the huge-for-their-species sassafras trees at this trail intersection. Turn left here, heading up the Homesite Trail.

1.8 Reach the fancy homesite in a level area atop a hill. You can see the home foundation, brick steps, and gardens amid the grasses. Observe the varied trees and shrubs planted here. On a clear day, easterly views extend far. Backtrack downhill to the trail intersection.

2.0 Turn left on the Ridge Trail.

2.1 Pass a spur trail leading right to an alternate parking area on the upper end of the developed part of the park. Continue walking the base of Chestnut Ridge.

2.3 Reach the right turn on the asphalt path to the trailhead parking area, finishing the hike.

The Mighty Chestnut

The American chestnut tree was once the dominant giant of the Appalachians. This tree formerly ranged from Maine to Mississippi and grew to massive proportions. The fruit of the chestnut was very important. Chestnut acorns were the staple food for everything from bears to birds. Of course, humans ate them, too. Remember the opening words from the Christmas favorite, "Chestnuts roasting on an open fire . . . "

The tree also provided some of the best wood for everyday use by pioneers. The smooth, fine-grained wood is easy to work, and it provided a nearly smokeless and radiant wood for heating and cooking. Chestnut was also coveted by the timber companies that harvested Appalachian ridges, as the massive virgin chestnuts yielded incredible board feet of wood.

Alas, the day of the mighty chestnut is gone. In the early 1900s Asian chestnut trees were imported to the United States, bringing a fungus with them. The Asian trees had developed immunity to the fungus, but the American chestnut was helpless. Before long, chestnuts were dying in the Northeast. The blight worked its way south, and two decades later the day of the chestnut was over.

But there is hope. To this day, chestnut trees sprout from the roots of the ancients and grow up, but always then succumb to the blight. Hopefully these chestnuts are building a resistance to the blight and will one day tower over the mountains again, long after we are gone. Scientists are expediting this process and experiments are under way to graft American chestnut trees with Asian chestnuts in an effort to develop a blight-resistant American chestnut. Then, once again, the name Chestnut Ridge will be an accurate one.

Slate Run Hike

This hike is steeped in human and natural history. Start at a living-history farm, where you can see central Ohio lifeways from days gone by. Then begin your hike, first traveling along clear creeks cutting steep hills under rich forests. Open onto wide grasslands, then grab a first-rate view from a ridge, down onto wetlands through which you will walk. Tour the wetlands, watching for wildlife. Backtrack across the grasslands before returning to Slate Run Farm. Make sure to allow time before or after your hike to tour the farm.

Start: Slate Run Living Historical Farm parking area
Distance: 6.8-mile double loop
Hiking time: About 4 to 5 hours
Difficulty: Moderate to challenging due to distance and hills
Trail surface: Gravel and natural surface
Best season: Year-round
Other trail users: Joggers and cross-country skiers
Canine compatibility: No pets allowed

Land status: Metro Parks
Fees and permits: None
Schedule: Open daily year-round, 6:30 a.m. to dark; living historical farm hours are varied
Maps: Slate Run Metro Park; USGS Canal Winchester
Trail contact: Metro Parks, 1069 W. Main St., Westerville, OH 43081; (614) 891-0700; www.metroparks.net

Finding the trailhead: From exit 46 on I-270, southeast of downtown Columbus, take US 33 east for 4.7 miles to the Canal/Winchester/OH 674 exit. Turn right on Gender Road/OH 674 and follow it 2 miles to the dead end into Lithopolis Road. Turn left on Lithopolis Road, then quickly turn right on Winchester Southern Road, staying with OH 674. Follow OH 674 for 4 miles and turn right into Slate Run Park. Enter the park and follow the signs to Slate Run Farm. Trailhead GPS: N39 45.231'/W82 50.845'

THE HIKE

There is no doubt that Slate Run Living Historical Farm is the number one draw at this Metro Park. However, the trail complex here rivals any other in the Metro Parks system. The trail system not only has 12 miles of total pathways, but also explores different environments, from open grasslands, to hills with views, to widespread wetlands, to steep glacial-cut ravines. This hike explores all these environments. The trek is nearly 7 miles long, so allow for plenty of time to enjoy the hike. Of course, you should also make time to visit the farm. To do both will take all day, but it will be a worthwhile day in your life.

You will leave Slate Run Farm on the Sugar Maple Trail. The path soon splits and the hike begins reconnoitering the hills and tributaries of the Slate Run Creek valley. You'd never know it by your drive into the park, but the trail soon plunges into steep, slaty ravines cloaked in lush woods of sugar maple, red maple, cherry, pignut hickory, and beech. It isn't long before you join the Five Oaks Trail, named for an oak tree that sprouted five trunks after it was initially cut down. Unfortunately, one of the five trunks has fallen prey to disease.

After wandering through steep, slaty hills, the path comes to a major tributary of Slate Run. Here an observation deck overlooks a sheer chasm, falling to clear waters flowing through a forested vale. You next drop to bridge this ravine. Con-

Looking over the Kokomo Wetlands.

tinue with more ups and downs before rejoining the Sugar Maple Trail. This path goes by Buzzards Roost Picnic Area, a major developed area of the park, with a playground, picnic shelters, and fishing lake as well as shorter nature trails.

Leave the Slate Run Creek valley for verdant uplands and the Bobolink Grassland Trail. A spur trail leads to a hilltop and a fantastic view from an observation deck, one of my favorite views in central Ohio. From here rake down upon the Kokomo Wetlands, a series of ponds, lakes, and vernal pools that offer a chance to see aquatic wildlife and experience the meshing of water and land. The Bobolink Grassland Trail leads you down to the 156-acre wetland complex, where a loop trail leads to all these aquatic features, highlighted by a pair of observation decks overlooking ponds and a long boardwalk crossing the neck of one lake. Some are permanent ponds, and others are seasonal wetlands. Waterfowl and other birds will be there in season. Make sure to look up at the observation deck you had visited earlier before completing your loop.

Next, backtrack on the Bobolink Grassland Trail. You won't miss the glacial erratic, a seemingly out-of-place sizable boulder left there by retreating glaciers. Rejoin the Sugar Maple Trail, enjoying a final woodland wander on a ravine edge above Slate Run before returning to Slate Run Living Historical Farm.

MILES AND DIRECTIONS

0.0 Start at the Slate Run Living Historical Farm parking area. Pick up the Sugar Maple Trail, located at the far end of the parking area, near the restrooms, and soon enter forest.

0.3 The Sugar Maple Trail splits. Stay right, dipping to span Slate Run on a wooden bridge, and climb.

0.4 This arm of the Sugar Maple Trail ends. Step onto the Five Oaks Trail, leaving right, and bridge a tributary stream with rocky shoals. The ups and downs continue.

0.8 Come to a trail junction and observation deck. Enjoy looks into another, larger tributary. A short spur leads right to the Shady Grove Picnic Area. Stay left and dip to cross the larger tributary. After climbing, open onto a successional meadow, then reenter younger woods.

1.4 Reach an intersection. The Five Oaks Trail leads left, but you stay right, rejoining the Sugar Maple Trail.

1.7 A spur trail leads right to the Buzzards Roost Picnic Area. Soon turn left and dip toward Slate Run.

1.8 Bridge Slate Run.

Slate Run Hike

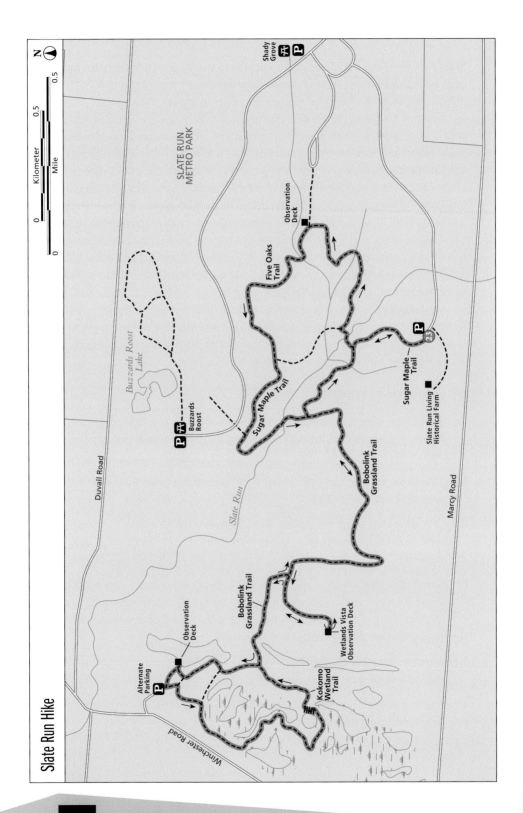

1.9 Meet the Bobolink Grassland Trail. Hike through forest, then open onto grasslands, turning westerly. Look south for the Slate Run Farm barn roof.

2.8 Take the spur trail leading left to an observation deck overlooking the Kokomo Wetlands.

3.1 Come to the observation deck just after passing the state record Osage orange tree. The view opens westerly onto the wetlands and beyond, and a field scope allows closer looks into the pools below. Backtrack to the main trail.

3.4 Return to the main track of the Bobolink Grassland Trail. Descend off the hill, gaining more views to your west.

3.7 Meet the Kokomo Wetland Trail. Turn right, making the outermost loop of the series of interconnected loops.

4.0 A paved spur trail leads right to an observation deck overlooking a pond. Continue the loop, coming near the Kokomo Wetlands park entrance, which offers alternate parking and picnicking. Continue on the outside of the loop trails in the wetlands. In places you are on an elevated trail bed with water on both sides of you, bordered by willows.

4.8 Cross a pond on a boardwalk. Part of the boardwalk has a bench and relaxation area.

5.1 Complete the Kokomo Wetland Trail. Begin backtracking easterly on the Bobolink Grassland Trail.

5.4 Pass the spur to the wetlands overlook. Stay left, cruising through grassland.

6.3 Turn right, rejoining the Sugar Maple Trail, and travel a ravine edge dropping to Slate Run.

6.6 Reach an intersection. Stay right with the Sugar Maple Trail.

6.8 Arrive back at Slate Run Farm, finishing the hike.

Slate Run Farm

Slate Run Living Historical Farm represents a working central Ohio farm from the 1880s. The farmhouse and most of the outbuildings were built on-site and are part of the original farm that went through several hands since its inception. A time line at the farm entrance details significant events at the farm, in Ohio, and around the world. You will pass pastures with animal breeds from the era, increasing the authenticity of the site. Even the orchards and heirloom gardens are typical of that time!

Volunteers and park employees reenact lifeways on the farm before tractors and gas-powered machines. Their activities depend on the season. As it was back in the 1880s, summer is the busy time, and winter can be slow. The farming is real and the fruits, vegetables, hogs, and poultry are sold to help pay farm expenses.

Special events are held at Slate Run Farm, but you can take a self-guided tour whenever the farm is open. Call ahead or check the Slate Run website for exact hours and programs. The Gothic Revival farmhouse, built in 1856, is impressive. Nearby, the summer kitchen and woodshed are where you may find reenactors making soap, chopping wood, or doing the laundry. Check out the root cellar and smokehouse. And, yes, there is an outhouse.

Larger buildings include the barn, built in 1881. The big red building is a sight to behold, and functional, too. The granary, hog shed, and machine shed are spread on the grounds for you to tour. Give yourself ample time to tour the farm (the park recommends allotting one to two hours), then make the hike. Bring lunch, since taking advantage of the history and beauty of Slate Run Metro Park will probably take you all day.

The historic house at Slate Run Farm.

Stages Pond State Nature Preserve

Stages Pond turns the argument on its head that Ohio's flatlands offer little for the nature enthusiast. A walk here divulges another side of central Ohio and presents opportunities for birders and other wildlife enthusiasts. First you will visit a smaller pond with a wildlife blind, then walk through former fields, now a transitional mix of ecotones, before reaching Stages Pond, created from glacial ice melt. Cruise past wetlands that change with the seasons before making a loop in tall woods that form a shady harbor among the meadows and croplands.

Start: Parking area at preserve front gate

Distance: 3.2-mile double loop

Hiking time: About 2 to 2.5 hours

Difficulty: Easy

Trail surface: Grass and natural surface

Best season: Year-round; may be hot in summer

Other trail users: None

Canine compatibility: Dogs not permitted

Land status: State nature preserve

Fees and permits: None

Schedule: Open daily year-round

Maps: Stages Pond State Nature Preserve; USGS Ashville

Trail contact: Ohio Department of Natural Resources, 2045 Morse Rd., Building C-3, Columbus, OH 43229; (614) 265-6561; www.dnr .state.oh.us, www.stagespond statenaturepreserve.info

Finding the trailhead: From exit 52 on I-270, south of downtown Columbus, take US 23 south for 14.7 miles to Hagerty Road / Pickaway CR 38. Turn left and follow Hagerty Road 1.6 miles to the preserve on your left. Park in the small lot at the front gate if possible. There is a larger parking area up the entrance road when the preserve gate is open. Trailhead GPS: N39 40.131' / W82 56.089'

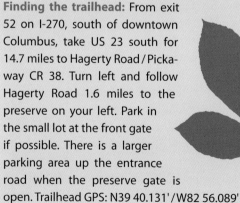

THE HIKE

t is hard to wrap my mind around the fact that the ponds and wetlands of this state nature preserve were created by a giant piece of melting ice! Of course, we have to start with the concept that thousands of years ago much of Ohio was covered with massive glaciers. When these glaciers receded, a big chunk of ice broke off at this particular spot in Pickaway County. Over time the ice melted, creating the depression that filled with water as the ponds and wetlands we see today. Back when Ohio was being settled, such wetlands were seen as impediments to agriculture. Attempts were made to drain part of this depression, but the glacial effects were mostly left as they were found. As Columbus grew the recognition of the natural importance of such areas as Stages Pond grew as well.

At the same time, other glacial relics were being altered and drained to improve agricultural output. And who can blame farmers for wanting to maximize the yield of their land? But Stages Pond was to have another fate, thanks to citizens who recognized the necessity of preserving such places. It all started with the Pickaway County Garden Club, when members decided to save Stages Pond. They began raising money to purchase this tract that held the 64-acre depression featuring Stages Pond, a kettle lake, in glacial nomenclature. They partnered with the Nature Conservancy and other garden clubs throughout the state. The money was raised and the land was purchased, then turned over to the state of Ohio and placed in its nature preserve system.

The 178-acre tract was dedicated in 1974 and leaves an intact landscape— and waterscape. Today the preserve is managed for native plant species, wildlife, and waterfowl. The ponds and wetlands attract migratory birds. The wooded portions of the preserve provide a refuge and nesting area for not only songbirds but also other forms of wildlife in an area mostly composed of open agricultural fields.

It isn't long before the hike explores its first wetland feature. You will cruise to an observation blind overlooking a pond. Waterfowl will be here in season. The three-sided wood structure, set amid white pines, has openings to view waterfowl. After this you backtrack and join the Meadow Trail, which travels through what once was cropland. While hiking through this mix of grass and woodland, look south across Hagerty Road and contrast tilled land with the terrain through which you walk. Depending upon the season it may be green with grasses and cedars, yellow with wildflowers, red with maples, brown and barren, or even white with a winter coat.

Reach Stages Pond, named for the property's original owner, William Stage. There is another waterfowl blind here. The hike then travels easterly through seasonal wetlands. Surprisingly, you climb just a few feet and enter lush forest. This provides yet another habitat at the preserve. The state nature preserve has an additional tract located northeast of the main parcel of land, and the two areas are connected in their corners. The White Oak Trail squeezes through this corner piece and makes a loop through some impressive flatwoods, featuring mature white oaks that have seen many a year come and go. Maple, walnut, and other trees form a large wooded lot that everything from squirrels to foxes to deer can utilize, especially considering the fields around them. In spring look for vernal pools among the trees as well as wildflowers aplenty.

The Moraine Trail leads south through more woodland back toward the trailhead. Boardwalks visit additional wetlands. The final walk amid brushy forest returns you to the main trail kiosk. From here it is a short backtrack to either preserve parking area.

Larkspur brightens the woodlot beside Stages Pond.

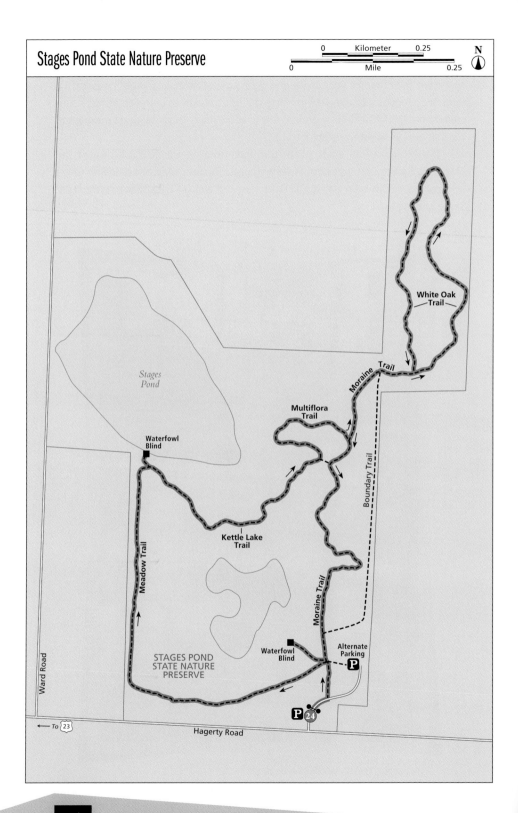

Kilometer
0   0.25
Mile
0   0.25

N

White Oak
Trail

Stages
Pond

Moraine Trail

Multiflora
Trail

Boundary Trail

Waterfowl
Blind

Kettle Lake
Trail

Meadow Trail

Moraine Trail

Waterfowl
Blind

Alternate
Parking
P

STAGES POND
STATE NATURE
PRESERVE

Ward Road

P 24

← To 23

Hagerty Road

MILES AND DIRECTIONS

0.0 Start by walking the gated asphalt road 300 feet to a sign indicating the trail system. Leave left from the road, following a grassy track north. Birdsong will already be prevalent in the warm season.

0.1 Reach a kiosk and five-way trail intersection. Walk toward the waterfowl blind, entering a dark white pine copse. After viewing, return to the kiosk and join the Meadow Trail, walking west.

0.6 The Meadow Trail turns north, hugging the western preserve boundary. Continue through a mix of trees and grasses. The boundary is lined with trees, while a farm lies on the other side.

0.9 Come to an intersection. Walk a short distance to Stages Pond and another waterfowl blind. Backtrack and then join the Kettle Lake Trail, heading easterly through seasonal wetlands.

1.2 Climb into full-blown forest, entering the preserve's woodlot.

1.3 Turn left on the Multiflora Trail and immediately bridge a little streamlet. Stay in the heavily wooded uplands. In winter you can gain glimpses of Stages Pond to the west. The brushy understory can be thick in summer.

1.5 Turn left onto the Moraine Trail. Head northbound, still in woods, and bridge a streambed.

1.6 Reach another trail intersection. Here the Boundary Trail heads right, south, back toward the parking areas. However, this hike stays straight, squeezing through a small easement to join a different wooded tract of the preserve, now on the White Oak Trail. You will travel through a fine example of Ohio's flatwoods, but the level terrain will be sloppy after heavy rains and in early spring.

1.7 Reach the loop portion of the White Oak Trail. Stay right, heading northbound through mature woods. Watch for animal paths coursing through the light understory and animal tracks in damp areas.

2.1 The loop turns south. Travel through more forest.

2.5 Complete the loop of the White Oak Trail, then backtrack to the Moraine Trail and begin walking southbound. The Boundary Trail provides a less interesting alternative back to the parking area.

2.6 Keep straight, passing the intersection with the Multiflora Trail.

2.7 Keep straight, passing the intersection with the Kettle Lake Trail. Traverse an extended boardwalk while still in woods. Watch for brush, briars, and vines.

3.0 Keep straight, passing the southerly intersection with the Boundary Trail.

3.1 Return to the main trail kiosk and the five-way trail intersection. From here backtrack toward Hagerty Road.

3.2 Reach the state nature preserve gate, completing the hike.

The Mighty White Oak

You will obviously see white oaks on the hike's White Oak Trail. And there are many. It is no surprise these big trees are here—white oaks are known for their longevity. Interestingly, oaks are technically part of the beech family. White oaks grow throughout the state of Ohio, with the greater Ohio River valley offering near-ideal growing conditions. The white oak's range covers most of the eastern United States, from Texas north to Minnesota, then east to Maine and south to Florida.

The high-quality wood has been prized by Americans for generations. Among other uses, it once was made into barrel staves, bringing about the all-but-forgotten nickname "barrel oak." Wildlife may love white oaks more than mankind, especially in an isolated woodlot like this one, set in agricultural lands of Pickaway County. The acorns are a valuable food source. Woodpeckers and turkeys are among the birds that partake of the nuts. Raccoons and chipmunks enjoy the nutrient-packed treat, too. Deer eat the acorns and browse on tender white oak twigs. In the same way we see the fields surrounding Stages Pond State Nature Preserve as food sources, wildlife sees the mighty white oak.

Shallenberger State Nature Preserve

This hike explores a protected state nature preserve in Fairfield County near the town of Lancaster. You will start out cruising the slopes of Allen Knob, which rises 240 feet above the surrounding terrain. The rich woods below the knob are a great spring wildflower destination. Next, travel to the top of Allen Knob, with its rock outcrops and partial views. The final part of the hike returns you to the trailhead.

Start: Shallenberger State Nature Preserve trailhead

Distance: 1.6-mile double loop

Hiking time: About 1.5 to 2 hours

Difficulty: Moderate; does have some hills

Trail surface: Natural surface

Best season: Year-round

Other trail users: None

Canine compatibility: Dogs not permitted in nature preserve

Land status: State nature preserve

Fees and permits: None

Schedule: Open daily year-round

Maps: Shallenberger State Nature Preserve; USGS Amanda

Trail contact: Ohio Department of Natural Resources, 2045 Morse Rd., Building C-3, Columbus, OH 43229-6693; (614) 265-6453; www.dnr.state.oh.us

Finding the trailhead: From exit 46 on I-270, southeast of downtown Columbus, take US 33 east for 21 miles to US 22. Take US 22 east a short distance toward Lancaster, then turn left on Becks Knob Road. Follow Becks Knob Road for less than 0.1 mile and reach the parking area on your right. Trailhead GPS: N39 41.489' / W82 39.429'

THE HIKE

N amed for the benefactor who recognized the special beauty of this location and subsequently passed it on to future generations, Shallenberger State Nature Preserve contains a pair of sandstone knobs that offer wintertime views. The preserve is a known wildflower haven, and it also harbors myriad vegetation affected by ancient glaciation. Though the trails are somewhat steep, the mileage is short; therefore, you might want to take your time exploring the flora of the preserve. As mentioned, spring produces scads of wildflowers, but the other seasons are desirable as well—fall offers a kaleidoscope of colors, and wintertime presents an opportunity to peer well beyond the knob. In summer you can enjoy the deep woods found at the preserve.

After starting the hike, notice the dedication plaque at the trailhead. Jay M. Shallenberger owned this property. He enjoyed the beauty of his land but didn't want to keep it all to himself. He actually saw Allen Knob as an outdoor education venue, and upon his death in 1971, willed the land to Fairfield County. Later, county commissioners transferred the property to the state of Ohio, and in 1973 Shallenberger's property became an Ohio state nature preserve.

The hike works its way along Allen Knob's angled slopes, which are cloaked in sugar maple, cherry, and shagbark hickory. We will save our climb to Allen Knob

The author waits out a rain beside a rock overhang near Allen Knob.

for the final highlight of the hike. Watch for impressive embedded boulders on the mountain slope. Most of the boulders are cloaked in moss, a result of being in the shade of tall trees. The north slope of Allen Knob is strewn with rocks. The trail explores fields of rocks from which rise tall straight-trunked tulip trees and paw-paw patches. This part of the preserve is especially rich with wildflowers in spring.

You'll pass a trail junction and then begin to circle beneath Rubles Knob on a second loop. A trail once went to the top of this stony peak but has since been abandoned. Instead, the trail traverses a lofty forest below Rubles Knob before returning to the base of Allen Knob. This second loop is also great for wildflowers. Bloodroot, mayapple, and hepatica are some early spring wildflowers that can be seen here. But even if it isn't spring, the deep mature woods are inspiring.

After completing the loop below Rubles Knob, you will start your climb to Allen Knob. The peak is somewhat level at the top. The erosion-resistant sandstone can be seen emerging from the thin soil and also forms outcrops along the edge of the knob. Unfortunately, tall trees obscure views from these outcrops, though in winter you can see beyond the vegetation, especially to the southwest and north-west. Several spur trails lead to the outcrops, where hikers vainly search for an open vista point. Note the mountain laurel thriving atop this knob; it blooms pink in late spring. Oddly, there is a circular depression in the center of the knob. I suspect it was man-made but can't find the reason for it. Come up with your own theories—perhaps it was a pit dug for the rock within, or maybe a pond.

After circling the knob top, you will descend via the wooden stairs. Make your final intersection, then descend through viney woods back to the trailhead. Along the way, watch for a huge triple-trunked tulip tree. Its base is massive.

MILES AND DIRECTIONS

0.0 Start at the upper end of the parking area. Pass a trailside kiosk and immediately enter lush mature woods.

0.1 The trail splits. Turn left and begin circling around Allen Knob. This is a lesser-used option—most people stay right, heading directly for Allen Knob. The trail traverses a slope and comes very near Becks Knob Road.

0.2 Pass a maple tree with widespread branches next to Becks Knob Road. The vertical limbs indicate it once stood in an open field. Turn easterly on the north slope of Becks Knob.

0.3 Bisect a boulder field. Look uphill and you will see the boulder field rises to a sheer rock face.

0.4 Reach a trail junction. Stay left and cross a tributary of Hunters Run, which flows below the northwest side of Allen Knob.

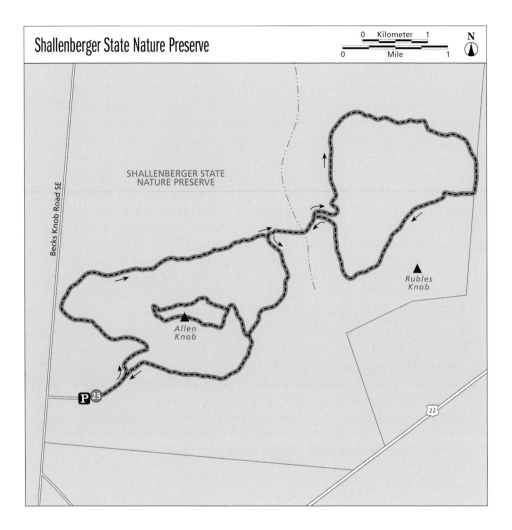

0   Kilometer   1

0   Mile   1

N

SHALLENBERGER STATE
NATURE PRESERVE

Becks Knob Road SE

*Rubles
Knob*

*Allen
Knob*

P 25

22

0.5 Stay left at the trail junction and begin the loop below Rubles Knob. This is an opulent wildflower area.

0.8 Come very near the boundary of the state nature preserve. You may see a closed trail that once led to the peak of Rubles Knob. Stay on the marked path below Rubles Knob.

1.0 Complete the loop below Rubles Knob. Stay left and reach the crossing of the tributary of Hunters Run.

1.1 Turn left, now working your way toward Allen Knob. The trail steepens.

1.2 Stay right at the junction to Allen Knob. The path angles up the slope of the knob, then comes along a sheer sandstone wall. Wooden steps aid your ascent to the rocky top of Allen Knob, where you begin a small sub-loop. Sandstone outcrops draw you to the knob's edge. The most prominent outcrop extends westerly from Allen Knob.

1.4 Complete the loop atop Allen Knob. Backtrack down the wooden steps off the knob. Ahead, turn right and make the final descent toward the trailhead.

1.6 Arrive back at the trailhead, finishing the hike.

The Mighty Tulip Tree

You will pass numerous tulip trees on the north slope of Allen Knob. Tulip trees were once more commonly known as poplars. Though it still often goes by the name yellow poplar, the correct name of the tree comes from the shape of its leaf, which resembles the outline of a tulip flower.

Tulip trees are easy to identify in several ways. First, you have the tulip-shaped leaves, which turn yellow in fall. When walking through a grove of tulip trees, the yellow leaves will cast a memorable hue upon the autumn landscape. The trunk of a tulip tree grows remarkably straight, whether it is on a steep slope like here at Allen Knob or growing on a level former farm field. The furrowed bark is a distinctive dark gray. In spring tulip trees will develop some of the largest tree flowers you will see. The cup-shaped center of the flower is bordered by rounded green petals.

Tulip trees grow throughout the Buckeye State. The Ohio champion tulip tree is in Summit County, at Sands Run Metro Park. The native range of tulip trees extends northeast to Rhode Island, west to the southern half of Michigan, and all the way down south to Louisiana and Florida. Old-growth tulip trees are among the most massive living things in the forest. They can reach heights of 200 feet and have a trunk 10 feet in diameter. Pioneers actually used hollowed-out tulip tree trunks as temporary homes when they settled wild regions.

Tulip trees are valued as a commercial hardwood, which is used for furniture, boxes, musical instruments, and in cabinetry. After you leave Allen Knob, look for the unique triple-trunked tulip tree, just one more example of how Jay M. Shallenberger did us right by preserving this special parcel of Ohio.

Hargus Lake Loop at A. W. Marion State Park

Make a circuit around attractive Hargus Lake at this classic, family-friendly state park. First, cross the dam that backs up Hargus Creek and creates Hargus Lake, enjoying the aquatic views from this perch. Begin circling along the shore of the impoundment, then pass through the park campground before turning up Hargus Creek. The final part of the hike wanders through the day-use area. Elevation changes are less than 100 feet, making it an ideal longer family hike or a good trail-running circuit.

Start: A. W. Marion Memorial parking area near the dam
Distance: 3.9-mile loop
Hiking time: About 2.5 to 3 hours
Difficulty: Moderate
Trail surface: Natural surface
Best season: Mar through mid-Oct
Other trail users: Trail runners
Canine compatibility: Leashed dogs permitted
Land status: Ohio state park

Fees and permits: None
Schedule: Open daily year-round
Maps: A. W. Marion State Park; USGS Ashville, Circleville
Trail contact: A. W. Marion State Park, 7317 Warner Huffer Rd., Circleville, OH 43113; (740) 869-3124; www.dnr.state.ohio.us

Finding the trailhead: From exit 52 on I-270, south of downtown Columbus, take US 23 south for 15.2 miles to N. Court Street. Turn left on N. Court Street and follow it 0.3 mile to Bell Station Road. Turn left on Bell Station Road and follow it 3.2 miles to Winchester Road. Turn right on Winchester Road and follow it 0.8 mile to OH 188. Turn left on OH 188 and follow it 0.1 mile, then turn right on Bol-Pontious Road. Follow Bol-Pontious Road for 0.5 mile to Warner-Huffer Road. Turn left on Warner-Huffer Road and follow it 0.3 mile, then turn right on Reigel Road. Follow Reigel Road for 0.2 mile and enter the park, immediately veering left on Ohio Natural Resources Road 2. Stay right as it makes a loop to soon reach the A. W. Marion Memorial and Hargus Lake Dam. Trailhead GPS: N39 37.726' / W82 53.157'

THE HIKE

The Hargus Lake Perimeter Trail is advertised by A. W. Marion State Park as being 5 miles long. It simply isn't so. Sometimes when trails are established, mileages are estimated or otherwise erroneously calculated. Somewhere along the way this path was determined to be 5 miles long, and the incorrect information has stuck and been passed along in park and other literature. A simple GPS measurement of the path shows the accurate mileage as a shade less than 3.9 miles. Round up to 3.9 miles, and you have the distance of the Hargus Lake Perimeter Trail. While hiking here one time, I ran into a young woman who had questioned her own trail measurement simply because the park advertised the distance as being 5 miles. The distance in no way adversely affects the hike itself. It's just that we all want to know how far we're going to hike before we do it, in order to be best prepared.

A large picnic area with restrooms overlooks the lake near the trailhead. The hike crosses the park dam. On a clear day panoramas open of the lake below and hills to the west. During the warm season, boaters will be fishing for bluegill, bass, and catfish. Worry not about motor noise, however, as only electric motors are allowed on the 145-acre impoundment. By the way, the park rents boats, should you want to tool around the water or drop a line yourself. Anglers must have a valid Ohio fishing license.

Enjoying Hargus Lake on a serene summer day.

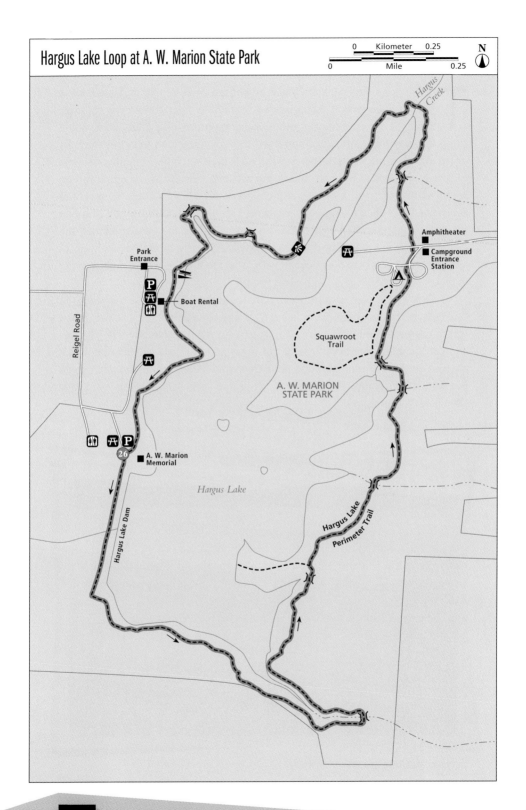

0   Kilometer   0.25

0   Mile   0.25

N

Hargus Creek

Amphitheater

Campground
Entrance
Station

Park
Entrance

Boat Rental

Squawroot
Trail

Reigel Road

A. W. MARION
STATE PARK

26

A. W. Marion
Memorial

Hargus Lake

Hargus Lake Dam

Hargus Lake
Perimeter Trail

Alley Park Hike

This hike makes a loop through extremely hilly and wooded terrain centered by a small lake. You will navigate a nest of sometimes confusing paths with an amazing number of trail intersections for the park's size. Start out by exploring pretty Lake Loretta, with the nearby nature center and covered bridge as a backdrop, before climbing into steep hills. Work your way toward little Twin Lake, then make a long curve on a high ridge, viewing impressive sandstone cliff lines and other geological features reminiscent of the Hocking Hills, including a rock house. Work your way back to the parking area, passing umpteen more intersections.

Start: Beginning of road leading to nature center

Distance: 2.6-mile loop

Hiking time: About 1.5 to 2 hours

Difficulty: Moderate; does have steep hills

Trail surface: Natural surface

Best seasons: Spring for wildflowers, winter for rock features

Other trail users: None

Canine compatibility: Leashed dogs permitted

Land status: Lancaster city park

Fees and permits: None

Schedule: Open daily year-round

Maps: Alley Park Trails; USGS Lancaster

Trail contact: Lancaster Parks & Recreation, 1507 E. Main St., Lancaster, OH 43130; (740) 687-6651; www.lancasterparks.com

Finding the trailhead: From exit 46 on I-270, southeast of downtown Columbus, take US 33 east for 26 miles to Tarkiln Road. Get off at the exit, turn left, and pass under US 33. Just ahead, turn left on Old Logan Road before you reach a traffic light and US 33 Business. Follow Old Logan Road for 1.4 miles, then turn left into Alley Park. Enter the park and veer right into the parking area. Trailhead GPS: N39 40.916' / W82 34.560'

M ost first-time hikers at Alley Park have no idea how steep the trails are, nor do they realize how many trail intersections they will have to navigate. But these hiking challenges are part of the spice in the entree here. Besides, the park isn't that big, so you won't get lost for long no matter what. And the hills are only so high, so you will eventually be going down regardless of which trail you take. Having said that, I recommend looking at the navigational aspects of hiking here as an adventure rather than a frustrating and confusing endeavor. There are so many intersections that even with this guide in hand, a map-loaded GPS, a rabbit's foot, and some tarot cards, you may lose sight of exactly where you are.

Moss-and-fern-covered boulders line the trails here.

For almost the entire hike, with a couple of exceptions, if you stay left at the trail junctions, you will be just fine. Luckily, park personnel have installed plastic-covered maps at many intersections, displaying exactly where you are. This helps immensely. Part of the Lancaster Parks & Recreation system, Alley Park features a fine nature center in which programs are held regularly, from nature study to square dancing. Check the Lancaster Parks website for program information.

Start your hike by walking up the road toward the nature center. You soon join the trail leading left across the dam creating Lake Loretta. This scenic impoundment is encircled by hills, which you will be hiking. In fall, tree colors reflect off the impoundment, doubling their grandeur. After leaving the lake you will take a series of trails aiming for Twin Lake. This is the worst area to get caught in confusing junctions, but the lucky hiker will eventually make it to the Meadow Trail and escape Twin Lake.

Once on the south side of the park, you will pass some sandstone bluffs, boulders, and overhangs, recalling Hocking Hills. Pass through a boulder squeeze. Ferns grow in the shade. Continue along the cliff line, then climb away. The sharp ups and downs make for a good training hike if you are heading to the main Appalachian chain.

Eventually join a piney ridgeline, where the hike mercifully levels out. Oaks and hickories add to the pines. You pass the Poplar Valley Trail, then the Alley Trail curves north, hemmed in by the park boundaries. Hopefully you won't miss the user-created trail leading to a rock house, lying on the west side of the ridge below. The rock house can be found after the junction with the Trillium Trail. You will make an obvious switchback, and after that the user-created trail heads south on an old roadbed just a short distance and then curves to the edge of a bluff where you can overlook the rock house.

Beyond the rock house the hike undulates northward and eventually turns east, once again hemmed in by the park boundary. You will come very near private property before making a final turn to close the loop. If the loop described isn't enough exercise, the numerous spur trails going up and down the ridges and hollows will provide more than enough strenuosity for even the most enthusiastic hill hiker.

MILES AND DIRECTIONS

0.0 Start by walking the gated road up toward the covered bridge and the nature center. You will see a restored cabin on your right. Turn left upon reaching Lake Loretta and cross the dam.

0.1 Leave the lake left, ascending sharply through oak hardwoods on the Alley Trail.

0.2 Pass a gate and service road leading left. Stay right, still ascending.

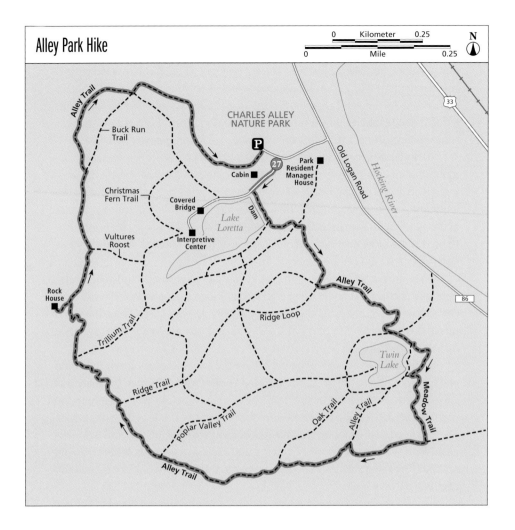

0.3 Come to a four-way intersection. Stay left here as the Ridge Loop leaves right.

0.5 Stay left to avoid a series of trail junctions that circle around Twin Lake. If you follow the left turn and end up at Old Logan Road, backtrack to the previous intersection and go left.

0.7 Join the Meadow Trail and begin climbing toward the south park boundary.

0.8 Come very near the south boundary atop a ridge. Here a grassy service road leads left. Turn right, heading westerly, and soon top out on a knob in a meadow.

0.9 Stay left at the intersection as the Meadow Trail ends. Rejoin the Alley Trail and come along some sandstone outcrops.

1.1 Stay left as the Oak Trail leaves right toward Twin Lake. Climb sharply away from the cliff line.

1.3 Stay straight at the junction as the Poplar Valley Trail drops right.

1.5 The Ridge Trail leaves right. Stay straight, still on the Alley Trail, and dive off the main ridge, passing near more impressive cliff lines and switchbacking to moderate the drop.

1.6 The Trillium Trail leaves right. This is an obvious good spring wildflower diversion off the main loop. Otherwise, keep straight with the Alley Trail and switchback uphill.

1.7 Once atop a ridge, a user-created spur trail cuts left to the rock house. The main loop keeps north.

1.9 Stay straight in a gap as the Vultures Roost Trail leaves right for Lake Loretta.

2.0 Stay left with the Alley Trail as the Buck Run Trail stays right.

2.3 Stay left again after meeting the other end of the Buck Run Trail.

2.6 Emerge in a meadow above the parking area. Descend to the park road and finish the hike.

Ohio's Covered Bridges

This hike travels very close to a historic covered bridge located near the Alley Park nature center. Known as the George Hutchings Bridge, it once spanned Clear Creek, as in Clear Creek Metro Park. The wooden structure, constructed in 1900, was moved here after being reconstructed by Lancaster park employees. Thirty percent of the bridge you currently see is made of materials from the original bridge. The bridge now extends over an arm of Lake Loretta. It has windows to let in light.

Ohio is second only to Pennsylvania when it comes to numbers of standing covered bridges. And Fairfield County, home of Lancaster and Alley Park, has the most covered bridges in the Buckeye State, eighteen in all. The bridges range from 33 feet to over 120 feet long! Most of these Fairfield County bridges were built between 1871 and 1906. Some crossed the many creeks running through Fairfield's Appalachian foothills, while others crossed the Ohio-Erie Canal. A few are on private property, but the rest can be seen by enthusiasts who like to head back in time. Appreciation for these bucolic yet functional wood structures seems to be increasing by the day.

This loop takes place at a scenic metro park that also has the special designation of state nature preserve. Start the hike cruising the forests and dales along Clear Creek, exploring bottoms and bluffs. Leave the riparian zone for wooded hills, making a solid climb, and hike through upland meadows managed for wildlife. Revel in a forest cruise atop Cemetery Ridge, passing a relic barn from when this nature preserve was farmland, eight score distant. Descend steeply to enjoy the Clear Creek bottoms one more time before returning to the trailhead.

Start: Creekside Meadows Picnic Area

Distance: 5.3-mile loop

Hiking time: About 3.5 to 4.5 hours

Difficulty: Moderate to difficult due to hills and distance

Trail surface: Natural surface

Best season: Year-round

Other trail users: None

Canine compatibility: Dogs not permitted in nature preserve

Land status: Metro Parks

Fees and permits: None

Schedule: Open daily year-round, 6:30 a.m. to dark

Maps: Clear Creek Metro Park; USGS Rockbridge

Trail contact: Metro Parks, 1069 W. Main St., Westerville, OH 43081; (614) 891-0700; www .metroparks.net

Finding the trailhead: From exit 46 on I-270, southeast of downtown Columbus, take US 33 east for 34 miles to Clear Creek Road, just after crossing into Hocking County. Turn right on Clear Creek Road/CR 116 and follow it 1.8 miles to the Creekside Meadows Picnic Area on your left. Trailhead GPS: N39 35.329' / W82 34.666'

THE HIKE

lear Creek Metro Park comes in at a whopping 5,300 acres, of which 4,769 are designated state nature preserve, making it the largest nature preserve in the state of Ohio. The park, despite its well-developed trail system, tastefully integrated amenities and historic preservation and exudes a wilderness aura. The glacially carved Clear Creek valley, complemented by tall hills and sheer bluffs rising from wide bottoms, presents a variety of landscapes and habitats rich with flora and fauna. The special characteristics of the Clear Creek valley were noticed decades ago and ultimately resulted in its becoming a nature preserve and metro park.

Clear creek really is clear—and gorgeous.

The park is popular with a variety of outdoor enthusiasts—from bicyclists who pedal its quiet roads, to anglers vying for trout and bass in the stream and Lake Ramona, to picnickers who relax at its attractive dining destinations, to hikers like us who ply the 15-plus miles of hiking trails. It isn't just people that appreciate and populate the preserve. Over 2,000 plants and animals call Clear Creek home, including 40 rare and endangered Ohio species. The valley, one of greater Columbus's most scientifically chronicled locales, was protected in a relatively pristine condition and is an excellent representation of Appalachian foothills within easy striking distance of Ohio's capital.

This loop hike explores the highs and lows of the area, offering a chance to visit differing habitats. The circuit begins at the Creekside Meadows Picnic Area, with tables, restrooms, and trailhead information. As you travel up the valley, Clear Creek Road is never far away, but it is not an intrusion. The trail even joins the road for brief periods as it is hemmed in by the sandstone bluffs and the crystalline stream, both of which you will appreciate. Clear Creek, a tributary of the Hocking River, alternately flows in rocky shoals and around gravel bars, and stills in pools. Fallen logs and wooded banks complement the scenery. It isn't long before you pass the first designated fishing access. These accesses are simply marked spur trails that connect Clear Creek Road and the stream itself, and cross the Creekside Meadows Trail. Whether you fish or not, the spurs avail easy access to the waterway.

The trail also passes through meadows on a mown track. In late summer, wildflowers and grasses will be rising higher than a hiker's head, making this an ideal time to do this hike. In other seasons the fields open to ridgetop vistas and views of the sandstone bluffs that flank Clear Creek.

The hike leaves Clear Creek on the Fern Trail, but the attractive scenery doesn't stop there. The rocky track passes multiple species of ferns as it climbs under hemlocks and birches bordered by massive mossy trailside boulders. A steady climb leads to a ridgetop covered in oaks, maples, and sourwoods. Eventually the forest gives way to upland meadows, which also display summer wildflowers and offer chances to observe deer and other wildlife. These meadows are not mere lawns, but are allowed to successively grow into a mix of fields and tree colonies, adding to biodiversity. They are periodically cut and the process is repeated. These uneven aged plant communities not only provide good food for nature's beasts but also for birdlife. Strips of woods divide the meadows from one another.

You will still be traveling these openings after joining the Cemetery Ridge Trail. Woods take over when the path turns east, tracing a roadbed that makes for pleasant and easy hiking. Gain glimpses into the Clear Creek valley and ridges to the south. The path is mostly canopied but at times is open to the sun overhead.

Along the way you come to a historic barn, part of the Williams family farm, established in 1837. The hewn wooden structure is now surrounded by forest, making it harder to imagine the tilled fields that once sprawled along the ridge. From here on the hike is mostly downhill. After crossing Clear Creek Road, you will make one more trip through bottomland meadows. Enjoy the riparian setting as the path overlooks Clear Creek a final time before returning to the trailhead, completing the circuit.

More to Clear Creek Metro Park

Greater Columbus residents speak most fondly of Clear Creek Park. It is acknowledged as a star of the Columbus Metro Parks system. The natural setting makes an outstanding base upon which to establish a park—and it has something for everyone. Hikers can choose from nine different paths, hiking them individually or creating loops, such as the one detailed above. There is even a historic component to the park, with the restored nineteenth-century Mathias Log Cabin and the Ed Thomas Cabin. Written Rock contains aboriginal outlines that have unfortunately been harmed by graffiti and subsequent sandblasting to remove said graffiti. The Mathias Log Cabin is used in the park's interpretive programs. Park naturalists have nature programs for kids aged 5 to 95. Check out the Metro Parks website (metroparks.net) for programs throughout the system.

MILES AND DIRECTIONS

0.0 Start at the Creekside Meadows Picnic Area. With Clear Creek Road to your back, turn right from the trailhead kiosk, joining the Creekside Meadows Trail. After a few steps, cross Starner Road and continue up the Clear Creek valley, with Clear Creek to your left. Enter hardwood forest on a mown path.

0.3 The trail comes directly alongside Clear Creek, with Clear Creek Road nearby. Look for sandstone bluffs on the far side of Clear Creek Road.

0.6 Reach a trail junction after stepping over a tributary of Clear Creek. Here the Hemlock Trail leaves right, across Clear Creek Road. The Creekside Meadows Trail soon joins and leaves Clear Creek Road twice.

1.0 Come to the Fern Picnic Area and trailhead after passing through a walnut-bordered wildflower meadow. The Creekside Meadows Trail ends at the parking area. Cross Clear Creek Road and join the Fern Trail, a rising footpath.

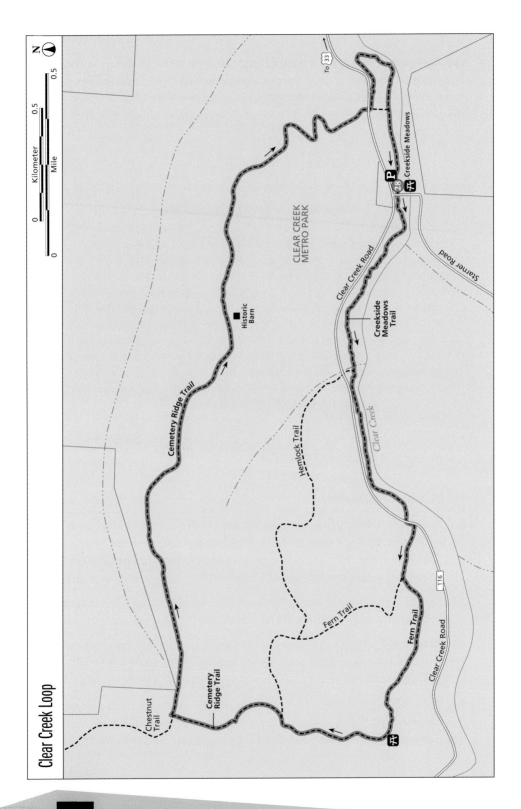

Clear Creek Loop

1.2 The Fern Trail splits. Most hikers stay right with the easier climb, but this hike leaves left, traveling sharply up a ridgeline. Oaks become more prominent in the trailside woodland.

1.8 Open onto the first of a series of linear upland meadows. Sumac, cherry, and dogwood trees rise amid the grasses.

2.1 Join the Cemetery Ridge Trail as the Hemlock Trail comes in from the right. Keep straight, still traveling through meadow.

2.4 Stay with the Cemetery Ridge Trail as it turns right after its intersection with the Chestnut Trail. Hike easterly in ridgetop hardwoods and scrub pines, and soon enter older forest.

3.1 Pass a gas well clearing.

3.6 A short path leads right to a barn built by settlers who farmed what are now woods. A closed track leads left and downhill at this same intersection. The Cemetery Ridge Trail keeps straight here.

4.0 Pass through a gap and come to another gas well clearing. From here the path narrows and reenters full-blown forest.

4.4 Drop off Cemetery Ridge underneath white pines. Switchbacks ease the downgrade.

4.7 Cross Clear Creek Road. Turn left at the intersection, making a final lap through bottomland fields. The path turns upstream along Clear Creek into a grove of walnut and locust trees.

5.1 Pass the other end of this mini-loop. Keep straight toward the Creekside Meadows Picnic Area.

5.3 Arrive back at the picnic area and trailhead, completing the hike.

🍃 Green Tip:
Please don't pick wildflowers or try to transplant plant or animal life from wildlands. State natural preserves do just that, preserving the life within them and providing a place for the natural beauty of the region.

Rockbridge State Nature Preserve

Visit the largest natural bridge in the Buckeye State amid this protected special swath of the greater Hocking Hills. Travel a right-of-way to reach the 200-acre preserve. Downhill meanderings lead to the significant arch. Walk over, under, and around it, reveling in numerous vantages. Make a side trip to the nearby Hocking River. Next, visit a rock house and low-flow waterfall on a separate loop before returning to the trailhead.

Start: Rockbridge State Nature Preserve trailhead
Distance: 2.7-mile multiple loops
Hiking time: About 2 to 2.5 hours
Difficulty: Moderate
Trail surface: Natural surface
Best season: Year-round
Other trail users: None
Canine compatibility: Dogs not permitted in nature preserve
Land status: State nature preserve

Fees and permits: None
Schedule: Open daily year-round
Maps: Rockbridge State Nature Preserve; USGS Logan, Rockbridge
Trail contact: Ohio Department of Natural Resources, 2045 Morse Rd., Building C-3, Columbus, OH 43229-6693; (614) 265-6453; www.dnr.state.oh.us

Finding the trailhead: From exit 46 on I-270, southeast of downtown Columbus, take US 33 east for 35.7 miles. Turn left onto Township Road 124/Dalton Road (Township Road 503 leaves right from the same intersection). This left turn is just past the rest area on US 33 and is not a signed exit with an off-ramp. The turn is after the signed right turn for Cantwell Cliffs but before the OH 180/Laurelville exit off US 33. Follow Township Road 124/Dalton Road as it runs parallel to US 33 then veers left away from US 33. Reach the trailhead on your left at 0.7 mile. Trailhead GPS: N39 33.982'/W82 29.965'

THE HIKE

Rockbridge stands as the largest of the twelve commonly recognized major arches in Ohio, though over sixty geologically classified features of this sort have been categorized during a statewide arch survey. Two of the major ones are here in Hocking County—Rockbridge and Rockhouse. This one, Rockbridge, measures around 100 feet long. Rising over an ever-widening tributary of the Hocking River, it averages 3 feet in thickness and is highest in its middle—over 20 feet above the ground. It was the erosion caused by the tributary that morphed this former rock house into the arch we see today. Ohioans are lucky to have access to this protected physical feature.

Arches are fascinating geological features and deserving of preservation.

From the trailhead, hikers walk an arrow-straight right-of-way to reach the state nature preserve, a swath of land rising from the south bank of the Hocking River. During the length of the right-of-way, you get a good taste of hilly rural Ohio landscape, fields, and forest less like the extensive granaries found in more level parts of the state. It is easy to note the contrast between the nature preserve and adjacent fields as you travel the preserve border. The hike soon leads into the drainage that created the natural bridge. At first you are in a regenerating forest of maple, dogwood, tulip tree, and scrub pine. This was likely a field several decades back.

Enter older, taller woods rife with beeches upon reaching a trail intersection very near Rockbridge. Before you know it, the arch comes into sight below. Most hikers will walk atop the natural bridge, even though it leads nowhere, then backtrack across it again. A maintained trail leads under the bridge. It is most impressive down here. You can see the length of the arch as well as its separation from the main sandstone wall. A rope discourages hikers from traveling into the rock house behind the arch, as generations of visitors have trampled sensitive plants and wildflowers. Photographing the arch can be challenging, and your success may depend on the time of year and light. Arches can be tough to capture as images.

The next part of the hike takes you down to the Hocking River and its adjacent floodplain. Follow the drainage that created Rockbridge into the bottomland, where maple ashes and sycamores rise regally above pawpaws and stinging nettle. The path cruises along the river shore. At lower water levels you can access gravel bars and get an up-close look at the Hocking. Interestingly, a sign indicating the state nature preserve is situated along the shore, attracting paddlers plying the Hocking River.

The hike climbs from the river bottom to an adjacent ridge as oaks increase in number. Once on the ridge you come to a trail intersection and a chance to visit a rock shelter with a low-flow waterfall. As evidenced by the footbed, most hikers blow off this second natural feature. If you are already here, why not see all the state nature preserve has to offer?

Follow the spur off the ridge, switchbacking down an old roadbed. Then the rock house comes into view. Here a sandstone lip has resisted the intermittent flow of a stream, and below it the land has eroded, creating the rock house. When the stream in the hollow is flowing well, the watercourse creates a bridal veil–type fall. At low flows the stream isn't more than a drip off the top of the stone shelter.

The hike next makes a small, inconspicuous loop before the confines of the state preserve force it to turn around. On your return trip note how the rock shelter isn't noticeable until you are directly on it. From there it is mostly a backtrack to the trailhead.

Paddle the Hocking

The Hocking River abuts part of Rockbridge State Nature Preserve. When you walk to the riverbank on the hike, you can see a sign indicating the preserve. The sign is directed toward the river so that paddlers on the Hocking can access and visit the arch here.

The Hocking River wanders for 95 miles through Ohio. It is born near Lancaster, in Fairfield County, then cuts a southeasterly course through the Appalachian foothills into Athens. From there the river winds to the Ohio River at the aptly named Hockingsport.

The river is well suited for paddlers, with Class I waters and small shoals most of its length. A few dams must be portaged. Officially the state's fourteenth-longest river, the Hocking has public ramps as well as an outfitter that provides boat rentals and shuttles. Anglers vie for smallmouth bass, rock bass, and bream. Some sections of the river have special smallmouth bass regulations designed to create opportunities to land a big one.

For more information about the Hocking River outfitter, which offers a trip that passes the Rockbridge area, visit www.hockingriver.com. A paddle on the Hocking will add an aquatic component to your visit to Ohio's largest arch.

Green Tip:
Use the sun to recharge backcountry electronics.

MILES AND DIRECTIONS

0.0 Start at the signed parking area for Rockbridge State Nature Preserve, with several parking spaces and an informational kiosk. Hike north along a grassy strip, an easement, between a field to your left and a wooded strip on your right.

0.2 Traverse a boardwalk over a wide intermittent streambed. Keep north along the easement.

0.3 Cross over a second boardwalk.

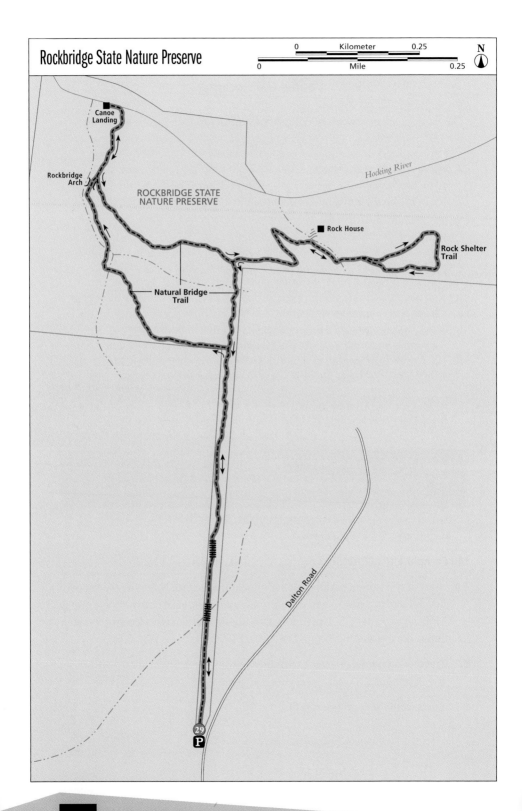

Rockbridge State Nature Preserve

0 — Kilometer — 0.25
0 — Mile — 0.25

N

Canoe Landing

Rockbridge Arch

Hocking River

Rock House

ROCKBRIDGE STATE NATURE PRESERVE

Rock Shelter Trail

Natural Bridge Trail

Dalton Road

29
P

0.4 Enter woods on a rocky, rooty track, still on the right-of-way. Climb a hill, reaching a resting bench at its apex.

0.5 Enter Rockbridge State Nature Preserve at a trail intersection. Head left on the Natural Bridge Trail, cruising the boundary between field and forest, divided by a fence. Watch for deer here.

0.7 Bridge a streamlet. Continue downstream in a spring wildflower haven.

0.8 Bridge the main streambed of the hollow. Keep downhill.

0.9 Come to Rockbridge, the natural arch, after keeping straight at a trail inter-section. A spur trail leads under the arch. View the rock house behind the arch, of which the arch was once a part. Beyond the arch, continue down toward the Hocking River. The trail dead-ends near a signed canoe landing on the river. Backtrack to the intersection above Rockbridge.

1.0 Return to the intersection. Head left, ascending the hollow, then climb a slope shaded by large red oaks and beeches.

1.3 The Rock Shelter Trail leads left and downhill, switchbacking on an old road. The Hocking River is visible through the trees.

1.5 Come to the rock shelter on your left. A spur trail leads to the shelter itself. If the water is flowing, you may hear it dropping over the shelter before you see it.

1.6 After crossing the stream above the rock shelter, the Rock Shelter Trail splits. Head left, uphill, ascending through upland hardwoods.

1.8 Finish the loop portion of the Rock Shelter Trail, then backtrack the way you came.

2.1 Complete the Rock Shelter Trail. Turn left, rejoin-ing the Natural Bridge Trail, and descend to a stream drainage before climbing sharply along an old fence row, now grown up with trees.

2.2 Complete the Natural Bridge Trail. Backtrack along the right-of-way.

2.7 Reach the trailhead, completing the hike.

Cantwell Cliffs Loops

Take a comprehensive tour of this sandstone canyon, where sheer cliffs drop to a gorge below. You will first walk the rim of the gorge, admiring the rock formations both immediately in front of you and below. Next, dip into the gorge itself, traveling a wildflower-rich basin before turning back to the cliffs. Check out a large rock house and waterfall in season before rejoining the ridge crest via the stairs of "Fat Woman's Squeeze."

Start: Conkles Hollow trailhead
Distance: 1.9-mile double loops
Hiking time: About 1.5 to 2.5 hours
Difficulty: Moderate
Trail surface: Natural surface
Best season: Year-round
Other trail users: None
Canine compatibility: Leashed dogs permitted

Land status: Ohio state park
Fees and permits: None
Schedule: Open daily year-round
Maps: Hocking Hills State Park Trails; USGS Rockbridge
Trail contact: Hocking Hills State Park, 19852 OH 664 South, Logan, OH 43138; (740) 385-6842; www .dnr.state.oh.us

Finding the trailhead: From exit 46 on I-270, southeast of downtown Columbus, take US 33 east for 35 miles to the community of Rockbridge and OH 374 (there will be a sign for Cantwell Cliffs on US 33). Turn right and follow OH 374 south for 5.8 miles to the trailhead on your left. Trailhead GPS: N39 32.401'/W82 34.545'

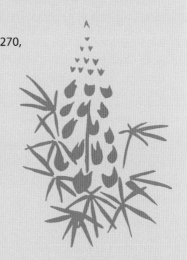

THE HIKE

There is a lot to see on this hike, so allow ample time to absorb both the dramatic scenery, such as the cliffs of Cantwell, and more intimate beauty, such as a cluster of ferns perched on a bluff or dainty wildflowers coloring the hollow of Buck Run. Of course, some things just can't be missed, like the huge rock house near Fat Woman's Squeeze and the portal of Fat Woman's Squeeze itself.

Cantwell Cliffs State Natural Area is bordered by state forest land, which enlarges its wild nature. The trail can be crowded on nice weekends, but a well-timed hike will yield not only solitude but also seasonal paybacks. In summer you will drown in a sea of green, especially in the lush hollow. During autumn the trail

Stone steps lead up "Fat Woman's Squeeze."

along the cliffs will take you eye-level with colorful trees that contrast with the gray sandstone. Winter will reveal the geological glory of the gorge, where sandstone walls, rock houses, and boulder gardens stand naked astride leafless vegetation. The waters of the gorge, Buck Run, will be flowing boldly in spring, and you can see dripping cascades spilling over the gorge rim feeding Buck Run, a clear stream gurgling down the hollow amid wildflowers aplenty.

The trailhead has a water spigot, picnic tables, a covered picnic shelter, and restrooms. It's a pleasant place to relax before or after your hike. The hike quickly reaches the Cantwell Cliffs Trail, then you cruise along the rim edge on a nearly level track. It is hard to keep your eyes on the path ahead—you will be finding yourself peering into Cantwell Hollow below. The trail courses through the forest, with the boulders below clearly visible. Hemlocks and pines continue to shade the Cantwell Rim Trail, and streamlets flow from the hills above, crossing the trail and dropping into the gorge. After rains and during freezes, the watercourses will be quite scenic, with veil-like cataracts morphing into frozen falls of white. During late summer and fall, the streams can run dry. Stay with the Cantwell Rim Trail for the full distance, avoiding the shortcut into the gorge. The sheer drop-offs lure you to the edge, where lush flora of mosses, ferns, fungi, and forest envelop the rock formations below.

Once you leave the rim, a network of official blazed trails and unofficial user-created trails can be a little discombobulating. However, stay with the blazed trails and you will be fine. Beyond that, it is difficult to become truly lost within the confines of the gorge or along the rim. Incredible fallen boulders stand in repose, while vertical sandstone bluffs rise and even overhang the woodlands where you walk. While hiking you will appreciate the extensive trail work leading into the gorge, with hundreds of stone, rock, and concrete steps leading over the uneven terrain. A more typical natural-surface footpath leads down Buck Run. Small tributaries, both intermittent and running, form an aquatic network feeding Buck Run. It is these tributaries, along with an ample dose of time, that eroded Cantwell Cliffs into what we see today. Hemlocks and hardwoods border the trail, and the sandstone cliffs are left behind. The crowds tend to stick near the cliffs, so you will likely have this lower loop to yourself even on a crowded day.

After returning to the cliffs, explore the sandstone walls, with their alcoves, rock houses, and remarkable rock formations. The rock house at the head of the hollow is amazingly large. Though the mini-maze of paths here can create confusion, you will easily find the steps slicing upward through Fat Woman's Squeeze. In reality, the break in the cliff line isn't quite as tight as advertised, but is a highlight of the hike nonetheless. A brief climb returns you to the trailhead.

Saving Ohio's Hemlocks

You will see many hemlock trees while hiking at Cantwell Cliffs. Unfortunately, Ohio's hemlocks are imperiled by the invasive bug known as the hemlock wooly adelgid. This critter from Asia has reached the United States and made its way down the Appalachian chain. So far Ohio, with its disjunct hemlock stands, has been spared widespread infestation of its shade-bearing evergreens. The wooly adelgid has been found on nursery stock trees brought into the Buckeye State, but they have been destroyed and the adelgid contained—so far.

Infected hemlocks become diseased with these bugs, whose signatures are tiny round white "golf balls" on the undersides of the tree's needles. Ninety percent of infected trees die within three to five years of infestation. East of here, in the main Appalachian range, entire forests have been altered when the hemlock tree has been eliminated, including places like Shenandoah National Park. The Hocking Hills area is a mainstay for Ohio's hemlocks, and keeping the adelgid out is a priority. Ohio state foresters are monitoring the hemlocks of Hocking Hills to halt any infestation.

The adelgid can be stopped with a soapy insecticide sprayed on the trees or injected in the roots. A Japanese beetle that feeds only on the hemlock wooly adelgid has been propagated and introduced in several states to stop the bug. If you see any sign of the adelgid on backwoods hemlocks or nursery stock planted in your own backyard, please report it to the Ohio Division of Forestry to help keep Ohio's hemlocks green and growing.

MILES AND DIRECTIONS

0.0 Start at the lower end of the parking lot loop. Join a wide trail under hemlocks and pines below the actual trailhead parking area, and soon reach a sizable shaded picnic shelter. The main trail leads left and downhill on a rooty track, mixed with stone steps, beyond the shelter.

0.1 Reach the edge of Cantwell Cliffs. The Cantwell Lower Loop Trail leaves left down the stone steps of Fat Woman's Squeeze. For now, stay right on the Cantwell Rim Trail, heading easterly on the canyon rim. Soon pass an alternate path back to the picnic shelter.

0.3 A shortcut trail leads left, descending a break in the cliff line. Stone steps make the path more discernable. Stay straight atop the canyon rim, bridging a small streamlet.

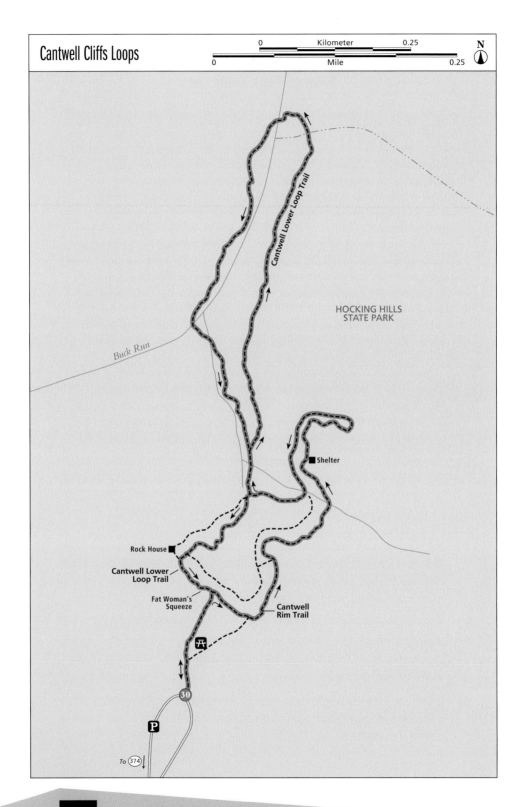

Cantwell Cliffs Loops

0 Kilometer 0.25

0 Mile 0.25

N

Cantwell Lower Loop Trail

HOCKING HILLS
STATE PARK

Buck Run

Shelter

Rock House

Cantwell Lower
Loop Trail

Fat Woman's
Squeeze

Cantwell
Rim Trail

To 374

0.4 Pass a small shelter house on your right. The Cantwell Rim Trail continues along the rim.

0.5 Turn into the gorge, dropping off the rim. The sandstone bluffs that you were on top of earlier rise to your left. The Cantwell Rim Trail crosses a perennial low-flow stream via a boardwalk.

0.7 The trail leads past a low-flow waterfall and rock house along the trail. Another trail leads left and runs at the base of the cliff line.

0.8 Come to a trail junction at the bottom of the hollow. Turn right, downhill, and head down the hollow of Buck Run. You will return to this intersection later. In a mere 300 feet, come to yet another intersection and begin the second loop on Cantwell Lower Loop Trail. Stay right, hiking through mixed hardwoods in the ever-widening hollow. This is a rich wildflower area in spring. The headwaters of Buck Run flow to your left.

1.1 Cross clear Buck Run. During normal flows this will be a simple dry-footed hop over the sand and gravel bed. Turn upstream.

1.4 Step over a tributary coming in on your right. Stay up the main hollow and cross Buck Run, which is very small at this point.

1.5 Complete the Lower Loop Trail. Continue straight up the main hollow, coming along a cliff line. Ahead, trace a trail using wood and earth steps, while a parallel path runs along the stream to your right. This is the area most visited by cliff explorers, and visitors have created a maze of unofficial paths. The official trail leads left along the cliff line. You can explore this area or continue up to another intersection. Here a trail leads right to visit the huge rock house at the head of the hollow.

1.8 After exploring the area, turn left up the steps of Fat Woman's Squeeze.

1.9 Reach the trailhead, after backtracking from Fat Woman's Squeeze, and complete the hike.

🐛 *Green Tip:*
Keep to established trails as much as possible.
If there aren't any, stay on surfaces that will be least
affected, like rock, gravel, dry grasses, or snow.

Conkles Hollow Hike

You won't believe you are in Ohio while on this geologically mind-blowing trek in a state nature preserve. First, climb the rim above Conkles Hollow, where rock outcrops provide inspiring views across a deep gorge. Pass a waterfall before circling back to the base of the canyon, then turn into the depths of Conkles Hollow, where rich flora grows among incredible cliffs, boulders, and rock houses. Finally, find a waterfall in the innermost depths of the gorge before backtracking out.

Start: Conkles Hollow trailhead
Distance: 3.2-mile loop and out-and-back
Hiking time: About 2 to 2.5 hours
Difficulty: Moderate, but does have a climb
Trail surface: Natural surface
Best season: Year-round
Other trail users: None
Canine compatibility: Dogs not permitted in nature preserve
Land status: State nature preserve

Fees and permits: None
Schedule: Open daily year-round
Maps: Conkles Hollow State Nature Preserve; USGS South Bloomingville
Trail contact: Ohio Department of Natural Resources, 2045 Morse Rd., Building C-3, Columbus, OH 43229-6693; (614) 265-6453; www.dnr.state.oh.us

Finding the trailhead: From exit 46 on I-270, southeast of downtown Columbus, take US 33 east for 36 miles to exit 33A, Laurelville/OH 180. Turn right off the exit and follow OH 180 west for 3.9 miles to OH 678. Veer left on OH 678 south and follow it for 3.9 miles. Stay straight as OH 678 becomes OH 374 south, and stay with OH 374 south for 3.4 miles. Turn left on Big Pine Road and follow it 0.1 mile to reach the parking area on your left. Trailhead GPS: N39 27.210' / W82 34.408'

THE HIKE

Conkles Hollow State Nature Preserve is situated in scenic Hocking Hills State Forest. The state forest lives up to its name, being quite hilly, with steep valleys cut by streams maximizing vertical variation. Conkles Hollow has been long recognized for its special natural qualities and was purchased for preservation by the state way back in 1925. Though busy in season, the hike is not nearly as popular as the trails around Old Man's Cave. Simply hike here during off times, and especially consider a trip when the stream and waterfalls of Conkles Hollows are frozen. Furthermore, the vast majority of the hikers take the 0.6-mile Gorge Trail into Conkles Hollow, skipping the 2-mile circuit around the rim of the valley. I recommend doing both.

An arched bridge takes you over Pine Creek and into Conkles Hollow, centered by an unnamed stream that—over eons—sculpted the land, eroding rock into what we see today. The hollow got its name from an early visitor's carved inscription on the west wall. His connection to the gorge is unknown other than one W. J. Conkle visited the place in 1797. The East Rim Trail leads to the lip of the gorge, where wind-fashioned pines grasp to outcrops that give hikers views into the gulf below. Mountain laurel, greenbrier, and stunted oaks populate thin

Outcrops stretch over the greenery of Conkles Hollow.

southwest-facing soils. The level path often travels over bare rock. At the upper end of the gorge, gain a top-down look on a waterfall from an observation deck. The West Rim Trail delivers views into the gorge, especially closer looks from sheer cliffs, around which grows vegetation more often seen points north.

The circuit finally leads back to Conkles Hollow and what most hikers consider the best part of the hike—the inner sanctum of the gorge. An all-access trail leads into the gorge, where erosion and time have produced an array of geological peculiarities, from overhanging caves, to ferny dripping rock walls, to precarious boulder gardens. The damp vale also supports wildflowers in spring. In summer a forest of sugar maple, black birch, and sycamore shade the path. Widespread fern fields carpet the understory. Your trip ends at the Lower Falls, where a stream falls into a stone cathedral that seems to transport you in place and time. On your way out, look for fascinating rock formations unseen on the way in.

Ohio's State Nature Preserves

In 1970 the Buckeye State developed a system by which special natural treasures could be left unspoiled for today's citizens and future generations. The mission of nature preserves is to establish a sanctuary for the flora and fauna within, rather than to simply be a recreation destination. However, most nature preserves are open to the public for what is known as "passive recreation," basically hiking and nature study. Other preserves are closed to the public but can be visited with a special permit.

Preserves protect places such as Conkles Hollow, with its amazing geology. Others include places like Compass Plant Prairie, which conserves a 16-acre site that is the only known spot in the state for this western prairie wildflower. Hueston Woods protects one of the largest remaining stands of old-growth forest in Ohio. Browns Lake Bog harbors wetland species normally found farther north.

You can help expand and protect Ohio's preserves by donating to the program. Simply find the check-off on your state income tax form. This is one of the few easy opportunities you have to direct your tax dollars where you think they should go, while simultaneously supporting Ohio's special natural communities.

Green Tip:
Avoid sensitive ecological areas. Hike, rest, and camp at least 200 feet from streams, lakes, and rivers.

MILES AND DIRECTIONS

0.0 Start at the lower end of the loop below the actual trailhead parking area, which has picnic tables and a restroom. Take the iron bridge over Pine Creek, entering Conkles Hollow State Preserve. Shortly join a boardwalk over sensitive wetlands, then reach a trail junction. Turn right on the East Rim Trail, climbing wood-and-earth steps to begin circling Conkles Hollow, saving the trip into the gorge for last. You will also be leaving the crowds behind. Ascend in hemlock and birch, gaining 200 feet in elevation. Rock outcrops soon become commonplace.

0.3 Join the gorge rim, turning northwesterly. The wooded valley of Conkles Hollow falls away.

0.4 Come to a rock outcrop bordered in pines, presenting views into the defile below. Continue cruising a level cliff line scattered with scrub oaks. More views open just ahead. Listen for water flowing through the hollow and for birdsong echoing in the gorge. At certain angles you can discern that the rim you are walking actually overhangs the land below.

0.5 Come to a second vista on a point. Continue along the cliff line.

0.8 The East Rim Trail crosses a perennial low-flow stream via a boardwalk.

1.0 A spur leads left to an observation deck overlooking the Upper Falls, spilling into Conkles Hollow. This ferny, moist, and shady area is cool in the summer and can be a spectacular ice spectacle in winter. In late winter and spring, the falls will flow their boldest.

1.1 Circle around the head of the gorge, now turning southeast on the West Rim Trail. White pines rise overhead, and views open below to fern fields and rock shelters. Unfortunately, a little road noise from OH 374 can spill into the trail corridor here. Ahead, watch for pedestal rocks distended from the main cliff line and for boulders fallen into the abyss below.

1.4 Partial views open through the trees across the gorge. A preponderance of mosses grows in this northeast-facing locale, which will be good for vernal wildflowers.

1.6 A spring gently flows across the trail and splashes over the rim. Grab looks at rock houses below.

1.9 Come very near OH 374 on your right. There is no official parking along the winding road here. Descend via switchbacks, boardwalks, and wooden steps from the rim into the base of the hollow.

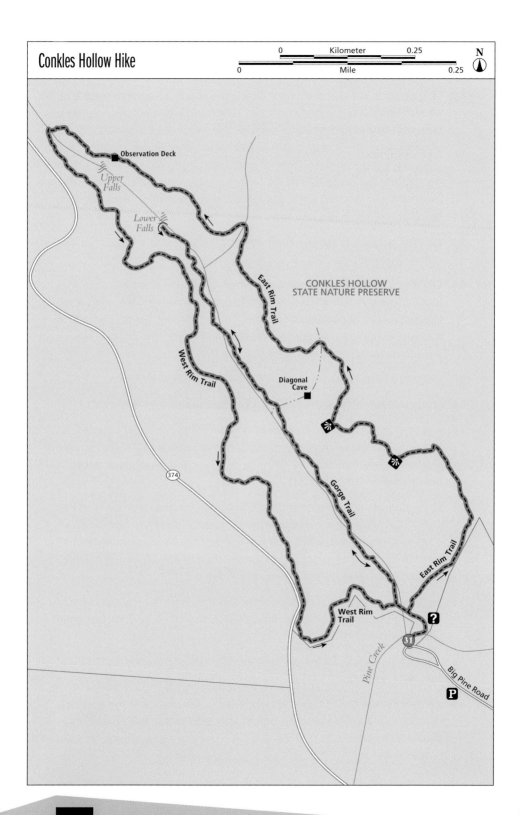

Conkles Hollow Hike

0 — Kilometer — 0.25

0 — Mile — 0.25

N

Observation Deck

Upper Falls

Lower Falls

East Rim Trail

West Rim Trail

CONKLES HOLLOW
STATE NATURE PRESERVE

Diagonal Cave

Gorge Trail

374

East Rim Trail

West Rim Trail

Pine Creek

31

Big Pine Road

P

2.1 Turn left onto the Gorge Trail. At this point the path is concrete, allowing wheelchair trail trekkers to explore Conkles Hollow.

2.2 Cross over to the right-hand side of the stream running through Conkles Hollow on Stewart Bridge.

2.4 A gentle uptick leads over a boardwalk and to Diagonal Cave, which is visible to the right of the trail. The cave roof has a diagonal angle. Access is closed to protect rare plants in this small side hollow. Please respect this closure even if you see others violating it. Ahead, on your right, come to an accessible rock house known as "The Grotto."

2.5 The concrete all-access trail ends in a rock jumble; one of the trailside boulders is known as "Slump Rock." Cross over to the left-hand side of the gravel-bottomed stream. The sheerest, highest bluff in Conkles Hollow rises on your left. More rock houses form ahead, and the trail twists deeper into the geological wonderland.

2.6 The Gorge Trail dead-ends in a semicircular rock amphitheater where a low-flow 20-foot waterfall spills onto a gravel floor. This spot is cool and dark even on the hottest summer day. Backtrack toward the trailhead.

3.2 Emerge at the circle below the parking area after bridging Pine Creek, completing the hike.

Conkles Hollow presents "gorge-ous" scenery.

Ross Hollow Loop

This is an excellent introductory hike to Tar Hollow State Park and Forest. It is long enough to enjoy the wildflowers, trees, and terrain of this hilly preserve, yet allows extra time to explore the rest of the park amenities as well as make the drive to and from Columbus. You will start out at Ross Hollow Campground and then ascend to Brush Ridge, winding in and out of small valleys that harbor scads of wildflowers. Reach a high point on Brush Ridge, with a picnic shelter nearby, then curve your way back down the hollow. Work around a hillside so steep you can't imagine this is Ohio before drifting into the trailhead.

Start: Shower house at Ross Hollow Campground
Distance: 3.5-mile loop
Hiking time: About 2 to 2.5 hours
Difficulty: Moderate due to distance and steep hills
Trail surface: Natural surface
Best seasons: Spring for wildflowers, fall for colors
Other trail users: None
Canine compatibility: Leashed dogs permitted
Land status: Ohio state park
Fees and permits: None
Schedule: Open daily year-round
Maps: Logan Trail; USGS Hallsville
Trail contact: Tar Hollow State Park, 16396 Tar Hollow Rd., Laurelville, OH 43135; (740) 887-4818; www.dnr.state.ohio.us

Finding the trailhead: From exit 52 on I-270, south of downtown Columbus, take US 23 south for 20 miles to the Circleville/Washington exit. Join OH 56 east for 14.6 miles, passing through Circleville, to reach OH 180. Turn right onto OH 180 and follow it west 0.6 mile to a four-way intersection in Laurelville. Keep straight, joining OH 327 south from Laurelville, and drive 7.3 miles to turn right into Tar Hollow State Park. Pass the park office at 0.8 mile, then continue toward the camping areas. At 1.8 miles, spur off to the Ross Hollow camping area, campsites 1–28, just before a sharp left turn toward the state forest fire tower. Drive a short distance to a large parking area, and you will find the trail starting near the camping area shower house. Trailhead GPS: N39 23.574' / W82 45.166'

THE HIKE

Tar Hollow State Park comes in at a modest 600 acres. However, it is completely encircled by 16,000-plus-acre Tar Hollow State Forest, which effectively enlarges the wild area. The missions of the state park and state forest are a little different. State parks focus on user recreation and resource preservation, while state forests focus on resource management first and recreation second. The Ross Hollow Trail is located entirely within the state park, which means you can hike it year-round without consideration of hunting seasons. But no matter when you come to Tar Hollow, make a complete day of it, as the setting is wonderful

Showy orchis is a prize wildflower find on the Ross Hollow Trail.

and there are other activities such as picnicking, swimming, camping, paddling, and fishing. In fact, Tar Hollow is an excellent alternative to the Hocking Hills on those ideal spring and fall days when you know the Hocking area will be overrun. I believe the scenery here at Tar Hollow rivals the Hocking Hills.

A hike on the Ross Hollow Trail will confirm this. Rich woodlands hug the Appalachian foothills, where steep valleys have been carved by clear rocky streams. The wildflowers are simply outstanding, and you will find the wide assortment of hardwoods deliver a kaleidoscope of color in fall. During winter the beauty will be more muted, yet the silence of the backwoods will prove a full immersion in nature. In summer a hike here can be but one of many park activities, especially if you spend a weekend camping and exploring this swath of the Buckeye State.

The hike challenges immediately as it sharply climbs the nose of a ridge before leveling out. Spring wildflowers will carpet the floor—bluet, trillium, bellwort, mayapple, and dwarf crested iris—and regal oaks rise overhead. It isn't long before you wind into your first small hollow. These tributary streams form wet-weather drainages divided by dry ridges. As you wind in and out of the hollows, more wildflowers will be seen along the rocky vales. "Hollow" is an Appalachian term for a valley or stream drainage. Over time, water "hollows out" these valleys from the ridges, giving rise to the name. The term is now on maps from Ohio to West Virginia, down to Georgia and Alabama.

The trail crosses old wagon tracks, woods roads, and timber routes, all in different stages of fading back into the forest. The way is clear if you simply follow the blazes. You do come near North Ridge Road, though it will be out of sight. Later, you will see a picnic shelter where two forest roads join. This is a scenic little knoll that is worth a stop.

As you curve around the head of Ross Hollow, tulip trees grow straight and tall. This state park wasn't always this way. Homesites once dotted the hills, but the steep terrain was unproductive for farming, and over time erosion became a problem. In the 1930s the land that became the state park and forest was purchased by the United States government and the locals ostensibly relocated to more productive areas. However, in reality, the residents of Tar Hollow, being hill people, stayed in the hill country they loved and resumed living as they always had, just in a different place. The Civilian Conservation Corps came in after the lands were purchased. They dammed the park lake and built many of the picnic shelters you see. By the way, the name Tar Hollow comes from a forest product in abundant supply here— pine tar. Pitch from pine trees was important to early Ohio residents in many ways, much like how we use oil today.

Your return trip down Ross Hollow stays on sloping, sometimes rocky terrain. The valley lies a good 250 feet below, and you can see north across Ross Hollow to the ridge you were walking earlier. This panorama delivers a clear visual representation of the word "hollow." Finally, the path slopes down toward Pine Lake. You never get to the body of water, however, though views of the impoundment open during leafless winter. This is where the slope you are walking becomes so steep, it is reminiscent of the Allegheny or Smoky Mountains. The path slowly and carefully works down the slant. Ross Hollow Campground comes into view, but you turn away and emerge onto the campground access road, using the road bridge to cross the unnamed stream that forms Ross Hollow. After bridging the stream, you are at the campground and trailhead, ending the hike.

More about Tar Hollow State Park

Ask your fellow greater Columbus residents if they have ever been to Tar Hollow State Park, and I bet the answer will be "No." This getaway is one of the most underutilized natural resources in central Ohio. Sure, it doesn't have the eye-popping natural features of the Hocking Hills such as Old Man's Cave and Cantwell Cliffs, but neither does it have the crowds. What it does have is extremely hilly terrain combined with remoteness and size that delivers an aura of being in the back of beyond, deep in the Appalachians. It's a relatively painless drive, and the park offers plenty to do. I recommend making a weekend of it.

Start off by bringing your camping gear. The park has several camping areas set deep in the hollows, where even a hot summer day is tolerable. You can enjoy nice sites with hot showers and running water. Check out Pine Lake, a 15-acre impoundment where only electric motors are allowed, keeping the atmosphere serene. Take a swim at the beach or launch your canoe or kayak onto the waters to sightsee or vie for panfish. Numerous shelters make picnicking a breeze and the settings are scenic, whether you are atop a ridge or down by a stream.

Take a drive to the nearby fire tower, and climb 73 feet to gain a view of the hills that stretch for miles. Ride your bike on the park roads, check out what ranger programs are going on at the nature center, or challenge your camping compadres to a game of miniature golf. No matter whether you come for a day, a weekend, or longer, your time will be well spent at Tar Hollow.

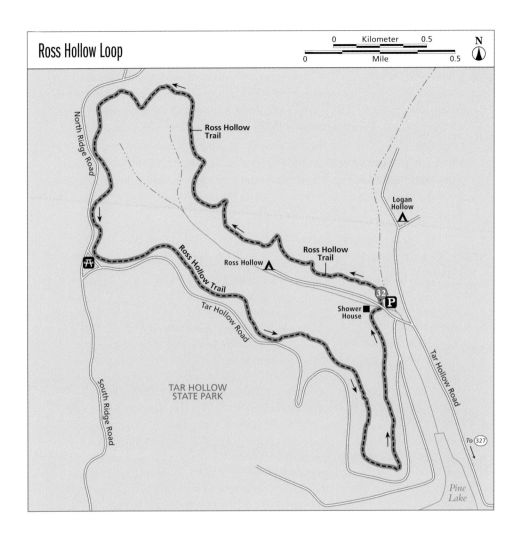

Ross Hollow Loop

Kilometer

Mile

N

Ross Hollow Trail

North Ridge Road

Logan Hollow

Ross Hollow Trail

Ross Hollow

Ross Hollow Trail

Ross Hollow

32
P

Tar Hollow Road

Shower House

South Ridge Road

TAR HOLLOW STATE PARK

Tar Hollow Road

To 327

Pine Lake

🍂 Green Tip:
*This trail is a great place to exercise the adage
"Take only pictures, leave only footprints," as there are
ample wildflowers to photograph in spring.*

MILES AND DIRECTIONS

0.0 Start by leaving the large parking area between the shower house and a creek to your right on the yellow-blazed singletrack Ross Hollow Trail. This initial climb is surprisingly steep, but short. Turn westerly into Ross Hollow, well above the campground.

1.2 Curve just below North Ridge Road. It remains unseen above, while the trail winds just inside the lip of Ross Hollow.

1.7 Come within sight of a picnic shelter located at the intersection of two forest roads. A user-created trail rises right and comes to the forest road and shelter. The singletrack Ross Hollow Trail keeps straight and curves southeast down the hollow.

2.4 Pass through a dense groundcover of privet just below another knoll. There was likely a homesite above the trail here.

2.5 Join the top of a ridge, wandering easterly underneath gray-trunked chestnut oaks. Hills drop sharply from both sides of the trail.

3.0 Curve into the hollow of Pine Lake on a slender footpath, barely hanging onto a declivitous slope. Gain glimpses of Pine Lake below. The 15-acre impoundment will be hard to see during summer, when the leaves are thick. Wildflowers are rife here in spring.

3.5 Complete the hike after using the campground access road bridge to cross the stream forming Ross Hollow.

This is the longest and most difficult hike in the entire guide. The hike is not to be feared, however—it simply takes time and planning to execute. Since the walk involves over 9 miles of hiking with combined elevation changes of 4,200 feet, you will be challenged. Start at the hike's lowest point near Pine Lake at Tar Hollow State Park, then make four distinct climbs followed by four descents as you stretch into the hills and hollows of adjoining Tar Hollow State Forest, a 16,000-plus-acre enclave perched in the Appalachians foothills south of Columbus. Along the way visit the Brush Ridge Fire Tower, which you can climb—if you have enough leg strength.

Start: Pine Lake parking area

Distance: 9.3-mile loop

Hiking time: About 5.5 to 6.5 hours

Difficulty: Difficult due to distance and elevation change

Trail surface: Natural surface

Best season: Year-round

Other trail users: None

Canine compatibility: Leashed dogs permitted

Land status: Ohio state forest and park

Fees and permits: None

Schedule: Open daily year-round

Maps: Logan Trail; USGS Hallsville, Londonderry, Ratcliffburg

Trail contacts: Tar Hollow State Forest, 2731 Stoney Creek Rd., Chillicothe, OH 45601; (740) 663-2538, www.ohiodnr.com/forestry. Tar Hollow State Park, 16396 Tar Hollow Rd., Laurelville, OH 43135; (740) 887-4818; www.dnr.state .ohio.us

Finding the trailhead: From exit 52 on I-270, south of downtown Columbus, take US 23 south for 20 miles to the Circleville/Washington exit. Join OH 56 east for 14.6 miles, passing through Circleville, to reach OH 180. Turn right onto OH 180 and follow it west for 0.6 mile to a four-way intersection in Laurelville. Keep straight, joining OH 327 south from Laurelville, and drive 7.3 miles to the right turn into Tar Hollow State Park. Pass the park office at 0.8 mile, then continue toward the camping areas and drive 0.4 mile farther. Look left for the parking at the spillway below Pine Lake. Trailhead GPS: N39 23.034' / W82 44.852'

THE HIKE

When scanning topographical maps of central Ohio, what is now Tar Hollow State Forest and Tar Hollow State Park stand out. The lines marking elevation changes are very tight here, indicating serious elevation change. During the Great Depression of the 1930s, someone came up with the idea to move poor hill-country Ohioans to better farming grounds. What is now the state forest and state park were poor lands—subsistence farmers were tilling narrow ridges and erosion-prone hollows, while the slopes themselves were often grazing lands also subject to wearing away. Despite these good intentions, the hill people ended up in a different place doing the same thing, but the residents of Ohio now had over 16,000 acres that became the third-largest state forest.

Today the land is managed for timber extraction, wildlife, and recreation. You will likely see all three components on your loop. The hike begins in the recreation-intensive Tar Hollow State Park, with its lake, campgrounds, and other amenities. Climb out of the actual Tar Hollow onto a ridge that encloses it. Stay up top long enough to catch your breath before descending back into the hollow. There is an acronym that Appalachian Trail thru-hikers use known as "PUDs," and it stands for "pointless ups and downs." This quick ascent and descent may conjure up the term.

This wildflower is commonly known as wild oat, though some call it bellwort.

After your first up and down, wander into Logan Hollow, which has a campground spanning its lower reaches. Soon leave the camping area but not before passing close to a couple of campsites. You will then work deeper up the hollow along a gorgeous stream flanked with spring wildflowers underneath a verdant forest. Follow the stream, crossing it time and again, and even going directly up the streambed as it shrinks smaller and smaller, then trickles no more. Top out on North Ridge Road. Congratulations, you have now made your second major climb of the day. Your reward is another trip into one of the scenic valleys hidden from the rest of the world by abrupt wooded slopes.

The path works around a private inholding before mountaineering another rocky ridge, this one with limited views to the north. Watch for the red wildflower known as *fire pink* atop this ridge. The tips of the cardinal-colored flower look like they've been clipped with pinking shears, hence the name. You've now made your third climb.

It isn't long before you are dropping into the interestingly named Slickaway Hollow. This is one of the most scenic spots in the state forest. A clear stream meanders through a high-walled valley rich in flora. Rock hop the main watercourse and its tributaries several times before meeting the South Loop, just before the Brush Ridge Fire Tower and an alternate trailhead. The fire tower is open for climbing and includes interesting interpretive information about Ohio's state forests and the history of fire towers in the Buckeye State.

After this final climb of the trek, the rest is a piece of cake. Enjoy the visual treats as you wind back down a wildflower-filled slope to reach the Pine Lake spillway and the hike's end. Upon completing this loop, you will agree it is more than worth the effort.

White trillium is one of Ohio's largest yet most delicate spring wildflowers.

MILES AND DIRECTIONS

0.0 Start by walking south from the large parking area, away from Pine Lake. Look for a sign indicating the Homestead Trail and walk toward it, then veer left on a singletrack path blazed in red. Do not follow the trail downstream, which crosses the stream flowing from Pine Lake. Instead, quickly rise to cross the main park road. You will likely see this road crossing on your drive in, as it is just before the left turn into the trailhead parking area. A singletrack path takes you uphill in the pines, then turns back near the main park road.

0.6 Level off in a gap after climbing steadily 300 feet to reach a hilltop. The rise moderates. Turn west near the park boundary. Sturdy white oaks shade the track.

0.8 Begin diving into Logan Hollow.

1.4 The Logan Trail passes next to a huge beech tree beside a streamlet. Step over the streamlet.

1.6 Reach a low point not much higher than when you started the trail. Park roads and picnic area facilities are in sight.

1.8 Step over a streamlet just a stone's throw above a campsite in Logan Hollow. Walk along steep hillsides.

2.0 Step over another stream just above more campsites. Leave Logan Hollow Campground.

2.2 Cross two streams, then enter upper Logan Hollow. Walk through ferny woodlands, exuding the back of beyond. Crisscross the stream as it meanders back and forth across the hollow.

3.0 After a sharp ascent, emerge at North Ridge Road. Cross the asphalt and look left for the trail. Enjoy a brief level respite in brushy woods.

3.1 Pop out on a doubletrack dirt road. Watch for the red blazes as you walk left along the road.

3.2 Pass a little pond to your left, likely an old farm pond, filling more and more with sediment each year.

3.3 Leave left from the roadbed, back on singletrack path. Dive into an unnamed valley carved by an unnamed stream flowing into Walnut Creek.

3.5 Step over the streamlet several times as the unnamed valley widens. Wildflowers are bountiful in spring.

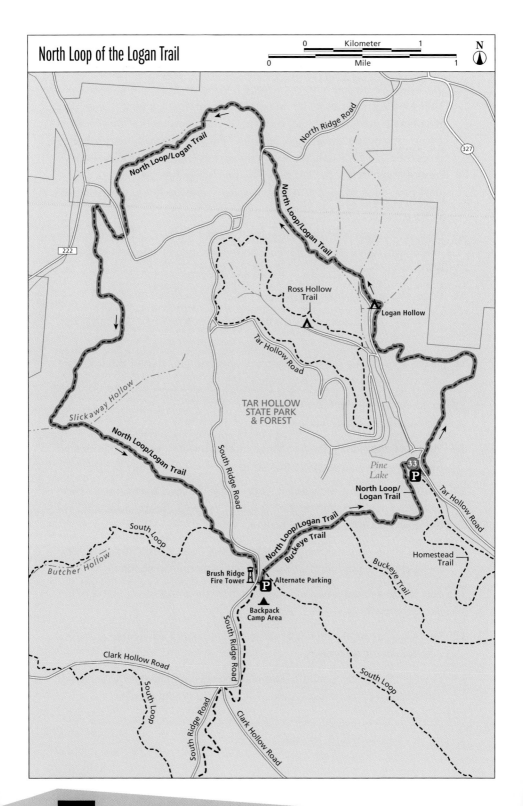

4.0 Make your last stream crossing near a private forest inholding, then curve left into a huge bed of periwinkles.

4.5 Step over Tar Hollow Road and rock hop a stream. Start angling up the side of a ridge.

4.8 Turn south, straight up the nose of a ridge. Look back for views to the north.

4.9 Crest out on a rocky ridge shaded in chestnut oaks.

5.3 Keep a close and careful eye on the red blazes as you pass through a series of grassy clearings and along or near grassy roadbeds.

6.0 Drop off the ridge you've been following, then plunge into Slickaway Hollow.

6.3 Turn into Slickaway Hollow and enjoy a gorgeous walk through flats astride a clear gravelly stream. Cross the waterway multiple times.

6.5 Curve into the right arm of the hollow. Ascend gradually and keep stream-hopping as the hollow contracts.

7.4 Meet the South Loop after a final push out of Slickaway Hollow. Stay left here, as the two loops of the Logan Trail run in conjunction. Pass over a grassy road, then walk under several old-growth northern red oaks.

7.8 Reach the fire tower and alternate trailhead. To continue the hike, walk toward the fire tower and look left for the red-blazed trail with a sign stating PINE LAKE, NORTH LOOP, LOGAN TRAIL. Descend on the singletrack path, running in conjunction with the Buckeye Trail.

7.9 The South Loop leaves right. Keep straight with the North Loop/Buckeye Trail as it runs parallel and along a doubletrack old logging road. Enjoy a well-deserved easy ridge walk.

8.5 The Buckeye Trail leaves right in a gap. Stay straight with the North Loop of the Logan Trail as it curves downhill as a singletrack path. Cruise an abrupt side slope.

9.0 Turn north into the hollow of Pine Lake. Keep descending.

9.2 Hit a roadbed and stay left, still following the red blazes downhill, to reach a bridge spanning the dam spillway.

9.3 Cross the grassy lawn below the dam, reaching the trailhead and completing the hike.

South Loop of the Logan Trail

Tar Hollow State Forest, deep in the Appalachian foothills, is the setting for this long circuit that dares hikers with 3,600 feet of elevation changes stretched out over 8-plus miles. But you will be well rewarded on this major hike. Start at the state forest fire tower, then work your way west into the mountain scenery of Butcher Hollow. Cruise along the serpentine course of Piney Run before rising to high, lonely hardwood ridges. Next, drop into Clark Hollow and the Pike Run watershed. Make a long, slow ascent in a gorgeous valley, aiming for the fire tower. Your hike ends with a bang as you rise very steeply to reach the trailhead.

Start: Brush Ridge Fire Tower

Distance: 8.8-mile loop

Hiking time: About 5 to 6 hours

Difficulty: Difficult due to distance and elevation change

Trail surface: Natural surface

Best season: Year-round

Other trail users: Equestrians for one short stretch

Canine compatibility: Leashed dogs permitted

Land status: Ohio state forest and park

Fees and permits: None

Schedule: Open daily year-round

Maps: Logan Trail; USGS Hallsville, Londonderry, Ratcliffburg

Trail contacts: Tar Hollow State Forest, 2731 Stoney Creek Rd., Chillicothe, OH 45601; (740) 663-2538; www.ohiodnr.com/forestry. Tar Hollow State Park, 16396 Tar Hollow Rd., Laurelville, OH 43135; (740) 887-4818. www.dnr.state .ohio.us

Finding the trailhead: From exit 52 on I-270, south of downtown Columbus, take US 23 south for 20 miles to the Circleville/Washington exit. Join OH 56 east for 14.6 miles, passing through Circleville, to reach OH 180. Turn right onto OH 180 and follow it west 0.6 mile to a four-way intersection in Laurelville. Keep straight, joining OH 327 south from Laurelville, and drive 7.3 miles to the right turn into Tar Hollow State Park. Pass the park office at 0.8 mile, then continue toward the camping areas. (Do not turn left and park at the spillway below Pine Lake. This is parking for the North Loop of the Logan Trail.) At 1.8 miles spur off toward the Ross Hollow camping area, then quickly turn left toward the fire tower. Drive another mile, then stay left again, following the signs for the fire tower. Drive another 1.5 miles to reach the tower. Parking is on the left just before the tower. The proper segment of the Logan Trail starts off the paved road as it curves right, away from the fire tower. Trailhead GPS: N39 22.509' / W82 45.780'

THE HIKE

The Logan Trail is a nearly 20-mile-long figure-eight loop that courses through Tar Hollow State Forest and Tar Hollow State Park. It is maintained by Boy Scouts from the Columbus and Dayton metropolitan areas. They often use it for long treks, whereupon they can earn a merit badge. I believe they deserve a merit badge just for keeping up this huge hiking asset to central Ohio. It is tough enough just to hike the trails, much less maintain them. So as you walk this loop, give a big thanks to the Boy Scouts. You may actually see some of them on weekends.

This historic fire tower stands at the trailhead.

The natural setting of Tar Hollow State Forest provides an ideal canvas upon which to lay a path. The ridgetops, cloaked in oaks, rise high and divide moist drainages where rocky watercourses dash for the lowlands beneath myriad hardwoods and wildflower displays rivaling any other part of the Buckeye State. This is the less strenuous of the two large loops that comprise the Logan Trail. That being said, it is still the second longest and second most difficult hike in this entire guidebook. But don't let that scare you—in fact, take it as a challenge and give yourself a full day to enjoy this scenic swath of Ohio's public lands.

The red-blazed Logan Trail leaves north from the fire tower. At this point the North Loop and the South Loop are running in conjunction. The singletrack path undulates through hardwoods, including some old-growth northern red oaks that will catch your eye. You will see blackened bases on many trees. Prescribed fire is a regular management tool here in the state forest, and is used to keep the understory light. By the way, you will also see logging practiced in the state forest. This generates revenue for the state forest system as well as provides timber products for us, including the pages of this guide. Think of all the paper-based products that we utilize every day. State forests such as this provide repositories for timber as well as areas where the natural landscape can be maintained for the maximum benefit of wildland species.

This stream in Clark Hollow cuts a serpentine course.

After the two loops diverge, the South Loop runs a ridge and then drops into Butcher Hollow. The deeper you get, the wilder the look and feel. Wildflowers are abundant, and rocky tributaries flow into the main stream of Butcher Hollow. The South Loop then follows upper Piney Run into the high country, meeting the Buckeye Trail. Enjoy some easy ridge-running as you pass a spur loop to Camp Dulen, an overnight camping area for Boy Scouts.

The path continues an extended period of traveling easterly along a high ridgeline, running roughly parallel to a power-line clearing. This clearing opens views to the south of hills and hollows fading into the distance. Next, the South Loop dives into Clark Hollow, switchbacking to ease the descent. The richly vegetated valley harbors wildflowers aplenty. You then turn up a tributary, once again enclosed by steep-sided hills. This unnamed stream gathers in little pools, gurgles beside gravel bars, and drops over small rock shoals.

Leave the valley and climb into oaks, working up the nose of a ridge. Climb over 300 feet in 0.4 mile before the ascent eases. When describing this hike, a not-to-be-named Tar Hollow State Park employee stated, "That last hill—it's a killer." The hill may not kill you, but it will leave a lasting impression of how craggy this place can be. Catch your breath while working north under a tall hardwood canopy. From there it's a simple ridgetop stroll, allowing time for reflection on a rewarding hike. Just look for a final left turn to reach the fire tower and the trailhead.

MILES AND DIRECTIONS

0.0 Start by leaving right from the paved road near the fire tower, northbound on the red-blazed Logan Trail. Do not take the Logan Trail leaving left that is signed for Pine Lake—that is the North Loop—and do not take the blue-blazed southbound Buckeye Trail. Pass old-growth red oaks.

0.4 The North Loop and South Loop diverge after crossing a grassy roadbed. Stay left with the South Loop and cruise westward atop a ridge.

1.1 Drop left from the ridge into Butcher Hollow. Switchback downhill on singletrack.

1.4 Reach the base of the hollow and continue downhill.

1.7 Cross the stream of Butcher Hollow twice in succession. The hollow widens.

1.9 Step over the stream again.

2.2 Turn left, easterly, away from Butcher Hollow, in an area of many white pines. Clark Hollow Road comes into view.

2.6 Cross Clark Hollow Road and a sycamore-bordered tributary of Piney Run. You will continue up the valley of this meandering stream.

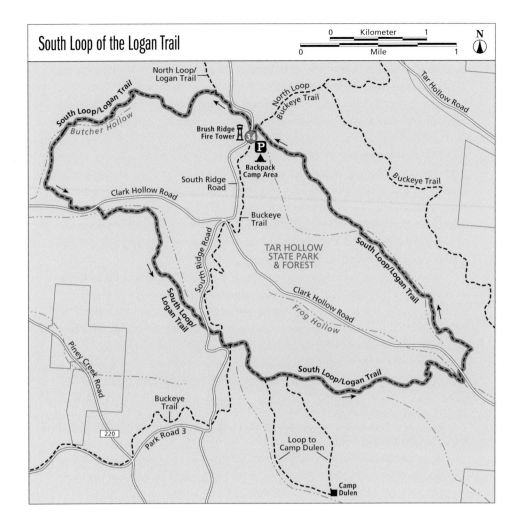

3.4 Stay left, joining a wide white-blazed bridle trail. Undulate along the ridge-line amid shortleaf pines.

3.8 Reach a clearing. Here the bridle trail keeps straight, while the South Loop leaves right as a singletrack path. Do not follow the doubletrack grassy road leading extreme right. Stay with the red blazes.

4.0 Cross South Ridge Road.

4.1 The Buckeye Trail comes in on your left. Here the South Loop and the Buckeye Trail run in conjunction.

4.2 Return to South Ridge Road. Stay left here, leaving South Ridge Road, and pass around a pole gate, continuing on a doubletrack path. The Buckeye Trail diverges right here.

4.6 Pass the first part of the loop trail down to Camp Dulen. Continue ridge-running east.

4.8 Pass the second intersection with the loop to Camp Dulen.

5.1 Open onto a power line. Stay left and don't go to the other side of the power line. You'll be running parallel to it for some distance.

5.7 The South Loop drops left off the ridgeline, switchbacking sharply on a very steep slope toward Clark Hollow.

6.3 Rock hop a streambed, then immediately cross to the north side of Clark Hollow Road after dropping 350 feet from the ridge above. This is the low point of the entire hike. Climb away, then turn into another valley, passing through an old homestead.

6.8 Reach an unnamed stream, then turn right heading up the valley. Look for evidence of old settlement in the flats.

7.6 Join a doubletrack trail and continue up the hollow, gently ascending. Foam-flower, phlox, wood betony, and other wildflowers can be seen in spring.

7.7 Rock hop the stream at the point where two tributaries converge. Ascend the nose of the ridge dividing these two tributaries. At points the trail gets so steep you'll consider using all fours—but you can easily make it on two legs.

8.1 The South Loop levels off. Undulate atop a ridge connecting to Brush Ridge.

8.7 Intersect the North Loop and the Buckeye Trail. Make sure to turn left here with the red blazes, heading southwest.

8.8 Reach the trailhead and fire tower, completing the South Loop.

> 🌱 **Green Tip:**
> *Recycle your old gear by giving it to someone or an organization that will reuse it.*

Great Seal State Park Loop

This longer trek explores Appalachian foothills rising from the iconic state park out-side Chillicothe. A great training hike, the circuit presents over 2,000 feet each of ascending and descending during its 8-mile length. Start near Lick Run, then climb Mount Ives, a solid pull. Curve around Bunker Hill, then head north for more hills and Rocky Knob. Wander through a rock garden on a spur before descending a deep hol-low and completing the loop.

Start: Lick Run trailhead

Distance: 8.2-mile loop

Hiking time: About 5 to 6.5 hours

Difficulty: Difficult due to hills and elevation change

Trail surface: Natural surface

Best season: Year-round

Other trail users: Equestrians and mountain bikers

Canine compatibility: Leashed dogs permitted

Land status: Ohio state park

Fees and permits: None

Schedule: Open daily year-round

Maps: Great Seal State Park; USGS Chillicothe East, Kingston

Trail contact: Great Seal State Park, 4908 Marietta Rd., Chilli-cothe, OH 45601; (740) 887-4818; www.dnr.state.oh.us

Finding the trailhead: From exit 52 on I-270, south of downtown Columbus, take US 23 south almost to Chillicothe and the exit for OH 207. Cross US 23 to the east side of the highway, then immediately turn right on Hospital Road and follow it 0.6 mile to Delano Road. Turn left on Delano Road and follow it 1.7 miles to Marietta Road. Turn right on Marietta Road and follow it 1.8 miles. Here the road splits (the road you are on becomes Hopetown Road and passes under US 23). Turn left at this split, still on Marietta Road, which you follow 0.7 mile farther to a four-way intersection with stop signs. Keep straight, joining Rocky Road (Marietta Road turns right here). Follow Rocky Road for 0.2 mile to Lick Run Road. Turn right on Lick Run Road and follow it 0.8 mile to the trailhead on your right. Trailhead GPS: N39 22.014' / W82 56.280'

THE HIKE

This park is well known for being the inspiration for the Ohio state seal. The hills upon which you walk are depicted on the signet. And what better Buckeye State scene? The forested sandstone heights set a hiker's heart to pounding on the drive in. Beauty is found not only in views from afar but also up close, in wildflower-loaded hollows and emergent stone outcrops poking through the steep tree-covered hillocks. The Lick Run area, where this hike takes place, is in the lesser-visited south end of the park and exudes bona fide ruggedness. The hills are abrupt; the trails have steep sections. The loop is a great training hike for those heading to the Great Smoky Mountains or the Alleghenies.

Unlike the northern end of Great Seal State Park around Sugarloaf Mountain, the trails on the south end are less of a maze. Lesser visitation means lesser user-created trails to confuse you. That said, it is always a good idea to pay attention to where you are at. The trails are decently signed, and some of the trail sections are posted with a letter corresponding to a letter on the map. So when you get to trail intersection "M," for example, simply check the map to confirm your position. You will share the trails with equestrians and mountain bikers, but none of the paths here in Lick Run are heavily used. The Lick Run trailhead offers shaded picnic tables.

Oaks grow in solid ranks on a hillside.

0   Kilometer   0.5

0   Mile   0.5

N

The hike first leads down the Lick Run drainage. Mount Ives rises steeply to your right, nearly 400 feet above! You will soon be making your way up there, joining Great Seal State Park's master path, the Shawnee Ridge Trail. Cruise a slender high ridge—the steep drop-off will now be below you. Oaks dominate here. Sassafras and hickories rise in dense flanks on the Bunker Hill Trail but are superseded on the west-facing slopes, where oaks grow in nearly pure stands. The forest changes as the Bunker Hill Trail bends around to the east side and back in the Lick Run drainage before crossing Lick Run Road.

The hike next wanders the margin between the steep hills above and the lesser-sloped lands below in the upper Dry Run drainage. Emergent rocks and ferns border drainages crossing the trail. This roller-coaster section typifies the last half of the hike, with hardly a level stretch. The circuit turns back south, passing a power-line-created view, and eventually takes the Rock Garden Loop atop Rocky Knob. Walk amid ferny outcrops and mossy boulders, intentionally going around or near as much stone as possible. The southbound direction resumes beyond the rock garden.

After exploring the high, the circuit takes you low, into a streamshed east of Rocky Knob. The hike dips into a valley filled with beech, cherry, and tulip trees, then winds in and out of tributary drainages. Cross back over to the south side of Lick Run Road, and a short backtrack leads to the trailhead.

MILES AND DIRECTIONS

0.0 Start at the Lick Run trailhead. From the parking area on the south side of Lick Run Road, with the road to your back, head left, southeasterly, on a connector trail to soon cross Lick Run. The stream can range from swift in spring to bone dry in fall. Cruise down Lick Run Hollow in deep hardwoods.

0.2 Meet the Mount Ives Trail (Trail #9) at intersection "M." Stay right here and soon turn south, angling up the slope of Mount Ives. Come near a fence line and the park boundary.

0.8 Reach trail intersection "N." Turn right, joining the Shawnee Ridge Trail, and climb very sharply for 0.1 mile.

1.3 Come to trail intersection "O" and the Mount Ives high point. Stay right with the Shawnee Ridge Trail, dropping off the shoulder of Mount Ives.

1.5 Reach a gap and intersection "P." Keep straight here, as the Lick Run Trail comes in on the far left and leaves right. Climb to quickly reach another intersection. Stay left, joining the Bunker Hill Trail. Hike along the mountain's mid-slope, completely circling the north side of the hill.

3.3 Return to the Shawnee Ridge Trail at intersection "Q." Turn left, dropping severely downhill nearly 200 feet in 0.2 mile.

3.5 Come to intersection "R." Stay right to cut your loop short; otherwise, turn left with the Shawnee Ridge Trail. Walk north along the lower slope of Bunker Hill.

3.8 Cross Lick Run Road in a gap, then come to intersection "J." Turn left on the Grouse Rock Trail; the Shawnee Ridge Trail keeps right. Arc into the Dry Run drainage.

4.6 A spur trail leaves left to Rocky Road. Stay right and curve south. Pass through a power-line clearing. A view opens to the west into the lowlands below.

5.0 Come to intersection "I" in a gap on Rocky Knob. Turn right, southbound, on the Shawnee Ridge Trail.

5.2 Turn right, joining the Rock Garden Loop. Walk west under hardwoods, weaving between rock outcrops.

5.7 Return to the Shawnee Ridge Trail, resuming a southbound track on a steep downgrade.

5.9 Reach trail intersection "K." Turn acutely left here, picking up the Rocky Knob Trail. Turn into a drainage east of Rocky Knob.

6.5 Turn south down an unnamed stream after making a couple of switchbacks.

7.1 A shortcut leaves right. Keep straight down the hollow.

7.3 Reach trail intersection "L." Turn right on the Mount Ives Trail. A user-created trail leaves left along an old roadbed past a pond 0.2 mile to Lick Run Road.

7.5 The other end of the shortcut at 7.1 miles comes in on your right.

7.8 Come to Lick Run Road. Walk left a few steps, then cross the road. Walk through bottoms and along a power-line clearing.

8.0 Come to your final intersection, intersection "M." You've been here before. Turn right and backtrack to the trailhead.

8.2 Reach the trailhead, completing the hike.

About Ohio's State Seal

The Ohio state seal was originally adopted in 1847. It features an agricultural field in the foreground, enhanced with a sheaf of wheat and a bundle of arrows. Behind the field flows the Scioto River, and behind the river farther still rise the hills lying within today's boundaries of Great Seal State Park. A rising sun lords over the scene. However, today's seal has changed from the original version. The seal adopted in 1847 also had a canal boat flowing down the Scioto River. The boat was removed in 1967, and the seal adopted its current form in 1996.

The seal is also numerically interesting. The rising sun has thirteen rays, symbolizing the original thirteen colonies that formed the Union. There are seventeen arrows in the bundle, noting Ohio as the seventeenth state in the United States. The arrows are said to also represent the aboriginal peoples who lived here before Ohio became a state.

Southwest Hikes

The entrance to Clifton Gorge is dramatic (hike 37).

The area southwest of Columbus is regarded as farm country, and it is—for the most part. But that doesn't mean the locale is devoid of quality hiking destinations, for it features the most unusual walk in central Ohio. This area includes downtown Columbus and southwestern Franklin County, western Pickaway County, and the famed Clifton Gorge in Greene County. Metro Parks has a strong presence here, as it does throughout greater Columbus. But let's start with Deer Creek State Park, down near Mount Sterling. The hike here uses hiker-only trails on a high peninsula overlooking Deer Creek Lake. Soak in watery vistas before making your way on an impossibly narrow land spine. Descend to the tip of a peninsula, where a gravel beach awaits, and gain more bluff views on your way back to the trailhead.

For two centuries visitors have been hiking Clifton Gorge, a place of superlatives. It is simultaneously a state nature preserve and a national natural landmark, and has a national scenic river flowing through its heart. The Little Miami River carved this rock and water wonderland. Behold rapids and pools echoing off vertical canyon walls. Hike below and above the gorge rim, and cruise the river past giant boulders in rich woods. Everywhere-you-look beauty is contained in the gorge. Climb out along the rim and explore its heights as well as take in views of the canyon below.

Two hikes take place at worthy Battelle Darby Metro Park. The first hike tours the banks of Big Darby Creek and sneaks under a historic railroad. Walk in lush forests exuding a backwoods atmosphere to the Ancient Trail, where you can view Fort Ancient Mound, a visible part of an aboriginal Ohioan village that once thrived there. Dyer Mill Loop makes a circuit in the lowermost reaches of Little Darby Creek. Walk up the valley, opening to a vista of the stream. The circuit next climbs to uplands, where alluring oak and walnut forests rise. It makes a fine family trek.

Scioto Audubon Metro Park has the most unusual hike in this entire guide. The setting is downtown Columbus along the banks of the Scioto River, with the high-rises of downtown forming a man-made backdrop. Hike astride the Scioto River and pick up a series of connector paths to reach the Central Activities Area, where you can climb a restored water tower for good views of a rock-climbing wall in the foreground and the Columbus skyline in the background. It is a fitting piece of the diverse mosaic of hiking trails in the region.

Trails like this lure the hiker to see what lies around the next bend.

Deer Creek State Park Vistas

This trek combines several interconnected hiker-only trails on a high peninsula over-looking Deer Creek Lake. Start on the Ridge Trail, passing a wildlife blind before open-ing onto a grassy hill above the lake and your first aquatic panoramas. The second loop, the appropriately named Lakeview Trail, presents better reservoir views. Then comes the Waterloo Trail, which takes you along a wooded flat and to more over-looks on the lake. The final trail, Adena Ridge, is the most scenic of them all. It leads along a slender hilltop jutting into the water. Vistas open as you descend to the shore and a point, where a gravel beach awaits. Your return trip from the beach travels along a bluff with still more views.

Start: Near Deer Creek State Park Lodge parking area

Distance: 3.0-mile triple loop, plus brief road mileage

Hiking time: About 2 to 2.5 hours

Difficulty: Moderate

Trail surface: Natural surface

Best season: Year-round

Other trail users: None

Canine compatibility: Leashed dogs permitted

Land status: Ohio state park

Fees and permits: None

Schedule: Open daily year-round

Maps: Deer Creek State Park; USGS Clarksburg, Five Points

Trail contact: Deer Creek State Park, 20635 Waterloo Rd., Mount Sterling, OH 43143; (740) 869-3124; www.dnr.state.ohio.us

Finding the trailhead: From exit 84 on I-71, southwest of downtown Columbus, take OH 56 for 3.5 miles to Mount Sterling and OH 207. Turn right onto OH 207 south and follow it for 4 miles, then turn left on Yankeetown Road and follow it for 2 miles to the Deer Creek State Park entrance on your right. Turn right and follow the signs to the lodge. Park in the lodge parking area. Just before you reach the lodge parking area, a road leads right to the park cottages. The Ridge Trail starts near the intersection of the road to the lodge and the cottage road. Trailhead GPS: N39 37.354' / W83 14.326'

THE HIKE

The heart of Deer Creek State Park is located on a large peninsula where Deer Creek once made a sharp bend. The lakeshore mimics this big bend in the creek, creating the peninsula. The park lodge overlooks the lake here and is where you start your hike. The series of shorter nature trails you walk are all situated along the peninsula and together can provide ample hiking mileage to reward your visit.

The Ridge Trail is the first of four paths you will be walking and is the longest. It travels through young ridgetop flatwoods before it makes a spur to a wildlife blind. In a small clearing you will see bird and animal feeders and sand pits for picking up animal tracks. Most people don't have the patience to wait in a blind, but your chances are best if you do so early in the morning or late in the evening. Leave the flatwoods and curve onto the peninsula slope. The pathway is much harder here, as you drop off a slope. Lake views begin to open through the trees; the water is well below. You can see the park marina and boat launch across the lake, as well as a picnic area. More views open ahead in cedars and grasses.

To complete the Ridge Trail, you will come so close to your vehicle that you can grab something you forgot before turning back in the woods and picking up

This sandy shoreline beckons bare feet on a warm day.

the Lakeview Trail. Once again enter flatwoods. This trail is much like the Ridge Trail except this one offers better and more continuous views of the impoundment below, especially when you cruise through open grassy areas. User-created trails connect the Lakeview Trail to the Ridge Trail. The Lakeview Trail presents multiple views, then returns back to the cottage access road. Here you can either turn right and walk the cottage access road to the Waterloo trailhead or drive the short distance.

The Waterloo trailhead is but 0.3 mile distant on the right, near the second "Extra Vehicle and Visitor Parking" lot. This road mileage is not counted into the overall trail mileage given. The Waterloo Trail is but 0.3 mile long and curves along the ridgeline opening west, soon ending at the cottages near the road's end. The hike finally joins the Adena Ridge Trail as it makes the most scenic track of all, continuing down the slender peninsula, presenting nearly constant views. It eventually reaches the very tip of the peninsula at the water's edge and a gravel beach. This is a picturesque spot, where you can swim, fish, or picnic. It seems the trail dead-ends, but you can actually make a loop. The return route climbs along a bluff line overlooking the east side of the lake, the only place where a vista in this direction opens. After emerging back at the cabins, you can simply follow the cabin access road all the way back to the lodge or hike the Waterloo Trail back partway.

MILES AND DIRECTIONS

0.0 Start your hike on the Ridge Trail. Look for the sign leaving the lodge parking lot. Cross the cottage access road and begin following a mown strip into young trees before entering full-blown forest.

0.1 The Ridge Trail splits to form a loop. Stay right and begin the loop.

0.4 Turn right, heading toward the wildlife blind and the small clearing it abuts. From here, backtrack to the main loop and continue to the right toward the lake.

0.7 Cross a normally dry drainage flowing off the peninsula. Sporadic vistas open from the slope.

0.9 Come close to the water, then climb the slope back to flatwoods.

1.2 Reach the cabin access road after completing the loop portion of the Ridge Trail. Now, look in the woods for the Lakeview Trail. It heads west to the ridge slope and then turns along the slope, passing through clearings with panoramas of the lake. User-created trails head out to other overlooks.

1.7 Complete the Lakeview Trail circuit. You can turn right and walk along the cabin access road or drive 0.3 mile to the Waterloo trailhead.

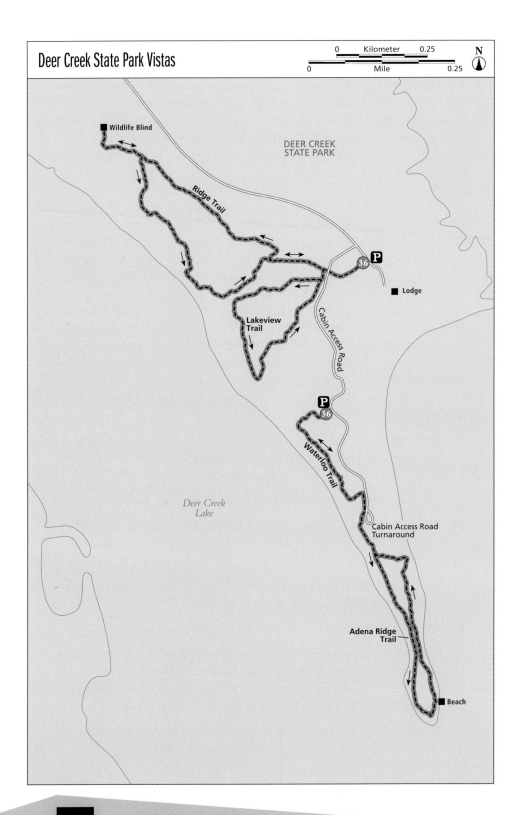

Deer Creek State Park Vistas

0   Kilometer   0.25

0   Mile   0.25

N

■ Wildlife Blind

DEER CREEK
STATE PARK

Ridge Trail

P
36

■ Lodge

Lakeview
Trail

Cabin Access Road

P
36

Waterloo Trail

Deer Creek
Lake

Cabin Access Road
Turnaround

Adena Ridge
Trail

■ Beach

Begin the Waterloo Trail. It quickly hits the peninsula slope, then turns south along the peninsula. It, too, has user-created spur trails dropping right toward the lake. Open onto the lower end of the cabin access road at another parking area. Turn right and head to the end of the cabin access road.

2.0 Join the Adena Ridge Trail as it leaves from the lower cabin access road turn-around, near cabin #21. Follow a well-worn path out the ever-narrowing ridge.

2.1 The Adena Ridge Trail splits. Stay straight, continuing down a high sliver of land.

2.4 Reach the edge of Deer Creek Lake and a gravel beach. This is a good place to stop. It seems the Adena Ridge Trail has come to an end, but the path actually continues along the east shore and then climbs along a bluff.

2.7 Complete the loop portion of the Adena Ridge Trail and backtrack a short distance to the cottage access road. *Option:* From here you can take either the Waterloo Trail or the cottage access road back to the beginning of the Waterloo Trail.

3.0 Arrive at the start of the Waterloo Trail. Follow the road back to the lodge parking area.

Green Tip:
Engage your local scout, church, or school organization to volunteer to clean and maintain trails. This can foster a lifetime of good land stewardship.

Ohio Squirrels

We all want to see wildlife while hiking in Ohio. It enhances the experience and establishes a connection between us and nature. So what do we end up seeing? As far as bigger mammals, that would undoubtedly be white-tailed deer. Overhead, we are often serenaded by birdsong, spotting birds in the trees and the skies above. Up there in the trees—and sometimes on the ground—we'll see what numerically stacks up as the number one animal spotted by hikers: the squirrel.

Often maligned, squirrels range throughout Ohio. And, yes, they are related to rats and are often, in fact, called "tree rats." Frankly, their road-crossing skills are indecisive at best.

Four species of squirrels call Ohio home. Flying squirrels are the rarest. They are quite small and really don't fly, but do glide using skin membranes that stretch along their outer legs. Red squirrels can be spotted in our cities and more remote areas. The red band of fur across its back gives this seed-gathering, pine-nut-and-fungi-eating squirrel its name.

The eastern fox squirrel is the biggest of them all, averaging from 1 to 3 pounds. Their size gives them away. They prefer hickory and oak nuts, but will also eat corn. This means that they seek a mix of forest and field for habitat. The scampering creatures emigrated from the Plains states after Ohio's once nearly endless forests were partially cleared for agricultural and urban use.

Eastern gray squirrels are the most widespread and commonly seen squirrel in Ohio and beyond. It's the one you will see raiding your bird feeder, tightroping along a limb, or running back and forth on the road, deciding which way to go. They dine on nuts, fruits, and even insects, and prefer hardwood forests. Gray squirrels were once so numerous in Ohio that they destroyed crops. Citizens were required to turn in skins of gray squirrels along with their tax payments in an attempt to reduce their numbers.

On your next hike or simply while relaxing in your backyard, take a second look at the squirrels. They comprise an interesting component in Ohio's web of life.

Clifton Gorge

Visitors have been hiking Clifton Gorge for two centuries. No wonder, as the Little Miami River flows in rapids and pools below sheer canyon walls. Footpaths travel both below and above the gorge rim. Your trek will take you along the river, past giant boulders in rich woods. Bridge the Little Miami River, a national scenic river, and continue downstream in an amazing environment that is deservedly designated a National Natural Landmark. Cross back over the Little Miami near John Bryan State Park, eventually gaining the rim of the gorge, which offers a different perspective on your return trip. Try to visit during off times, as the state nature preserve can be crowded on fair-weather weekends.

Start: OH 343 Trailhead just west of Clifton
Distance: 4.4-mile loop
Hiking time: About 3 to 3.5 hours
Difficulty: Moderate
Trail surface: Natural surface
Best season: Year-round; notable spring wildflowers and fall colors
Other trail users: None
Canine compatibility: Dogs not permitted in nature preserve

Land status: State nature preserve and park
Fees and permits: None
Schedule: Open daily year-round
Maps: Clifton Gorge State Nature Preserve; USGS Clifton
Trail contact: Ohio Department of Natural Resources, 2045 Morse Rd., Building C-3, Columbus, OH 43229-6693; (614) 265-6453; www.dnr.state.oh.us

Finding the trailhead: From exit 54 on I-70, near Springfield, west of downtown Columbus, take OH 72 south for 6.6 miles to Clifton and OH 343. Turn right on OH 343 and follow it west 0.6 mile to the trailhead on your left. Trailhead GPS: N39 48.003'/W83 50.191'

THE HIKE

This is one of my favorite places to hike in the entire state of Ohio, much less the greater Columbus area. Cut by fast-melting glaciers, the gorge appears seemingly out of nowhere in the nearby bucolic agricultural lands. Protected as a state nature preserve since 1970, Clifton Gorge gives hikers the opportunity to enjoy geology, water, and the life that lies along this stretch of the Little Miami River. I strongly urge you to come here throughout the year, as the gorge will present a different face each season. The verdant woodlands deliver a cornucopia of color in fall, and the moist bottoms contained within the gorge are a wildflower paradise in spring. Rock formations stand out in winter, and the river lures hikers in summer.

Hikers are visible below from the gorge lip.

Starting from the parking area, you still have no idea there's a gorge here, but your hike soon leads down stairs into the rock-bordered vale through which the little Miami River noisily flows. Once in the gorge, sheer walls to your right and the river to your left constrict passage. Furthermore, wooden trailside fences protect sensitive areas and keep hikers on the trail. Even though you expect to see them, the cliffs will impress. Dark boulders and huge rocks that have fallen from the gorge rim are scattered in the trailside woods. Tall sycamores overhang the shoals of the waterway, and moss grows on anything that isn't moving. You will soon pass Steamboat Rock, a notable boulder that makes it easy to imagine the name's inspiration.

The bluffs range upwards of 100 feet above you, and occasional drainages flowing off the rim cut across the path. Other features lay ahead, such as Slump Block Cave and the Blue Hole, a large pool below a narrow whitewater rapid known as Amphitheater Falls. Note piled brush left over from flood events. You will soon move over to the south side of the gorge, crossing the river on a bridge. Continue down the irregular forest floor aided by steps and wooden walkways. The ever-changing waterway is never out of earshot. Spring branches trickle over the trail. Massive ancient boulders continue to impress, as do occasional big trees. A couple of tributary waterfalls add to the scenery.

Your return trip begins with a footbridge crossing to the north bank. The bulk of recreational facilities at John Bryan State Park is downstream and down trail. This trek turns upstream, back into the preserve, and enjoys more continual trailside beauty. The woods are big here. The trail on this side of the gorge is more level and graded, since it follows the old Pittsburgh-Cincinnati Stagecoach Trail, a historic track that affirms the passing of many visitors through this gorge over the course of two centuries. While hiking this part of the valley, watch for evergreen hemlock stands, rare in these parts. Watch also for the large trail-side boulders that have tumbled off the gorge rim above you.

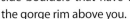

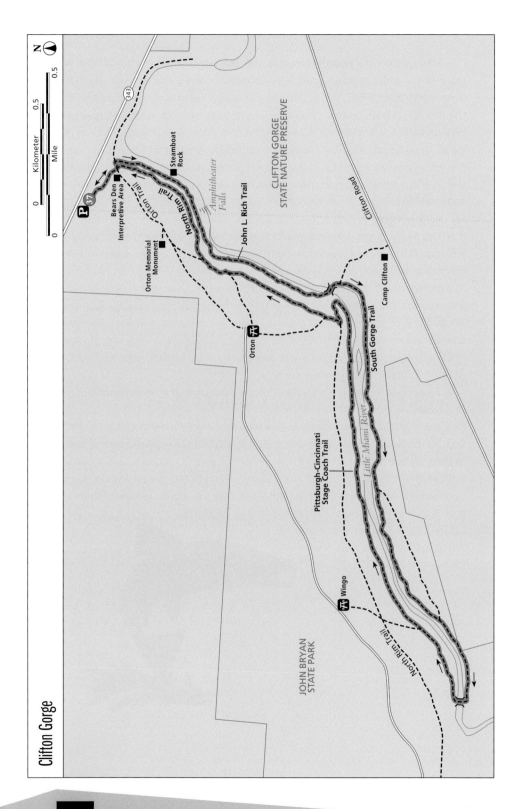

Clifton Gorge

N

Kilometer
0   0.5
Mile
0   0.5

343

P 37
Bears Den
Interpretive Area

Steamboat
Rock

Orton Trail

North Rim Trail

Amphitheater
Falls

John L. Rich Trail

CLIFTON GORGE
STATE NATURE PRESERVE

Orton Memorial
Monument

Orton

Clifton Road

Camp Clifton

South Gorge Trail

Little Miami River

Pittsburgh-Cincinnati
Stage Coach Trail

Wingo

North Rim Trail

JOHN BRYAN
STATE PARK

Soon you will be atop the gorge rim. A rocky trail bed leads through a break in the rim and you are on the cliffs. This conveys a different perspective and adds to your appreciation of the preserve. There are a few spots where you can carefully look over the rim, not only seeing the river but also seeing the hiking trail you were on earlier. After returning to the Bears Den Interpretive Area, you may want to follow the wheelchair-accessible asphalt path upstream to the Narrows, the aptly named tight section of gorge that also has a cataract worth viewing. However, the trail here is pinched in by OH 343. At the far end of the Narrows stands a plaque commemorating Clifton Gorge as a national natural landmark.

Rock climbing is not permitted within the state nature preserve. However, there are designated rock-climbing and rappelling sites at John Bryan State Park. The state park also has camping, picnicking, and more hiking trails to enjoy, and it features a nearly 10-mile multiuse trail that is popular with mountain bikers. The nearby town of Yellow Springs is home to Antioch College and a thriving urban hipster downtown where you can grab a bite or some coffee and do a little people watching.

MILES AND DIRECTIONS

0.0 Starting at the southeast corner of the parking area, take the asphalt path through flatwoods of maple, pine, and cedar.

0.1 Reach the Bears Den Interpretive Area and a trail intersection. The Narrows Trail, a paved path, leads left, and the North Rim Trail and Orton Trail leave right. Take a few steps left toward the Bears Den, then take the stairs into the gorge on the North Gorge Trail. Soon reach the gorge bottom and proceed downstream in magnificent scenery.

0.3 Reach Steamboat Rock. This massive fallen boulder recalls a steamboat flowing down the Little Miami River. Continue on rocky, uneven trail.

0.4 A spur trail leads right to Slump Block Cave, then up to the rim. A major rapid, Amphitheater Falls, flows below the rockfall shelter.

0.9 Reach a trail intersection. Here the Pittsburgh-Cincinnati Stagecoach Trail continues downstream. A connector trail heads right up to the North Rim. Our loop leads left to cross the footbridge on the South Gorge Trail. Enjoy the river views from atop the footbridge, then continue downstream along the south bank of the Little Miami River. Pass a spur trail to 4H Camp Clifton.

1.5 The trail splits. Stay right on the narrower footpath along the river. The other route is easier and wider. Watch for islands in the Little Miami and also for stream braids that flow only during high-water events.

1.9 Rejoin the main path. A feeder stream comes in just past the intersection, creating a small waterfall. Ahead, another branch drops off an overhang just above the river, forming a waterfall.

2.0 Turn right, crossing the Little Miami River on a long footbridge. Once across the river, turn right up the river on the Pittsburgh-Cincinnati Stagecoach Trail.

2.4 A spur trail leads left up to the Wingo Picnic Area. Continue straight up the gorge.

3.4 Return to the junction where you were earlier, when you crossed over to the south side of the gorge via the bridge. This time turn left and climb away from the Little Miami River, switchbacking uphill toward the North Rim Trail. You have now returned to the state nature preserve.

3.5 Reach the North Rim Trail. Turn right, heading north in a drier forest of oak, redbud, and hickory. Just ahead, a spur trail leads left to the Orton Picnic Area. Soak in the river views below. Be watchful as you enter a mini-maze of official and user-created trails connecting the Orton Memorial and the nearby picnic area. Just stay along the rim of the gorge and you will be fine.

3.9 A spur trail leads right down into the gorge. Stay along the rim.

4.3 Return to the Bears Den Interpretive Area. This is your chance to visit the Narrows. If you want to add this short trek, keep straight on the asphalt path along the rim. Otherwise, turn left and backtrack toward the OH 343 parking area.

4.4 Emerge at the OH 343 parking area, completing the hike.

Battelle Darby Double Loop

This hike explores Metro Parks' largest park, Battelle Darby. First, saddle along the banks of Big Darby Creek, then pass under a historic railroad to begin a loop on the Terrace Trail. Walk in lush forests exuding a backwoods atmosphere. Just before returning to Big Darby Creek, you will join the Ancient Trail. This second loop cruises bottomlands along the stream, then climbs to a field where you can see the Fort Ancient Mound, a visible part of an aboriginal Ohioan village that once thrived there. Return back through the valley of Big Darby Creek.

Start: Alkire Road trailhead

Distance: 4.2-mile double loop

Hiking time: About 2.5 to 3 hours

Difficulty: Moderate

Trail surface: Gravel and natural surface

Best season: Year-round

Other trail users: Joggers

Canine compatibility: No pets allowed

Land status: Metro Parks

Fees and permits: None

Schedule: Open daily year-round, 6:30 a.m. to dark

Maps: Battelle Darby Creek Metro Park; USGS Galloway

Trail contact: Metro Parks, 1069 W. Main St., Westerville, OH 43081; (614) 891-0700; www .metroparks.net

Finding the trailhead: From exit 7 on I-270, west of downtown Columbus, take US 40 / Broad Street west for 5.1 miles to Darby Creek Drive. Turn left on Darby Creek Drive and follow it 3.7 miles to Alkire Road (passing the Cedar Ridge entrance to Battelle Darby Park). Turn right on Alkire Road and follow it 0.6 mile to the trailhead on your left, just before the bridge on Big Darby Creek. Trailhead GPS: N39 53.599' / W83 12.995'

Battelle Darby Creek Park is strung out over a 20-mile segment of Big Darby Creek in disjunct parcels. Most park segments don't have trails but simply protect the banks and tributaries of Big Darby Creek. However, the section of park along Alkire Road has a quality trail network, and it is in this network that you make a double loop.

The hike starts at a combination canoe access and hiking trailhead. You will take the Indian Ridge Trail, which connects parcels of Battelle Darby Park lying north and south of Alkire Road. This is also an important aquatic intersection. Here Little Darby Creek and Big Darby Creek merge their waters, increasing the aggre-

Ohio's flatwoods community can be colorful in fall.

gate flow and making Big Darby Creek more paddleable from this point down-stream. An Ohio state historical marker details the stream's importance not only to aboriginal transportation and cultivation, but also for biodiversity above and below the water.

You will head south on the Indian Ridge Trail, passing under the Camp Chase Railroad Bridge. Note how its pilings were added onto and the bridge raised. At one time the railroad dipped to the span over Big Darby Creek but then had to climb out. This ascent from the creek bridge proved taxing to the locomotive steam engines, so the bridge was raised to keep the rail line elevated, making pas-sage easier. The railroad was originally constructed in the 1850s but had to stay west of Big Darby Creek until 1870, when the river bridge was complete, thus con-necting to Columbus. Of course, this isn't the original bridge from 140-plus years back. Imagine a wooden structure with numerous trestles, probably looking fragile by today's standards. At one time the railroad was quite busy. The line provided transportation between Cincinnati and New York City for decades, connecting numerous cities in between. For natives of the Buckeye State, the railroad linked Cincinnati, Columbus, and Cleveland before moving on to New York.

After joining the Terrace Trail, you will pass the Indian Ridge Picnic Area. Beyond that the hike crosses the threshold of deep woods. Here sugar maples, shagbark hickories, northern red oaks, red maples, and other majestic hardwoods form a conclave of wild woodland that takes you away from the hustle and bustle of roads and buildings.

The east end of the Terrace Trail travels through flatwoods. A keen eye will spot drainages dug to help dry out the level terrain, likely when this was cultivated land generations ago. You will eventually drop back into the Big Darby Creek flood-plain before picking up the Ancient Trail, which wanders through lowlands on an elevated track under river birches. These wetlands are periodically inundated dur-ing high-water events, when Big Darby Creek runs high and brown. Notice braided high-water stream channels and perhaps wood debris piled on the upstream side of trees.

The Ancient Trail climbs back from the bottomland, then begins its loop, cir-cling around an aboriginal Ohioan village. The first part skirts the edge of a walnut-studded bluff, with Big Darby Creek flowing below. Then you reach the Fort Ancient Mound. Like many other archaeological burial sites, it is now but a low hill covered in grass. However, this is the centerpiece of what is known as the Voss Site. Imagine an entire Indian village covering the adjacent field 1,000 years back in time. Luckily, this is one more protected site where Ohio's pre-Columbian past can be preserved.

The grassy trail continues south, mixing in meadow and woodland before turning back north. You will stay on the edge of forest. Take note of the nonna-tive planted red pines beside the trail, and view the Fort Ancient Mound from afar. Before long you are backtracking to the trailhead and the hike is complete.

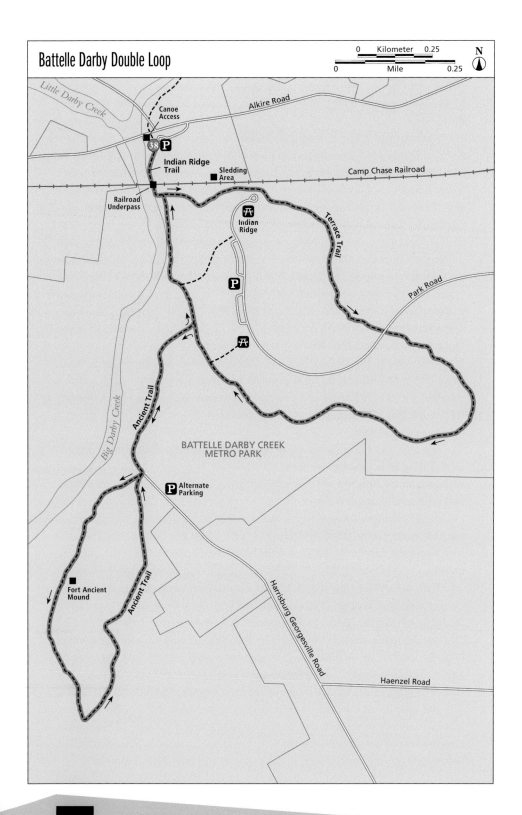

Kilometer 0.25

Mile 0.25

N

Canoe Access

Alkire Road

38 P

Camp Chase Railroad

Indian Ridge Trail

Sledding Area

Railroad Underpass

Indian Ridge

Terrace Trail

P

Park Road

Ancient Trail

BATTELLE DARBY CREEK METRO PARK

Little Darby Creek

Big Darby Creek

P Alternate Parking

Fort Ancient Mound

Ancient Trail

Harrisburg Georgesville Road

Haenzel Road

MILES AND DIRECTIONS

0.0 Start at the Alkire Road trailhead. Walk toward the end of the auto turn-around and pick up the Indian Ridge Trail, heading left toward the Indian Ridge Picnic Area. Make sure to look upstream at the confluence of Little Darby Creek and Big Darby Creek.

0.2 Come to the Terrace Trail after passing under the Camp Chase Railroad Bridge. Stay left here, as the Terrace Trail runs roughly parallel to the railroad. Three spur trails lead right, connecting to the Indian Ridge Picnic Area.

0.8 Dip to hop a streamlet just before crossing the access road to the Indian Ridge Picnic Area. Reenter deep woods.

1.4 Stay right at an old farm gate that leads to a field. The trail stays along the margin of field and woods for a short period.

1.6 Drop into the Big Darby Creek floodplain, cutting through a ravine originally created by glacial melt.

1.8 A spur trail leads right to a picnic shelter. Keep straight in bottomland of cottonwood, sycamore, and ash.

1.9 Come to a three-way trail junction. The Terrace Trail continues straight, back toward the trailhead. You will take this later. For now, pick up the Ancient Trail as it leaves left in bottomland and heads downstream along Big Darby Creek.

2.1 Bridge a stream by culvert, then climb away from the floodplain.

2.2 Come to the loop portion of the Ancient Trail. Harrisburg Georgesville Road comes in on your left, and there is alternate trailhead parking here. Stay right with the Ancient Trail, continuing in a strip of woods. Ignore any chain gates leading away from the main loop.

2.5 Come to the Fort Ancient Mound.

2.8 The Ancient Trail turns back north near a chain gate. Wander through a mix of woods and field.

3.4 Complete the loop portion of the Ancient Trail. Continue north, backtracking upstream in the Big Darby Creek floodplain.

3.7 At the trail junction, turn left, picking up a new portion of the Terrace Trail. Hike through more Big Darby Creek bottomland.

3.8 Pass a shortcut leading right to the Indian Ridge Picnic Area.

4.0 Complete the Terrace Trail. The Chase Railroad Bridge is just ahead, above you. Backtrack on the Indian Ridge Trail to the Alkire Road trailhead.

4.2 Reach the Alkire Road trailhead, finishing the hike.

The Voss Site

During this hike you will pass the site of an ancient Indian village occupied from AD 1100 to 1440. The only obvious sign of the people of the Fort Ancient Culture is an elevated burial mound. (By the way, the greater Fort Ancient Culture is named for the impressive mounds and earthworks on the Little Miami River near Cincinnati.) This is one of the most northerly sites of the Fort Ancient Culture. The peoples who lived here grew corn, squash, and beans on the very field you see today. The location of the village is no accident. The villagers supplemented their agriculture with foods from Big Darby Creek—fish, mussels, turtles, and waterfowl attracted to the stream. They also hunted for land creatures such as turkey and deer.

The Ohio Historical Society has excavated part of the Fort Ancient Mound as well as adjacent areas. However, modern technology has enabled archaeologists to re-create the village layout using remote sensing to distinguish land uses. Magnetic anomalies in soil composition enable archaeologists to differentiate between a burial pit and a refuse pit, between a homesite and a garden, between the central plaza and a field. These anomalies help establish a pattern to the village remains and determine the arrangement of the village. While hiking here, imagine this locale alive with the people of the Fort Ancient Culture.

Dyer Mill Loop

Located within Battelle Darby Metro Park, this hike makes a circuit in the lowermost reaches of Little Darby Creek. The loop leaves an attractive picnic area and heads up along Little Darby. It then splits and keeps up the valley, opening to a vista of the stream. The circuit next climbs to uplands, where alluring oak and walnut forests rise. Pass through a meadow before returning to the trailhead. Overall, the hike isn't hard, despite a few hills. It makes a fine family trek, especially combined with a trailhead dining experience.

Start: Little Darby Picnic Area off Gardner Road
Distance: 2.5-mile loop
Hiking time: About 1.5 to 2 hours
Difficulty: Moderate
Trail surface: Natural surface
Best season: Fall for leaf color
Other trail users: Joggers and cross-country skiers
Canine compatibility: No pets allowed
Land status: Metro Parks

Fees and permits: None
Schedule: Open daily year-round, 6:30 a.m. to dark; closed to hikers when cross-country ski conditions are favorable
Maps: Battelle Darby Metro Park; USGS Galloway
Trail contact: Metro Parks, 1069 W. Main St., Westerville, OH 43081; (614) 891-0700; www .metroparks.net

Finding the trailhead: From exit 7 on I-270, west of downtown Columbus, take US 40/Broad Street, west for 5.1 miles to Darby Creek Drive. Turn left on Darby Creek Drive and follow it 3.7 miles to Alkire Road (passing the Cedar Ridge entrance to Battelle Darby Park). Turn right on Alkire Road and follow it 0.6 mile, then turn left on Gardner Road, just before the bridge over Big Darby Creek. Follow Gardner Road for 0.2 mile, then turn left into the Little Darby Picnic Area. Trailhead GPS: N39 53.711'/W83 13.235'

THE HIKE

S amuel Dyer erected his mill on Little Darby Creek in 1805, at the confluence where Little Darby Creek flows into Big Darby Creek, now the site of Battelle Darby Metro Park. Settlements sprung up around Dyer's corn- and wheat-grinding operation, which later became the community of Georgesville. The mill went through a succession of owners, including a fellow named Gardner, who gave his name to the road you now drive to reach the trailhead. The mill remains are long gone—such is the fate of wooden structures built on flood-prone streams.

Georgesville was originally established along the east bank of Big Darby Creek, but when what is now the Camp Chase Railroad passed through, the rail line established a railroad station on the west bank of Big Darby Creek. The town of Georgesville followed suit. Aboriginal Ohioans recognized this area as a good place to live, too, having settled at the junction of Big Darby Creek and Little Darby Creek 1,000 years earlier. Although Dyers Mill never did turn into a city like Columbus, Samuel Dyer does have a trail named for him 200 years later, and that is a pretty good outcome if you ask me.

The trailhead has picnic tables, a covered picnic shelter, and restrooms. A small nearby pond makes for an ice-skating locale during the cold season. The Dyer Mill

You can almost smell the crisp fall air while looking at this photo.

Trail is also designated for cross-country skiing, so be aware that the trail is closed to hiking when cross-country skiing conditions are favorable. The main loop is bisected with a couple of shorter trails that allow you to shorten or lengthen the hike.

After passing through a wildflower-covered meadow, the trail climbs a hill and comes to the loop portion of the hike. Drop to the banks of Little Darby Creek in a riparian zone. A short spur leads to a picnic table overlooking the attractive and clear stream, a designated state and national scenic river. The hike then cruises an extensive section of bottomland, where ash, sycamore, walnut, and other hardwoods shade the forest floor. Enjoy your lowland walk before turning away from the creek. The forest changes to typical central Ohio upland woods: northern red oak, maple, cherry, white oak, and sugar maple. Traverse the edge of the stream valley before turning away from the watershed altogether.

Next, you get to enjoy a rolling prairie environment. A shortcut trail leads through the prairie, but the main loop keeps north, nearing Gardner Road, before turning right and exploring some interesting forestland of widespread oaks atop an often-grassy understory. The Dyer Mill Trail turns south and closes the circuit, and it is but a simple backtrack to reach the trailhead. If you find this hike too short, the Darby Creek Greenway extends north from the Cedar Ridge entrance of the park, heading 4.7 miles one way almost to US 40/Broad Street. A network of shorter trails emanates from the Cedar Ridge Picnic Area. Pet lovers can take their dog on the 1.6-mile Wagtail Trail. The Turkey Foot Trail is yet another loop trail that makes its own circuit. Still another hike—included in this guide—loops through the part of Battelle Darby Park south of Alkire Road.

MILES AND DIRECTIONS

0.0   Start at the Little Darby Picnic Area. With your back to the parking area, facing Little Darby Creek, look right for the signed trailhead and grassy path. Bisect a small restored prairie, then enter woods.

0.3   Reach the loop portion of the hike after climbing a hill. Stay left, heading clockwise with the loop. The trail dives off the hill, then crosses a streamlet and reaches Little Darby Creek in bottomland.

0.4   Reach a trail intersection. A yellow-blazed shortcut trail leaves right, and a short spur leads left to a picnic table beside Little Darby Creek. Stay straight on the main Dyer Mill Trail.

0.8   Climb away from the creek into upland hardwoods and eventually pass into younger trees.

1.3   Reach a trail intersection beside an open prairie. Here a shortcut trail leads right back toward the trailhead. Continue on the main trail in rolling terrain. Land swales allow far looks across the prairie.

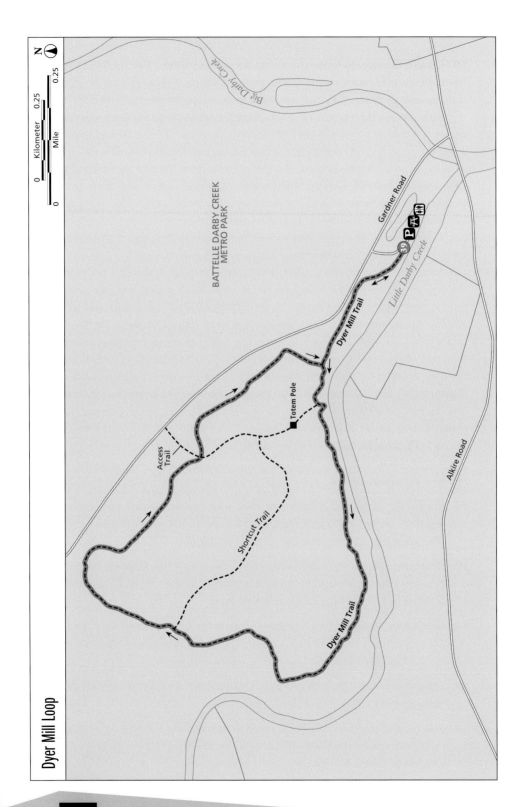

Dyer Mill Loop

N

Kilometer
0   0.25

Mile
0   0.25

Big Darby Creek

BATTELLE DARBY CREEK
METRO PARK

Gardner Road

Little Darby Creek

39

Dyer Mill Trail

Access Trail

Totem Pole

Shortcut Trail

Dyer Mill Trail

Alkire Road

1.9 Come to a four-way trail intersection. A spur leads left to Gardner Road, and the yellow-blazed shortcut trail leads right. Keep straight, still on the Dyer Mill Trail. Enter walnut-oak forest, then cross a wooden bridge over a streambed. The trail then turns right, away from Gardner Road, and descends.

2.2 Complete the loop portion of the Dyer Mill Trail. Turn left and backtrack to the trailhead.

2.5 Arrive back at the Little Darby Picnic Area, finishing the hike.

Of Mast

The word *mast* has many meanings. Most often a nautical notion, the word is associated with sailboats (the mast is what holds a sail up to the wind). The word also means the aggregate food that grows on trees; for example, acorns and nuts eaten by wildlife, from birds to squirrels to deer.

Several mast-bearing trees can be found along this hike. Look for white oaks in the woods beside the path. Interestingly, oaks are technically part of the beech family. Wildlife may love white oaks more than man does. Woodpeckers and turkeys are among the birds that partake of the nuts. Raccoons and chipmunks enjoy the nutrient-packed treat, too. Deer eat the nuts and browse on tender white oak twigs.

Scattered among the oaks is the black walnut. Ohio lies in the northeastern segment of the tree's range. Walnuts can be identified by their finely toothed compound leaves. This hardwood is coveted so much for furniture that individual trees are sometimes cut and stolen. Walnuts have provided edible fare for Ohioans a thousand years distant up to today. Historically, a black dye was made from their husks. Open up a walnut and you will be sure to get your hands and clothes black from the inner husk that surrounds the actual nut; in fact, it is a rite of passage for children to ruin clothes from opening black walnuts. Squirrels and other wildlife avidly consume the nuts.

Here at Battelle Darby Creek Park, walnuts and white oak acorns are but two examples of mast, which feed the wildlife that call this river valley home.

Scioto Audubon Metro Park Walk

This is the most unusual hike in the entire guide. The setting is downtown Columbus along the banks of the Scioto River. Start your adventure at the Grange Insurance Audubon Center to join the Scioto Greenway Trail. Follow it southeasterly astride the Scioto River, enjoying distant vantages while often shaded by a tunnel of trees. Pick up a spur trail to an observation platform where you can look upriver and downriver. Backtrack toward the Audubon Center, then take the Scioto Greenway Trail northbound, still skirting the river. Pick up a series of connector paths to reach the Central Activities Area, where you can climb a water tower for good views of a rock-climbing wall in the foreground and the Columbus skyline in the background. From here it is but a short trek over a boardwalk and other connector paths back to the Audubon Center.

Start: Grange Insurance Audubon Center

Distance: 2.1-mile loop

Hiking time: About 1.5 to 2.5 hours

Difficulty: Easy

Trail surface: Mostly asphalt

Best seasons: Fall and winter for best views

Other trail users: Bicyclists, joggers, anglers, and school groups

Canine compatibility: Leashed dogs permitted

Land status: Metro Parks

Fees and permits: None

Schedule: Open daily year-round

Maps: Scioto Audubon Metro Park; USGS Lancaster

Trail contact: Scioto Audubon Metro Park, 395 W. Whittier St., Columbus, OH 43215; (641) 891-0700; www.metroparks.net

Finding the trailhead: From exit 105 on I-71 in downtown Columbus, take Greenlawn Avenue east for 0.7 mile to S. Front Street. Turn left on S. Front Street and follow it 0.3 mile to W. Whittier Street. Turn left on W. Whittier Street and follow it to its dead end at the Grange Insurance Audubon Center. Trailhead GPS: N39 56.758' / W83 0.554'

THE HIKE

The transformation from no man's land to parkland has brought added hope—and people—to the banks of the river Scioto in downtown Columbus. As you drive into the park, the Grange Insurance Audubon Center catches your eye, as does the lacework of paths wandering through the park. Then you see the large water tower with its viewing platforms, and of course the climbing wall stands out. From one end of the park to another—and beyond—the Scioto Greenway Trail runs along the river and is your main hiking venue here. By the way, if the mileage isn't enough for you, simply take the Scioto Greenway Trail until your legs wear out.

Take a look around the Audubon Center before starting your walk. It is an incredible park facility, and gives a whole new meaning to the term *nature center*. After you have explored the building, it's time to explore the park. A short connector path leads to an observation deck and the Scioto Greenway Trail. As you cruise along a slough of the Scioto River, city sounds and that of bordering interstates drift into your ears. A canopy of trees—ash, hackberry, and willow—shade the asphalt path. Walking this greenway gives you a taste of all the other greenway possibilities in greater Columbus: This one goes for over 9 miles, the Alum Creek Greenway stretches 29 miles, the Olentangy Greenway is 18 miles, and the Blacklick Creek Trail is 15 miles. And there are more, and they are growing and connecting.

The park climbing wall in the fore and the Columbus skyline in the yon present quite a view from the park.

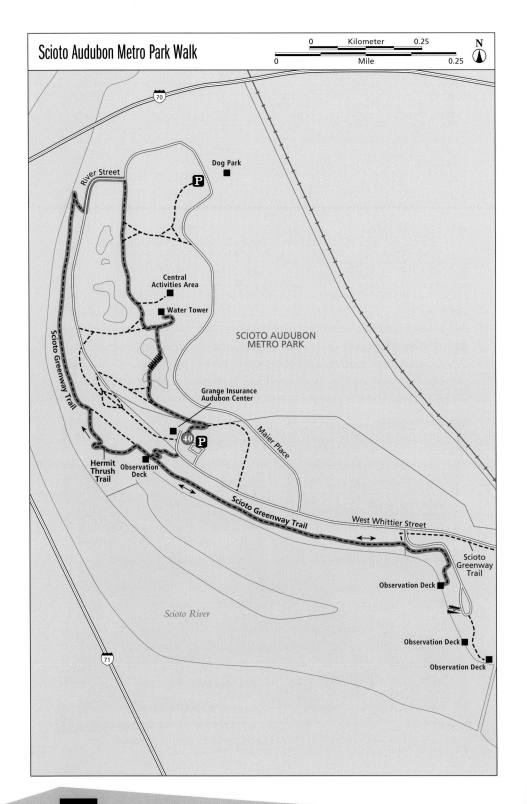

Scioto Audubon Metro Park Walk

0   Kilometer   0.25

0   Mile   0.25

N

I-70

River Street

P

Dog Park ■

Central
Activities Area ■

■ Water Tower

Scioto Greenway Trail

SCIOTO AUDUBON
METRO PARK

Grange Insurance
Audubon Center

40 P

Maier Place

Hermit
Thrush
Trail

Observation
Deck

Scioto Greenway Trail

West Whittier Street

Scioto
Greenway
Trail

Observation Deck ■

Scioto River

Observation Deck ■

I-71

Observation Deck ■

Pass some fishing accesses just before leaving the greenway for a narrower asphalt path heading toward the boat ramp and observation decks. Enjoy a view from the observation deck before backtracking to the Grange Insurance Audubon Center. Now walk a little soft path, the Hermit Thrush Trail, as it winds through a restored riverside habitat. Resume curving around the Whittier Peninsula, with the Scioto River to your left. You'll leave the greenway before reaching the interstate overpass and join a network of interconnected paved trails that wander among the wetlands and facilities of this Metro Park. Certainly stop by the Central Activities Area, where you can check out people using the 35-foot climbing wall, and also cruise up to the observation decks on the water tower for a favorable vantage of the park and beyond.

When returning to the parking area, make sure to cross the boardwalk over a pond, often occupied by waterfowl. Elevated rocks in the middle of the pond prove too tempting to birds, and some are almost always perched there.

MILES AND DIRECTIONS

0.0 Start by leaving the Grange Insurance Audubon Center and taking a winding path down toward the river. Meet the Scioto Greenway Trail; there is an observation deck just ahead overlooking the waterway. Turn left, heading southeast on the Scioto Greenway Trail.

0.4 The Scioto Greenway Trail splits left and runs along West Whittier Street. Stay right with an asphalt path that continues curving along the river.

0.5 Soon reach an observation deck and fishing area. You can look down on the park's boat ramp and out to the Scioto. Backtrack to the Scioto Greenway Trail, then backtrack to the Grange Insurance Audubon Center.

1.0 Arrive back at the Audubon Center. Take the Scioto Greenway Trail northwest just a few feet, then split left on the mulch-surfaced Hermit Thrush Trail. Pass through meadow, brush, and tree habitat favorable for birds.

1.1 Rejoin the Scioto Greenway Trail. The wooded riverbanks fall away to your left. Enjoy occasional cleared river views, especially at contemplation benches.

1.5 Leave acutely right from the greenway before it passes under the interstate ahead. Climb into the network of interconnected asphalt paths and wind toward the water tower, passing little wetlands. Ahead, pass a spur leading to the Central Activities Area.

1.9 Climb to the observation platforms on the tower. Soak in park and city views, then head toward the trailhead via the boardwalk over a pond.

2.1 Arrive back at the trailhead, finishing the hike.

Hike Index

About the Author

Johnny Molloy is a writer and adventurer based in Johnson City, Tennessee. His outdoor passion started on a backpacking trip in Great Smoky Mountains National Park while attending the University of Tennessee. That first foray unleashed a love of the outdoors that has led Molloy to spending most of his time hiking, backpacking, canoe camping, and tent camping for the past three decades. Friends enjoyed his outdoor adventure stories; one even suggested he write a book. He pursued his friend's idea and soon parlayed his love of the outdoors into an occupation. His efforts have resulted in more than forty-five books—so far. His writings include guidebooks on camping and paddling, comprehensive guidebooks about specific areas, and true outdoor adventure books covering the eastern United States. Molloy has also authored these FalconGuides:

A FalconGuide to Mammoth Cave National Park
Best Easy Day Hikes Cincinnati
Best Easy Day Hikes Greensboro and Winston-Salem
Best Easy Day Hikes Jacksonville, Florida
Best Easy Day Hikes New River Gorge
Best Easy Day Hikes Richmond, Virginia
Best Easy Day Hikes Springfield, Illinois
Best Easy Day Hikes Tallahassee
Best Easy Day Hikes Tampa Bay
Best Hikes Near Cincinnati

Molloy writes for various magazines and websites and is a columnist/feature writer for his local paper, the *Johnson City Press*. He continues to write and travel extensively throughout the United States, endeavoring in a variety of outdoor pursuits. His non-outdoor interests include American history and University of Tennessee sports. For the latest on Johnny, please visit johnnymolloy.com.

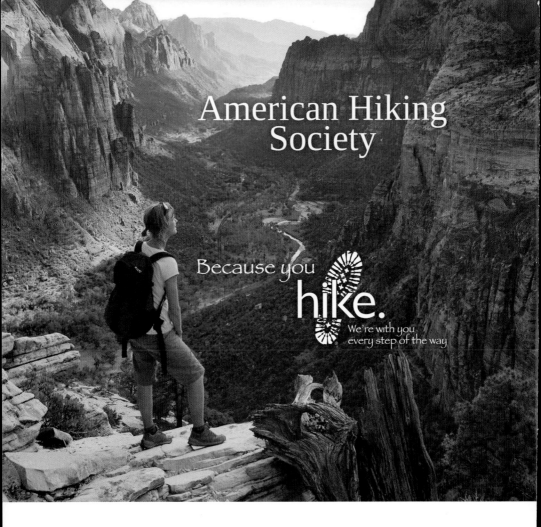

American Hiking Society

Because you **hike.**
We're with you every step of the way

A s a national voice for hikers, **American Hiking Society** works every day:

- Building and maintaining hiking trails
- Educating and supporting hikers by providing information and resources
- Supporting hiking and trail organizations nationwide
- Speaking for hikers in the halls of Congress and with federal land managers

Whether you're a casual hiker or a seasoned backpacker, become a member of American Hiking Society and join the national hiking community! You'll enjoy great member benefits and help preserve the nation's hiking trails, so tomorrow's hike is even better than today's. We invite you to join us now!

American Hiking Society